OLD TRAFFORD

100 YEARS AT THE HOME OF MANCHESTER UNITED

OLD TRAFFORD

100 YEARS AT THE HOME OF MANCHESTER UNITED

THE OFFICIAL STORY

IAN MARSHALL

SIMON &
SCHUSTER

London · New York · Sydney · Toronto

A CBS COMPANY

First published in Great Britain by Simon & Schuster UK Ltd, 2010
A CBS COMPANY

1 3 5 7 9 10 8 6 4 2

Simon & Schuster UK Ltd
1st Floor
222 Gray's Inn Road
London
WC1X 8HB

www.simonandschuster.co.uk

Simon & Schuster Australia
Sydney

A CIP catalogue for this book is available
from the British Library.

Hardback ISBN: 978-1-84737-911-5
Trade Paperback ISBN: 978-1-84737-912-2

Typeset by M Rules
Printed in the UK by CPI Mackays, Chatham ME5 8TD

To Mum and Dad, for the brilliant move of taking
me to Old Trafford back in 1973, and for so much more.
Who would have guessed it would come to this?

Contents

Acknowledgements

Writing and researching this book has been a joy, and has been made all the more pleasurable by the help, support and enthusiastic co-operation I have received in the process. There are many people I must thank.

At Manchester United: the club's official statistician, Cliff Butler, is a man who knows more about the Reds than most of us have forgotten; property manager George Johnstone gave a fascinating insight into the challenges of maintaining and improving the stadium; head groundsman Tony Sinclair was passion personified when talking about the piece of turf on which all the action takes place; media commercial manager James White helped provide access to all areas as well as much useful advice; and finally, curator Mark Wylie was an invaluable guide to the club's history and the wealth of resources contained within the museum.

Among the former players, Jack Crompton, Harry Gregg, Brian McClair and Wilf McGuinness were all generous with their time and their recollections of Old Trafford through the ages. Their enthusiasm for all things United was infectious – McClair had recently played in front of 35,000 in a Sport Relief charity game on the pitch and admitted he was 'like a little kid' having the opportunity to perform there once again. Like many millions around the world, I can only envy these players' great good fortune.

At Simon & Schuster, thanks must go to Ian Chapman, Jo Edgecombe, Mike Jones and Rory Scarfe not only for giving me the opportunity to write this book, but also for their support and patience during that process. Thanks also go to Ian Allen, the copy editor, who did such a diligent job on my prose.

I must thank Ivan Ponting for all his advice and guidance, which was invaluable, and also Steve Bartram for his help. Thanks also go to all those fans I spoke to about Old Trafford for sharing their memories and thoughts.

Finally, thanks to my wife Sugra and our young daughters Kiri (whose OT debut took place even before she was born) and Sophia for their understanding when work took me away, either to research the book in Manchester or from all the other things they would have rather I'd been doing, especially during the holiday period.

Ian Marshall
Eastbourne, August 2010

Introduction

Looking down on the pitch from high in the North Stand, the players look almost insignificant, surrounded by the huge area of the lush green grass of the Old Trafford turf. Twenty-two men line up in their neat patterns, waiting for a twenty-third to blow a whistle to bring a start to the action. An air of anticipation crackles around the ground. Looking across the pitch, a wall of faces reaches up into the dark night sky. They are just some of the 75,000 or so of us who have come from all over the world to see what will happen on the floodlit field below us. Below them, Sir Alex takes his seat in the dugout, chewing gum at the ready, making sure his players are alert to potential threats, play to the plan, take their chances and so send us all home happy. The whistle blows; the match begins.

For the next ninety minutes, all our attention, hopes and fears are focused on what the men in red do. A misplaced pass over ten yards is greeted with groans, someone a few rows back has an elderly relative who could have done better; a fifty-yard cross-field ball brought instantly under control to set up an attack brings forth cheers and admiration; we are out of our seats, hoping for a goal. We want our eleven men to succeed, yet when they fall short of the perfection we expect of them (but know we could never achieve ourselves), we feel personally affronted: they have let us down. When things go well, we believe we have played our part; our cheers, our comments have somehow filtered their way through to the players, our voice distinct among all the others. We are out there with them.

We have come to Old Trafford because we believe we can make a difference, because of the excitement of live action and drama where the plot is never known beforehand, and because it is where we belong. It is the theatre of *our* dreams. We are joined together, the lucky ones who have been able to get a ticket, knowing that countless millions around the world would gladly change places with us now. We know our dreams could come true tonight, with a goal, a victory. We don't want to wake up from this dream.

How have we come to this situation, where United have over 333 million fans, and the players can be mobbed in almost any country you care to think of? Obviously, the global reach of the Premier League plays its part, with satellite TV beaming matches around the world, and the internet bringing us all closer together. Then there is the unparalleled success brought to Manchester United during Sir Alex Ferguson's reign as manager; in sport few things appeal as much as victory. So all of this has helped United achieve a worldwide fame that was both unimaginable and impossible just thirty years ago. But even then, there was still United, still Old Trafford. The modern United couldn't have existed if it weren't for the old United before it.

Old Trafford reflects Manchester, and United still retains strong links to the city of Manchester despite the global nature of its fan base. The building of the stadium in 1910 reflected the pride and ambition of the city in the Edwardian era, the final flourishing of imperial confidence before the horrors of the First World War. Troubled years on the pitch between the wars were echoed by the depression that hit northern cities at the same time. During the Second World War, Old Trafford was twice bombed, sharing in the destruction that was visited upon both homes and factories. After the war came a desire to rebuild things and make the city a better place, with hope for all. The vision of Matt Busby helped provide that on the pitch, while the directors of the club rebuilt Old Trafford and made it a venue worthy of the heroes who had fought and endured horrors that no one should have to face.

With all of Europe anxious never to have to suffer in such a way again, efforts were made to draw the nations together. Football played its part in this, inventing new competitions. United were at the heart of it, Busby insisting that the club should be able to compete in the European Cup. Yet the dawn of a new era also brought tragedy, with the Munich disaster bringing a realisation about how fragile we all are, even our heroes. It was the legacy of the Babes, above all else, that made Old Trafford the iconic venue it has remained for the rest of its hundred-year existence. This was Manchester's team, not the red half, that had been struck down; this was the core of England's World Cup squad that had lost their lives, so it was England's tragedy too. If ever the link between club and city needed cementing, then this was surely the time that it happened.

Now, Manchester United has become a club that reflects the growing confidence and aspirations of the city. Manchester is a prosperous and vibrant place, stylish and trendy. The red shirt of United is a fashion statement around the world, immediately identifiable from Bangkok to Buenos Aires. Manchester knows it is one of Europe's great cities; United reflects that image. And Old Trafford is the club's natural home; it is unthinkable that it should be anywhere else. Like the city, it is much changed in recent years – slicker, smarter, more modern – but it is still the same place, still has many of the same people working there as before it all changed, still attracts the same people. Old Trafford and Manchester remain woven together.

Old Trafford tells the story of not just the ground itself, but also of the people who have helped make it into the landmark that it is today. It will go back to the days of United's first great era, in the Edwardian period, when the club's directors decided that a team that had been champions of England and FA Cup winners deserved to have a stadium to reflect their status as one of the nation's leading clubs. It will explain why the club moved to Old Trafford in the first place, and how the grand vision of the club had to be tempered by the financial realities.

The 'lost years' between the wars were a period of gentle decline on and off the pitch, all of which would change after the ground was bombed and a new start became necessary. Even then, however, there was a belief that United must stay at Old Trafford. We will hear about those who were involved in rebuilding the ground, and from those who were there on and off the pitch when United finally came home. Thereafter, the story will be told through the eyes of those for whom Old Trafford has been a part of their lives, for it is these people who can best sum up why this particular stadium means so much to so many.

We will go behind the scenes at the club to find out how it works on a day-to-day basis to ensure that the experience of the fans who come to cheer on their team is as pleasant and comfortable as possible, far removed from the days of crowded terraces, hampered views and the threat of violence. With United the centre of constant media attention, we will see how they are accommodated (when you watch United play on television, the camera angle on the action is perfect to make the viewing experience as good as possible). We will see how the facilities for the players are designed to help them perform to their best. We will find out the stories that will bring the place vividly to life. Above all, *Old Trafford* will celebrate the first hundred years of glory, of the hopes and dreams of fans and players, and look forward to the years ahead as United look to triumph again in the decade to come.

1

Old Trafford 2010

One hundred years after United first played at Old Trafford, the descendants of the team that turned out on that wet day in February 1910, as well as families of the stadium's architect, Archibald Leitch, and the man who provided the money for it, United's chairman John Henry Davies, are gathered in the club museum to mark the anniversary. For some of them, it is the first time they have ever been to the ground, and the club is making them very welcome, with a special tour of the stadium and a lavish lunch before they have the chance to watch the current version of Manchester United take on Fulham.

The family of Sandy Turnbull, who scored the first ever goal at Old Trafford and was killed during the First World War, have brought with them a copy of his contract with the club from 1912. The standard document is barely two pages long, and the agreement between the secretary-manager, James Ernest Mangnall, and Turnbull gets straight to the point: 'The Player hereby agrees to play in an efficient manner and to the best of his ability for the Club during the season 1912–1913.' Turnbull agreed to turn up wherever he was required to train or play, and to 'do everything necessary to get and keep himself in the best possible condition prior to and during' the season. If Turnbull were to be 'palpably inefficient or shall be guilty of serious misconduct or breach of the disciplinary Rules . . . the Club may on giving 14 days' notice . . . terminate this agreement and dispense with [his] services'. The club still retained the right to transfer him thereafter and keep any fee received, and there was no mention of any appeals procedure. For this, Turnbull was to receive £4 per week, and a handwritten add-ition confirms that he would be due a 'benefit after 5 years' service with a minimum of £500'.

David Stacey, grandson of left-back George, has brought some of his family photographs. He wants to correct the record on one matter: George Stacey was born in 1881, not 1887 as had previ-ously been thought. He recalls how his grandfather had worked at the local Westinghouse factory in Trafford Park while still a player for United, perhaps during the war. After hanging up his boots, he moved back to his home village of Thorpe Hesley, near Rotherham, to become a miner and run a sweet shop, eventually retiring from both activities at sixty-five. George was the owner of a pet Manchester terrier called Jack, who would often come on the bus to training with him. On those occasions he was left behind, Jack would occasionally wait for a bus and follow his master to training, with the drivers and conductors all recognising who he was and who he belonged to.

In other words, it was all very different a century ago from today.

Another of the guests remembers going as a young girl to the funeral of Billy Meredith in 1958 and seeing him lying in his coffin. Ted Roberts, grandson of Charlie, United's captain, is keen that the true story of his forebear is told, and how important it is that people realise the role he and Meredith had in setting up the Players' Union; United's first Captain Marvel deserves nothing less.

Susan Davies, whose great-grand-uncle was John Henry Davies, the man whose vision and money created Old Trafford, is hoping to meet other family members that have been lost in the interim. But the whereabouts of other members of the family is just as much a mystery as what became of the wealth of the Davies family, who were among the richest in Manchester a century ago.

Outside the ground, two and a half hours before the kickoff, the smell of chip fat at the top of Sir Matt Busby Way carries on the air, despite the best efforts of the blustery wind to blow it away. Early crowds are already milling around the stadium, many looking at the stories in the Munich Tunnel of the players and officials who lost their lives on that tragic day in 1958. United's worldwide support is clear, with many foreign tongues to be heard as you walk round. A group of Polish fans sing of their love for Edwin van der Sar. For the stars of 1910, foreign travel was a rarity; the team's tour of the Austro-Hungarian Empire in the summer of 1908 a rare experience that left many of them shocked after they came under attack when they humiliated local sides.

A surprising number of people are visiting Old Trafford for only the first or second time. When you're five, as is Edward Stevens from Cheltenham, perhaps it's not so unexpected. He and his big brother, Tom, aged seven, reel off their favourite players: Rooney, Scholes, Giggs and Rio all get a mention. They give some of their chants an early practice run; the match can't start quickly enough for them. But then Willie Lohan is here for the first time as a seventieth birthday present from his son, Mark, having travelled down from Renfrew near Glasgow. At United, Mark says, 'the club is well run, and you don't get the trouble and swearing' and none of the hatred that often fires Scottish football. And there's the small matter of a fellow graduate from the Govan shipyards, Sir Alex, to cheer on – one local boy who definitely made good.

For Bob Tinker and Kenneth Townsend, it's far from their first time at the ground. They've had season tickets next to each other since 1967, so they must have seen around a thousand games each in that time. Bob comments: 'I spend that much time here, my wife thinks it's my postal code.' As he lives 'five roads up', M16 probably is his postal code. Aged eighty and eighty-one, they've been through it all with United. 'I came here with my father when I was six years old,' recalls Bob. 'The only thing I remember then is you could wander around – the crowds were about twenty-six thousand – and you used to ask people for cigarette cards and silver paper.' He can still proudly reel off United's line-up for the 1948 FA Cup final. Kenneth has similar memories of his early days following the Reds: 'I went upstairs on the trolleybuses looking for cigarette cards – Stanley Matthews and Mortensen, and all that.'

With just over two hours to go before the match begins, the coach bearing the United squad arrives at the corner of the South and West Stands, and as the players make their way into the heart of Old Trafford, a crowd of about 500 watching them breaks into a chant of 'Rooney! Rooney!' At this stage, most of the accents you hear do not belong to Manchester, unless it's the people selling merchandise around the ground. Cliff Butler, the keeper of the Red flame at Old Trafford, has a theory why: 'Now you get a lot of day-trippers who come from far away; their relatives ask them to pick up something from the Megastore, they have to eat something here, and it's all part of the experience.' If you're a local, coming here every match, you don't need to be here so early, taking in the whole atmosphere, as it's almost part of your DNA.

The match gets under way; 75,207 are crammed into Old Trafford hoping for a Mother's Day treat. After a brisk start, United begin to lose some of their rhythm; passes go astray. Fulham, who beat the Reds 3–0 at Craven Cottage back in December when United's patched-up defence struggled to cope, rarely threaten, though a long-range shot from Clint Dempsey goes whistling over van der Sar's goal. Towards the end of the half, with the referee turning down a Wayne Rooney penalty claim, the Reds begin to look more fired up; certainly, Sir Alex is out in the technical area having a word with the fourth official.

Dimitar Berbatov starts and finishes a great move, but heads just over from six yards. The pressure is beginning to mount. Rooney drives one in from the edge of the box, only for it to be turned away. That's more like it; the crowd senses the change in momentum.

The half-time whistle goes just as United seem to be moving up through the gears. The players go back to their changing room to get a gee-up from Sir Alex. There's a title to play for.

Within thirty-one seconds of the restart, Berbatov, Nani and Rooney link up again, as they've been doing throughout the game. Nani's pass in from the left is steered home by Rooney from twelve yards, in a surprising amount of space, to continue his incredible run in front of goal. Fulham are still working hard, and suddenly, somehow, Bobby Zamora is through on goal, but Nemanja Vidic gets back to make a stunning covering tackle, just as Zamora seems certain to score.

Chance after chance comes United's way, but with six minutes to go Fulham are still in it and could easily nick a late equaliser. Then Michael Carrick hits a long, diagonal pass from well inside United's half; the ball floats over Berbatov's right shoulder and somehow he brings it under instant control with the outside of his right foot. It is a truly breathtaking and beautiful piece of skill, but there are still two players to beat. He accelerates past them and puts in a perfect cross to Rooney. On this form, there's no way he can miss: 2–0. That's thirty-two goals for him for the season, and he goes over to thank the man who made it so easy for him. For this is a team at United, however much focus one man may receive. Game over. But there's still time for one more, as Berbatov nods in a header from Ji-sung Park's inch-perfect cross. It's the goal his performance deserves.

Just as United had done one hundred years ago, the Reds have scored three goals, but this time their opponents haven't made any response. Satisfied fans make their way out of the stadium at the beginning of its second century. If the years that follow bring anything like the tragedy, drama, excitement and success of the first hundred years, Manchester United supporters are in for a roller-coaster ride. Who knows? Maybe Tom and Edward Stevens will still be around to recall what Old Trafford was like when it was just 100 years old?

2

Meredith & Co

The Edwardian era was a boom time for football, with crowds growing year on year and players gaining national fame for the first time. But, at the beginning of this period, Manchester United very nearly went out of business; indeed, when King Edward VII ascended the throne in January 1901, the club was still known as Newton Heath and was massively in debt. Yet, by the time he died, in May 1910, United was arguably the best football team in the land and, in Old Trafford, certainly had the best stadium. The transformation that took place in those years was as dramatic as any in the club's history, and it was the building of Old Trafford that helped cement United's place as one of the biggest clubs in England – whatever the team's position in the league. One thing, however, hadn't changed: Manchester United was still hugely in debt.

The club had long since shed its ties to the railway company that had given it its name back in 1878. Having moved about three miles south from its original ground at North Road, Monsall, in 1893 the Heathens set up at Bank Street in Clayton, close to the present City of Manchester Stadium, to begin their second season in the First Division of the Football League. The first season had not gone well, and Newton Heath had required a play-off, known as a Test Match, to stay in the top division.

If Bank Street was an improvement, it was only a small one. About the best that could be said for the pitch was that it was flat. However, when it rained, it quickly became a quagmire. The ground was surrounded by the local chemical works and soap factories, with some thirty chimneys belching out smoke. The club struggled on the pitch as well as off it. Newton Heath was relegated in 1894, and could not win promotion before the century was out. Some work was done to improve the ramshackle stands, but in truth it was only ever going to be a case of pouring good money after bad. With attendances regularly falling below 3000, and debts of £2760, mostly owed to contractors who had worked on the ground, the situation was serious. After a game, the club's directors would sometimes be seen counting out the attendance receipts, deducting the running expenses, and then paying players what they could from the balance left over. When one of the club's directors, William Healey, who was also owed over £200, went to court and was granted a winding-up order, the end seemed imminent.

Newton Heath's captain, Harry Stafford, had helped keep the club running with a series of fundraising events that ensured the Heathens could meet their day-to-day expenses. But things could not go on like this, and it was when he met a wealthy local businessman, John Henry Davies, director and chairman of Walkers and Homfrays Brewery and the Manchester Brewery Company, that the situation finally took a turn for the better. Davies, one of the wealthiest men in Manchester, who had married into the Tate family (of Tate & Lyle fame) and so enhanced his wealth further, was intrigued by the prospect of supporting his local football club.

Although Davies had had little if any association with football beforehand, he was a supporter of other sports in the city, such as cycling, and was involved with various charities. An astute businessman, he realised that the club had potential, given the increasing amount of leisure time available to workers, who were also beginning to see a little more of the fruits of their labours in terms of higher wages. He also no doubt saw the football club as an effective way of promoting his brewery interests. All of which meant that the popularity of football could surely only increase. Indeed, this was a period when many businessmen were investing in leisure activities for the Manchester population, with billiard halls, amusement parks, an ice rink and the impressive Victoria Baths all being built.

So, at the end of the 1901–02 season, when Newton Heath finished fifteenth out of eighteen in the Second Division (its worst performance yet), a meeting was held at New Islington Hall in Ancoats on 24 April. Davies and a group of new investors decided that the time had come to make some radical changes. They ousted the old board and took control themselves, with Davies in charge. First of all, it was decided to change the team's colours from white shirts and navy shorts to red shirts and white shorts; then, with the club's links to Newton Heath a distant memory, it was agreed that the name should change to Manchester United. With the debts now sorted out thanks to Davies, there were great hopes at the start of the 1902–03 season and a big crowd of 15,000 came to the first home fixture, against Burton United. Despite investing in ground improvements and new recruits, results didn't pick up, so Davies (like many club owners since) knew he needed to change the manager – or 'secretary-manager' as they were often known in those days – and brought in Ernest Mangnall after his predecessor, club secretary Jim West, resigned in September 1903.

Mangnall was brought in from Burnley on the recommendation of director John 'J.J.' Bentley, and would prove to be the first of United's triumvirate of great managers, the predecessor of Sir Matt Busby and Sir Alex Ferguson. He was a fitness fanatic, and a believer (as was so often the case in those days) in training without the ball, so that players would be 'hungry' for it come match-day. He also kept strict discipline over his team.

Mangnall quickly realised that the playing staff was not strong enough, and by the end of the 1903–04 season had brought in many of the players who would go on to be the biggest stars of the period: the enormous Harry Moger was in goal; the famed half-back line of Charlie Roberts, Alex Bell and Dick Duckworth all joined. As many managers since have understood, the key to success is making sure the foundations of the side are strong, and between them these four would play more than 1100 times for United. His ability to talent-spot was a further crucial element in his success.

Despite these signings, promotion did not come immediately, United finishing third in 1904–05 before finally going back to the top division after finishing runners-up in 1905–06. As United entered its fifteenth season in the Football League, it was about to enjoy its third campaign in the top division.

Before the new season began, however, United had a windfall when Manchester City was caught out by the FA in a series of illegal payments. Instead of paying their team the maximum wage of £4 per week, they were often paying £6 or £7. Eighteen players were banned from playing for the club again, and five directors were expelled. City planned on auctioning off their players, but before the bidding got started, Mangnall had stepped in and signed up the best of them, including Sandy Turnbull and Billy Meredith, to provide a great attacking line-up to add to the stalwart defence that was already in place. Although the new recruits were banned from playing until January 1907, which meant United had to settle for a mid-table finish that season, everything was set up for a strong challenge in 1907–08.

In autumn 1907, United was established as a limited company, which helped provide Davies with more funds to develop the team and the facilities. United won thirteen out of fourteen games at the start of the season, with Sandy Turnbull scoring an incredible nineteen goals in that time. That campaign, United's crowds averaged 22,315, a figure they'd exceeded on just three occasions two seasons earlier. Once United hit the top of the table, they were never likely to be caught and ended up winning the league by a massive margin of nine points.

Often Bank Street was unable to cope with the crowds attracted to see the best team in the land. In those days, the FA Cup was seen as the more important trophy, rather than the league title. So when United took on Aston Villa in the Cup in 1906, ticket prices were put up, over 35,000 squeezed into the ground, and gate receipts were £1460. But some 10,000 fans had had to be locked out of the ground. With football attendances on the rise everywhere (league attendances rose by about 10 per cent between 1905–06 and the following season, and this trend had continued), and United now crowned champions, Davies could see that the club was missing out on a potential goldmine. Imagine what the club could achieve if it had a ground with a capacity like the Crystal Palace? Imagine how much better the team could play if it had a pitch that wasn't a mud bath? Imagine how much more fans would pay if they could see better football in more comfortable surroundings, without having to hold their noses at the smog and fumes coming out of nearby factory chimneys? Davies could imagine all of this, and he thought he had the solution. He began to think about moving United to a new stadium.

Fortunately, Davies believed he had the perfect site for Manchester United: sixteen acres of land owned by the Manchester Brewery Company in Trafford Park, between the Bridgewater Canal and the Cheshire Lines railway. As early as 1907, he had been considering this move. At the time, this seemed an extremely bold decision, for it was taking the club from its heartland of support in Clayton in the east of Manchester to an area southwest of the city that was still developing. Nearby Sale and Altrincham were sparsely populated, and there was no guarantee that the fans would follow the club across the city – a journey that would take plenty of time. But, with so many people working nearby, he hoped they would want to come to the ground after they finished working at lunchtime on a Saturday. In any case, this was Davies's club, and he was going to do with it as he liked: he'd changed the name, changed the team colours, now he was going to change its location. But moving to Trafford Park was not only convenient for him, it was a statement of intent. For this area of the city, more than any other, had been responsible for the boom in Manchester's economy during the previous fifteen years; it was the Silicon Valley of Manchester.

At around the time the club had been founded as Newton Heath in 1878, Manchester was a city in relative decline. Its cotton industries may have been the biggest in the world, but progress was being hamstrung by the cost of importing raw cotton and exporting the finished goods, most of which came through the port at Liverpool. Dock charges there were so high that business was being damaged. The building of the Manchester Ship Canal, completed in 1894 at a cost of £15 million, would utterly change all that. The canal was so big that only five ships in the world at that time could not navigate its waters. Now ships could sail all the way to Manchester to the new port there, reducing costs dramatically. Within a few years, Manchester docks would be handling far more cotton than Liverpool, helping to make the city the largest banking, commercial and transport centre outside London. It could certainly be argued that the intense rivalry between the two cities has its origins in this period when Manchester took charge of its own destiny, damaging the economy of Liverpool in the process.

The canal and docks drew in other businesses around them, and when the 1183-acre Trafford Park estate was put up for sale by Sir Humphrey de Trafford, the council thought it could be developed into Manchester's equivalent of Hyde Park. While the council pondered its options, Ernest Terah Hooley bought the estate for £360,000. His general manager, Marshall Stevens, devised an idea to use the land as the world's first industrial estate – an area that would be separate from where people lived, used for factories and warehouses. The Trafford Park Estates floated in August 1896 and quickly attracted the UK's largest flour mill, while British

Westinghouse Electric Co built the biggest engineering works in the country there. Ford Motor Co arrived in Trafford Park in 1910, and within three years would become the biggest car manufacturer in Britain. Manchester United's Old Trafford ground was a part of all this: the most innovative and successful example of urban development ever, the driving force behind the city's economic boom. What the area lacked in nearby population, it more than made up for with good roads, as well as rail and tram links.

It wasn't just United that was able to build expensive new facilities. All around the city, the first decade or so of the twentieth century saw the fruits of this new wealth. The Opera House on Quay Street (completed in 1912) cost £40,000 to build, the same as the Hospital for Skin Diseases on the same road, which had been built a few years earlier. The police and fire station on London Road (1904–06) had cost £142,000. Everywhere you looked, the results of the boom were there for all to see.

How could it be otherwise when mill owners were earning between £20,000 and £60,000 a year? (Remember, at this time, footballers were well-paid working-class figures earning just over £200 a year.) Their civic pride demanded that they help Manchester have the impressive buildings its status deserved. They were able to do this because Lancashire supplied 60 per cent of the world's cotton trade, with over 620,000 people employed in mills in the northwest. The UK exported 7 billion yards of cotton each year; its nearest competitor, Japan, just 156 million. And Manchester was at the centre of all this success and dominance. So, of course, when Lewis's department store was opened in 1915, it had the UK's first escalators outside London, and inside was a sprung marble dance floor. Manchester expected nothing but the best for itself and its inhabitants. Manchester United was just as ambitious.

Davies and the United board approached Archibald Leitch to design the stadium at Old Trafford. He was already the most famous architect of sports stadiums in England, having worked at grounds such as Stamford Bridge, Anfield and White Hart Lane among others. Born in Glasgow in 1865, he worked at a local engineering company, where he trained as a draughtsman, and gradually got to know some of the city's most influential engineers. His first stadium commission had come in his native Glasgow in March 1899, when he was asked to design a new stadium at Ibrox Park, the home of his favourite team, Rangers. When completed, it had a reported capacity of almost 80,000 fans, the biggest in the UK.

In April 1902, part of the stand at Ibrox collapsed, resulting in twenty-six fatalities and over 500 injuries. Despite this, Leitch continued to be commissioned to extend and improve football stadiums around the country. Davies, supported by J.J. Bentley, knew he was the most experienced stadium architect in the country, and could put into practice all the lessons he had learned from his previous commissions, as well as from looking at other recent developments, such as White City, built for the London Olympics in 1908.

First of all, unlike many other grounds of the time, there would be no compromise on the nature of the venue: it would be a football stadium pure and simple, with no running or cycling track to distract people or to distance the crowd from the action. It was the first modern stadium of the twentieth century. The aim was to give it a capacity of 100,000 (with 36,000 of them due to be under cover in the Main Stand, either seated or standing), though this was later reduced to 80,000 when costs rose from the original estimates of £30,000 to double that sum. As such, it could rival any venue in London and lay claim to be the biggest and best in the country. With few houses in the vicinity, Leitch had the scope to respond to the ambitions of Davies and the United board. With the railway line running nearby, a tramline already in place that ran from Clayton, and good roads out of Manchester, there was every chance for people to get to the ground relatively easily.

Leitch contacted the board of Cheshire Lines to see if they would build a station next to the ground, and in return for the extra revenue this would bring in, loan United £10,000. The railway company worked out that the new station would attract perhaps £2750 a year in extra fares, not just to the football ground, but also to the cricket ground (already long established) and White City pleasure gardens. However, they declined the opportunity either to build the station or loan the money. It was a curious and short-sighted decision that would take a generation to be corrected.

Athletic News reported how the ground would be excavated to a depth of nine feet, so as to reduce the overall height of the containing wall to just thirty feet, with the lower part of the terracing built into solid ground and starting from slightly below pitch level, the middle portion backed by the excavated earth, and the top of the terrace 'built entirely of ferro-concrete – which is as hard as rock and non-inflammable'. At this time, when many stands were simply earth or cinder banks, concrete terracing was a relatively new phenomenon. The terracing, a hundred tiers high, was dotted with Leitch's crush barriers (a recent development he had devised) to prevent overcrowding. Underneath the terracing, a large, covered passageway twenty feet wide ran round the entire ground, to ensure that people could stay dry until they went up on to the stands. From the passageway broad staircases gave access to a sixty-foot-wide opening on the terraces in the centre of each stand. Meanwhile, there was plenty of space outside the stadium for people to gather before a game and not get crushed.

For those who wanted to sit down to watch the game, there would be a covered Main Stand with fifty tiers of seats. Unusually for the day, there was no standing paddock in front of them, so those in seats could get close to the action. Off the corridors below this stand were Old Trafford's special extras, including a billiard room for the players, tea rooms, a gymnasium, as well as the referees' quarters and a laundry. Special thought went into ensuring everyone could easily access their seats, with the least disruption to others, by having numerous entrances at different levels of the stand.

Leitch, as he had done before, worked with the contractors Humphreys of Knightsbridge on the construction of the stadium, the dimensions of which were 630 feet long and 510 feet wide, with the terracing 120 feet wide. The builders were to find that United was not particularly good at paying its bills, and lawyers were eventually called in to ensure the money started flowing through. They would have to wait many years before they were completely paid off.

Little is known about the precise timetable of the building work, as the surviving board minutes say almost nothing about the progress of developing Old Trafford. What they do show is that on 10 June 1909 the club groundsman was to be sent to the new ground 'as soon as the laying of the turf is commenced there'. As the new stadium came into being, followers of Manchester United eagerly anticipated the opening of their team's new home.

3

The Day the Bank Collapsed

For the 45,000 or more fans that made their way to watch United's first game at Old Trafford on 19 February 1910, their world was completely different from what modern-day supporters experience. The contrast between the players of 1910 and 2010 is even greater.

That day's *Manchester Guardian* (priced at a penny) gives a very clear idea of how things were. Almost unbelievably, there was barely a mention of the game about to take place against Liverpool that afternoon, or about the inauguration of the new stadium. Sport was yet to be so integral a part of the media's interests. Instead, the main headline (on page six) revealed how a petition with some 2000 signatures, gathered in three Salford seats during the recent general election, had been handed to the local Liberal MP, Mr Byles, calling for women to be given the vote. Mr Byles declared himself 'entirely in sympathy' with their demands.

Showing in the theatres that day were *Cinderella* at the Theatre Royal, John Galsworthy's *The Silver Box* at the Gaiety, while *The Miracle* was on at the Palace. The small ads, which filled much of the first few pages, had the usual range of jobs and accommodation on offer, though of course at that time many of the jobs were in domestic service. A large number of adverts offered to provide elocution lessons, or to teach dancing and deportment. Clearly Manchester's citizens were keen on self-improvement. Retailers were displaying their wares assiduously, with Mappin & Webb having a range of watches on sale, starting at around £5, while a Singer Modele de Luxe bike would set you back £10 10s. A letter from a local civil servant, explaining that clerks' salaries were around £75 to £83 per annum, shows just how expensive these things were. Despite that, the Manchester Motor Show was drawing in big crowds, giving people the opportunity to see a Bleriot Monoplane and cars that were priced at up to £1000. The eight-horsepower four-seat Rover was a more realistic £235, but still well out of the price range of all but the very wealthiest.

And football players were not among that group then. Relatively recently the maximum wage had been introduced to football, and the paper carried news of an agreement between the Football League and the Southern League that this would be maintained at £4 per week (£208 per annum).

In those circumstances, it was perhaps not so surprising that the following Monday's paper could report on how overcrowded the trams were as they headed out to Old Trafford, and how many were forced to walk to the ground from the centre of Manchester. As they walked, small boys entertained the crowds by turning cartwheels in the hope of earning a ha'penny. It was a cold and very windy day, but when the fans got into the ground (some without paying) they were confronted with a pitch 'as spick and span, as smooth, and as green as a billiard table' – quite a contrast to what they had been used to at Bank Street. Indeed, the stormy weather had already claimed one major victim a couple of days previously, when a stand at Bank Street had been destroyed. United had got out just in time.

In fact, they had originally planned to play their first game at the new ground four weeks earlier, against Tottenham Hotspur. Instead, the old ground said farewell to the Reds with a 5–0 victory to the home side. Three days before the first game, with all the main work now completed, John Henry Davies and his directors visited the stadium for an official inspection, accompanied by the local press. The final figures for the ground capacity were now confirmed as 12,000 seated in the Grand Stand, where it was noted that the seats' covering could be removed at the end of the match and taken indoors until next required, as well as room for 40,000 on 'the sixpenny side' as part of a capacity of 70,000 who could stand. More alarmingly, just ahead of the game, Stretford Council announced it did not have sufficient capacity to provide enough extra trams to the area, so some people were going to have to make their own way to the ground.

A band played on the pitch in front of the covered stand before the game, where the paper's reporter was sitting on a 'plush tip-up seat'. The fans around him were mostly dressed in dark overcoats, but some – a group led by Louis Rocca known as 'Rocca's Brigade' – were wearing red and white suits or carrying umbrellas in the team's colours. Rocca would go on to become United's chief scout and assistant manager. There was a real sense of anticipation. The cost of tickets ranged from five shillings for the best seats, down to sixpence for those standing. Many also paid a penny to buy the match-day programme, which showed United in mid-table not far behind that day's opponents, Liverpool. The publisher and editor of the programme, a Mr Gibbons, saluted the efforts of the club and its board on the transformation that had brought United to this stage. He noted how the ground had excellent facilities for the players, including a gymnasium and a reading room – 'so in the latter we may have some of our chaps preparing for barristers or MPs'.

The first game did not disappoint as a spectacle, even if the result did. United dominated the early play, with Sandy Turnbull having the honour of scoring the first goal at Old Trafford with a low header. Tom Homer then made it 2–0 when he followed in on the rebound from a Harold Halse shot. Liverpool pulled a goal back before left-winger George Wall scored the best goal of the match. Thereafter, Liverpool dominated and went on to win 4–3, sending the fans home in low spirits as the rain began to fall. The *Guardian*'s man in the stands concluded that the players would have to adapt to playing on such fine surfaces for 'these "swell" grounds need some living up to'. With match-day receipts of £1200 (as against a weekly wage bill of £134 10s), there was clearly going to be money to spend to ensure that the players reflected their surroundings.

But life was not easy for even the starriest of footballing names at this time. As we have seen, their weekly wage of £4 was easily better than most working men at the time; the Old Trafford ground staff, for example, earned between 28s and 35s per week. (Women's pay was even worse – the club's board minutes later that year noted that a Mrs Ryder had been taken on as office cleaner on 7s 6d per week, though she was subsequently able to supplement her earnings by making teas for 10s every time the board met.) But, given the short period a player could expect to perform at the top level, thanks to heavy pitches or heavy boots causing serious injury, this was hardly going to set up someone for life.

The clubs had recently introduced the maximum wage to ensure they maintained strict control over their players – once a club had the player's registration, he could not play for anyone else without their approval, meaning that the clubs effectively 'owned' their players. If they didn't want to sell them, they were going nowhere – there was no chance to leak a story to the back pages to alert other clubs that a player might be open to a transfer. As part of any transfer deal, the player would take a cut of up to £10, but as this was the equivalent of just two and a half weeks' wages, there was no obvious incentive to go looking for a transfer, especially as players would often be awarded a benefit match if they stayed with one team for five years.

The idea of a benefit match was that the player could earn the entire gate receipts from that game, a sum that could run to hundreds of pounds. For example, when goalkeeper Harry Moger was due his benefit in autumn 1908, the board accepted his choice of the fixture when the benefit should apply and also guaranteed that he would receive a minimum of £500 (roughly two and a half years' pay) by making up any shortfall on gate receipts. These rules were strictly enforced by the FA and the Football League.

However, clubs still managed to attract good players from rival teams, and often the only way to do this was to provide unofficial inducements. For example, in April 1904, Charlie Roberts, who would go on to become the club's first great captain, was transferred to United from Grimsby. In signing him up, United had to fight off interest from across the city. Nowadays, it would be easy to understand why a player might prefer the red half to the blue; but in 1904 City would finish the season as FA Cup winners and runners-up in the First Division. What was more, as was subsequently discovered, City had a track record for paying illegal inducements. Instead, for a fee of £400, Roberts came to United, who finished third in the Second Division. Either Roberts was excited by the challenge offered by United, or else the club made him an offer he couldn't refuse.

Football clubs therefore found themselves in a difficult position: the maximum wage helped them maintain control of their players and finances, but it restricted their opportunities to strengthen their position against rival sides. They looked for ways to get round the regulations. For example, United would often go to the coast for training ahead of a game. This wasn't simply a matter of providing players with clean air to help with their fitness; it was a hidden perk.

So when United won the league title in 1907–08, the club applied to the Football League to award the players a bonus, but were turned down. Instead, the players were taken on a summer tour of Europe (organised by Thomas Cook), visiting Paris, Prague, Vienna and Budapest. In reality, this was (or should have been) little more than a grand holiday with lavish hospitality equivalent to about three months' pay. In Budapest, United won so easily that even Moger the goalkeeper scored, from a penalty. It didn't entirely go smoothly, however. After another crushing victory in Prague, the Czech fans threw bottles at the United side as they left the pitch, bricks came flying through their changing-room window after the match, and on the journey back to their hotel, George Stacey (reputed to have the hardest shot in the game at that time) recalled how even their carriages were turned over by the enraged supporters.

The following season, United went on to win the FA Cup. For the trip down to London, the board agreed that the players' wives would be invited too. The players stayed in a hotel in Epping Forest, before beating Bristol City 1–0 in the final held at the Crystal Palace, thanks to a Sandy Turnbull goal. The 'treats' this time carried fewer risks, as the players were taken on a trip to Hampstead Heath and shopping on Oxford Street as well as having the opportunity to visit the music-hall star George Robey at his home in Finchley. Apparently no magnums of Krug were consumed, but nine months later United half-back Dick Duckworth and his wife had a baby.

The club wanted to give its players £20 each as a bonus, but the FA refused to sanction this payment, because United had fielded under-strength sides in the run-up to the final. The fact that they'd had to play four games in five days at one stage in the fortnight preceding the final was not deemed sufficient reason for what would now be seen as necessary squad rotation. This seemingly harsh response was largely due to the FA's concerns about the way United operated; in the FA's opinion, the club was being run on an extravagant basis. So while the FA declared an amnesty for all clubs who were guilty of illegal payments, United were singled out because of the role of Davies, who was effectively funding the club out of his own pocket. Even a century ago, football finances were a hotly debated subject.

But these 'treats' were just that, at the gift of the board, and the players wanted more control of their own destiny. So it was that a Players' Union was formed, holding its first meeting at the Imperial Hotel in Manchester in December 1907, to try to improve the conditions and opportunities for footballers, calling for the abolition of the maximum wage. The £4 wage had been set as long ago as 1901, since when the popularity of the game had increased hugely, but the players had not seen any of the benefits. The players also wanted greater freedom to change clubs, either with the abolition of transfer fees or with the players receiving a greater share of the transfer fee than the £10 they were currently entitled to.

Initially, some clubs supported the union, United among them, as they believed they would be able to attract better players if they could offer more money. But the Football League demanded that the clubs renounce the union and instigate a new form of contract that tied in players even more tightly.

One of the union's other claims revolved around the recently introduced Workmen's Compensation Act, which provided workers with some minimal form of insurance payment if they were injured while at work. With injury such a high risk to their career, and no support likely to be forthcoming from a club if a player's career was ended, the Players' Union wanted this piece of legislation applied to football. Astonishingly, the football authorities and clubs refused to accept this, arguing that football was not work, merely a leisure activity for which the players happened to receive payment.

Backed by the FA, the Football League and the Southern League, the clubs stood firm against the union's demands. Unless the players withdrew from the union, they would not be able to play for their clubs, and as the clubs held their registrations, players could not go elsewhere to earn a living from football. The FA insisted that the new player contracts for the coming 1909–10 season included a clause that each player would renounce his membership of the union. Faced with this heavy-handed response, during the summer of 1909 most footballers abandoned the union and gave in – except for United's players, where Charlie Roberts and Billy Meredith had been influential figures in setting up the organisation. So the FA suspended the entire FA Cup-winning side. The players dubbed themselves The Outcasts, and prepared to strike.

The resilience of the United players began to draw support from elsewhere. Footballers who had pulled out of the union now returned to it, realising that they had the support of the fans. Now it was the turn of the FA to back down and a muddled compromise agreement was reached, which left both sides feeling they had achieved something, even if the operation of a maximum wage and the transfer system would remain unchanged for another fifty years. A year later, for the 1910–11 season, the maximum wage was increased from £4 to £5, but only after four years' service at a club.

After losing their first game at Old Trafford, United went on to win their remaining seven home fixtures of the 1909–10 season, scoring nineteen goals in the process and conceding just four. The players had clearly responded well to their excellent new facilities. The quality of the ground impressed even those based in London, for the FA asked if they could hold one of the FA Cup semifinals that season at the new ground. It was to be the first of many the stadium would host, and Barnsley beat Everton 3–0 in front of a crowd of 40,000. However, the response of the fans to the new venue wasn't quite as consistent, with attendances varying wildly between 50,000 and 5000. Given the enormous cost of building Old Trafford, the club urgently needed the crowds to remain high. Then, as now, the best way to draw in new support was to sign an exciting striker, and Ernest Mangnall found just the man in Enoch West.

The club board minutes for July drily announced the arrival of 'E.J. West' from Nottingham Forest for a fee of £775 plus interest, as well as adding: 'Resolved that a telephone should be arranged for the club office with an extension through to the enquiry office.' There was more summer business to conclude. The rights to produce and sell the match-day programme were sold for £100 per season; two seasons before, these same rights had been sold for £40. Clearly the expectation all round was that the crowds were going to be much higher, and a club that had recently won two trophies was able to demand more.

For those who complain about how football has changed, with every tournament and club constantly plugging their 'official partners', they might also be surprised to learn that a Mr Leach paid £30 to be United's official sweet and chocolate seller for the first full season at Old Trafford. In truth, it is simply a case of the numbers getting bigger. Season-ticket rates were set at £2 2s for the chairs, and £1 2s 6d for the 1s 6d seats. And to ensure the crowds were well entertained, the Irwell Old Prize Band was to be paid £2 per match.

United's hopes for the 1910–11 season got off to the best possible start, with the first four home games producing four wins for the Reds. The second of these attracted the biggest crowd yet to Old Trafford: the first Manchester derby to be held at the ground drew in 60,000 fans. Sandy Turnbull scored United's first goal, but it was new signing 'Knocker' West who got the winner, following in the rebound after the City keeper failed to hold Dick Duckworth's fierce shot.

As the campaign drew on, it increasingly became a two-horse race between United and Aston Villa, the defending champions. United's 2–0 home win over Villa in December gave the Reds an early advantage, but they faced them again in their penultimate match of the season. A stormy 4–2 victory for Villa gave the Midlanders the edge, as they needed only a draw at lowly Liverpool while United had to beat third-placed Sunderland at Old Trafford. On a cold, wet and windy day at the end of April that deterred all but the hardiest fans from attending, United eased through 5–1 despite having gone a goal down early on. Ernest Mangnall had come up with a tactical ploy, however, and played Billy Meredith in a slightly more withdrawn role on the right. This not only created extra space for him to operate in (his crosses set up three goals), it also gave more space to Sam Blott on the other wing. Despite these tactics, United's victory was much aided by two Wearsiders having to go off in the second half through injury – no substitutes were allowed in those days.

Meanwhile, Liverpool had beaten Villa 3–1 – United were champions again. Those few fans that had made their way to Old Trafford celebrated wildly the first occasion when the trophy had been won at the ground. Had United fans realised how long they would have to wait until the next occasion they would be champions, many more would certainly have made the effort. As it was, most observers agreed that it was a well-deserved title, as United had suffered a series of injuries to key figures such as Charlie Roberts, Harold Halse, Dick Duckworth and George Wall at various stages of the season. Surely, with that being the case, this was merely the first of many trophies to be won at the new stadium?

To mark the occasion, the board decided that the players 'should be taken on a motor drive to Chester' and follow it up with a celebration dinner at the Midland Hotel. Given that an inexpensive car cost roughly the same as a player's annual salary, this was perhaps a more exciting reward than it may seem today.

Despite the poor attendance of just 10,000 for the title decider at Old Trafford, the crowds during the season had averaged 27,158, up about 40 per cent on the previous two campaigns and 16 per cent higher than in their last title-winning season. But it was the FA Cup that drew in the biggest crowds, and United's only home FA Cup fixture that season was a cracker, against Aston Villa: the two best sides in the land. George Wall scored the winner off the underside of the bar in a tense 2–1 victory that was seen by 65,101 fans paying record receipts of £2464. This was what Old Trafford had been built for, and the hope now was that such packed houses would be a regular feature in the future, so the club could quickly pay off the debts that had accumulated during the building of the stadium.

But the attendance record was to last only a few months, for on Wednesday 26 April, just three days before the title decider, Old Trafford hosted its first FA Cup final, a replay following a goalless draw between Bradford City and Newcastle United at the Crystal

Palace the previous Saturday. The ground had been operational for barely a year, yet already it had established itself as one of the premier venues in the country and certainly the best in the north of England.

Manchester was invaded by fans from the two cities, with Yorkshire and Geordie accents to be heard everywhere. The *Guardian* wondered 'how . . . did so vast a crowd contrive to escape its work for half or a whole day?' Clearly the concept of a 'sickie' was unheard of among the pressmen of the day. But the paper raised another point, suggesting that more finals ought to be held in the north, as it was clubs from that region that tended to dominate the competition.

The official attendance was 66,646, paying record receipts of £4478 – a bumper return. However, as a spectacle, the match was hampered by a strong wind blowing straight down the pitch, making it hugely difficult to play into. Despite this, it was Bradford who scored in the first half and, with the wind behind them in the second half, seeing it through was a relatively straight-forward process. Somewhat surprisingly, the *Guardian* admired Bradford's 'cruder tactics, but more life and spirit', saying these were preferable to the 'increasing elaborateness of play' shown by Newcastle. It concluded: 'Perhaps Bradford's victory is not a bad thing for the game.' English suspicion of flair and talent, as opposed to workmanlike effort, is nothing new.

Despite beating Swindon Town in the Charity Shield 8–4 early in the following season, with Harold Halse scoring six goals, United's campaign in 1911–12 never really got going. The team was beginning to show signs of ageing, and Ernest Mangnall didn't have the funds to rebuild. The crowds fell considerably, averaging just under 20,000 in the league. However, a quarterfinal FA Cup tie against champions elect Blackburn Rovers did draw a crowd of 59,300. As usual, prices were raised for the glamour tie, and, despite a miners' strike that was causing hardship across all industries, receipts were an impressive £3114. The game ended in a 1–1 draw, but United lost the replay at Ewood Park and their season was over.

Seeing the way things were moving, and knowing that the club did not have the funds to rebuild the side, Ernest Mangnall left United during the summer – for their greatest rivals, Manchester City. It was as devastating a blow as when Billy Meredith had crossed the city to join United in 1906. Soon, others from that great team, such as Charlie Roberts and Alex Bell, would leave the club. United received transfer fees of £1500 and £1000 respectively for them, but it had been the players' demands for a second benefit match that had been the cause of them being let go. For United was now struggling financially.

The board minutes for the first few months of the 1910–11 season give some idea as to why this was the case. On 19 September, it was noted that Davies loaned the club £1000; there was a further loan from him of £1000 on 9 November; on 15 November he guaranteed a further £5000 of the club's debts. The following week, Mangnall was asked to negotiate the transfers 'of several of our players . . . owing to the present financial position'.

The club was still paying the builders of Old Trafford, who held debentures that were only slowly being bought back by United. By the end of the season, it was decided that United needed to attract new investors and so the club sent out 20,000 circulars trying to draw interest in the prospectus for a rights issue. When the board looked at the figures, they were so bad that the club had to give the land on which Old Trafford was built to the Manchester Brewery and lease it back, with an option to buy it back at the original purchase price of £10,150. It still wasn't enough: Davies agreed not to take any of the interest owed to him that year, estimated to be around £1031. On top of which, in May and June 1911, Davies loaned the club a further £3000. As the average gate receipts at this time were roughly £500, and often less, these were enormous amounts. Without the Davies piggy bank to raid, sometimes almost on a weekly basis, the club could have gone bankrupt. No wonder he hadn't been receptive to Mangnall's request to go on a big spending spree to rebuild the team.

Indeed, Davies still had plans for further improvements to Old

Trafford, including a new entrance to the ground from the Salford side and the building of a bridge. This work was budgeted at £4000, but, along with a new car park, it would be a further decade before the work was completed.

New secretary-manager J.J. Bentley was a hugely experienced figure, having held a similar position at Bolton Wanderers, as well as being a referee, a member of the United board and president of the Football League for sixteen years to 1910. However, he struggled to win over the changing room, falling out with Sandy Turnbull, which led to a players' revolt. As a consequence of the pressure, his health began to deteriorate. Events on the pitch did little to help him, with United finishing a creditable fourth in 1912–13, but falling back to fourteenth the following season.

By then more serious matters were afoot, as war broke out in summer 1914. It was decided to continue with the full programme for 1914–15, and during this campaign John Robson was brought in to focus on the managerial side of the role, while Bentley took a step back to the secretarial position. United finished eighteenth that season, winning only one game away from Old Trafford all season (their last away fixture, against Chelsea). But it was a 2–0 home victory over Liverpool at the beginning of April that would raise eyebrows, when unusual betting patterns were discovered, causing bookmakers to refuse to pay out. In those days, it was rare to bet on the scoreline, but many had placed bets on United to win 2–0, and as Liverpool had barely mustered a sweat against their rivals it seemed that the match had been fixed. Billy Meredith certainly felt something was afoot, while Robson left the ground while the game was still in progress, apparently in disgust at what he was seeing.

The FA and Football League looked into the matter, and decided that three United players – Sandy Turnbull, Enoch West and Arthur Whalley – as well as four from Liverpool had colluded to fix the result and clean up at the bookies, though West was the only one to have played in the match. With the players' futures looking uncertain because of the war and the fact that their pay would be suspended at the end of the season, perhaps it was inevitable that some would try to ensure they had a little extra to tide them over. All protested their innocence but were banned from the game. However, after the war, because of their military service, all bar West were pardoned.

But before professional football finished for the duration of the First World War, there was one small matter to settle: the winner of the FA Cup. And once again Old Trafford was chosen as the venue – the only time in the entire twentieth century that the final was held outside London, excluding replays. It had been decided that the final would cause too much disruption in London, so an alternative venue was required. Known as 'The Khaki Final', because of the large number of fans watching in their military uniform, the match was comfortably won by Sheffield United, who beat Chelsea 3–0 in front of almost 50,000 fans. Hopes for a bigger crowd were dashed by a combination of wartime travel restrictions and the foggy conditions. But by then, people's minds were moving on to other things.

4

The Lost Years

When football got back to normality for the 1919–20 season, it was to a very different world. The war of 1914–18 had changed so much; Old Trafford had even been used by American servicemen to play baseball. More seriously, all football clubs had suffered tragedy, with players injured or killed in the battlefields of war. Sandy Turnbull, scorer of the first goal at the stadium, was United's most famous victim, killed in action in France in May 1917. For those who did survive, the war had often taken away their best years as a player or their desire to play – after all, what role had sport to play when one had lived through and seen so many horrors?

Some work had been done on improving the side during the war, when a series of regional leagues had been set up. Clarence Hilditch, at centre-half, and full-backs Charlie Moore and John Silcock gave the team a base to build on. Between them, they would go on to play almost 1100 games for United. But the war years had meant United's debts had continued to increase, with little revenue to cover their ongoing costs. There was no chance the club could go out and spend lots of money to provide the spectacle the fans and the stadium required.

United needed to find almost an entire new squad; only Billy Meredith and Wilf Woodcock were anything like regulars in the team in both seasons either side of the war. Meredith was not only now forty-five years old, he was also in dispute with the club, as he wanted a free transfer to join Ernest Mangnall at City and was claiming he was still owed money from his testimonial. He was eventually paid £774 by the club in January 1920, but the board was still holding out for a fee before allowing him to leave.

In the interim, many players had been sold. John Robson continued as the man in charge and he had a major rebuilding job on his hands. He had to do it without the support and involvement of J.J. Bentley, his predecessor as secretary-manager who, for all his shortcomings as a manager, was one of the game's most admired and effective administrators. Bentley died in September 1918, and with him went thirty years of Football League experience, for he had been around since its founding in 1888.

Even more serious than his loss was the decision of John Henry Davies to take something of a step back from the day-to-day running of the club (though his financial involvement with the club continued for the rest of his life). The man whose vision and energy – not to mention his wallet – had built Old Trafford had now had enough. It seemed he had finally brought some financial stability to the club, as United made a profit of £29,591 in the first two seasons after the war. But the boardroom without these two giants of the club was a much lesser place.

Attendances were up across the country, despite the fact that most clubs had put up their prices, thanks to a brief post-war economic boom and the fact that increasing numbers of people had Saturday afternoons off and access to cheap rail fares. United charged £3 3s for season tickets for the seated area of the stadium, though interestingly women were charged only £2 2s (the saving did not encourage that many to come). Entrance to the ground for all matches was £1 1s for the season. At Old Trafford, United's average home league attendance rose from 12,211 in 1914–15 to 26,786 in 1919–20 – the best since their title-winning campaign of 1910–11. But on the pitch, United had to settle for a mid-table finish, and there was no FA Cup run to inspire the fans. The weekly wage bill rose during the first season after the war from about £160 per week in August to almost £200 by December.

The following season, when there were three divisions for the first and only time, crowds increased even more, averaging 37,072. Five times Old Trafford drew in 50,000 or more and, on 27 December 1920, a record league attendance was set at the ground that would last until 2006–07. The money was pouring in: a game against Spurs in October 1920 generated gate receipts of £3136.

It was around this time that Davies made a surprising offer to Manchester City, asking if the club wanted to come and play their first-team games at Old Trafford, without having to pay any rent or a share of the gate receipts to United. The reason for the offer was that City's dilapidated Hyde Road ground was becoming an increasingly dangerous venue for the fans after its main stand burned down; its capacity was often reached, whereas Old Trafford was a modern stadium that could hold many more spectators. It was only a temporary measure, as City was in the process of looking for a venue for a new ground.

It was a bold proposal, and United would undoubtedly have benefited, because the idea was that United's reserve games would have been played at City's Hyde Road ground. Because of its location in the middle of a big working-class area, Hyde Road drew far bigger crowds for reserve games than Old Trafford, which was less convenient for fans to reach, so they tended to opt only to go to first-team games. The difference in gate revenues was marked. United generated just £75 for a reserve-team fixture against Bury at that time, yet City could easily earn £450 and pull in crowds of 14,000 for its equivalent matches. The new arrangement would have helped transform the reserve team from being a loss-making enterprise into one that could even make a profit.

It didn't take long for the City board to come back to Davies and his colleagues at United. Their response was a firm but polite 'no thank you'. Unlike the modern rivalry across the city, this wasn't because of the political sensitivities, but was down to the practical problems of City fans being forced to travel across Manchester to watch their team. City had also recently spent money on covering its stands, so feared (should it ever rain in Manchester!) more of its fans would get wet at Old Trafford, which was mostly open to the elements. In 1923 City moved to a new stadium of their own at Maine Road.

In all, 70,504 came to see United take on Aston Villa in that record-breaking match during the Christmas break, paying gate receipts of £4824; this pattern was repeated across many football grounds. However, whereas a decade before this would have been a top-of-the-table clash, now it was a game between two sides that were both off the pace. Villa ended up 3–1 winners, and after that game things were never as good again for United. There was a noticeable falling-off in attendances, so by the final game of the season just 10,000 turned up to see United beat relegated Derby to finish in thirteenth place.

However, this wasn't only due to poor weather or fans' disappointment at United's performances. Stronger factors were at play, as the post-war economic boom came to a shuddering halt. As so often throughout the club's history, United's fortunes mirrored those of Manchester. For Cottonopolis's dominance of the world cotton trade was under serious threat, and by 1921 the industry was already in decline. The seeds of this fall had been sown before the war, when the UK had exported some £6.5 million of textile machinery per year. At the time it seemed that no one could threaten Manchester's position, but the war had restricted Britain's ability to export its goods, allowing local producers to step in. Once war was over, and trade could resume more normally, foreign nations wanted to preserve their own smaller industries and the markets became closed off. British mills cut their prices, but it wasn't enough and soon they were going out of business and being closed down. With higher unemployment came a reduction in people's spending power; food and shelter were the first priorities, and football became a luxury fewer could afford.

Fortunately, by this stage United was no longer in debt to Humphreys Ltd, the builders of Old Trafford, with the final payment made in April 1921. The company had been receiving a share of the gate money for some time now to speed up this repayment. Now the club just had one major creditor to pay off: Davies. He was owed the grand total of £28,371 and the club agreed that until this debt was repaid he would receive interest of 7.5 per cent a year, a significant increase from the 5 per cent he'd been getting only a few months previously.

The changing economic climate wasn't immediately apparent; the club's bank account in May 1921 was healthily in credit. But the signs were becoming clearer. In November that year, the club agreed that the Salford Unemployed Workers Committee could take a collection at the ground during a match. A couple of weeks later, the Lord Mayor's Unemployment Fund was collecting at a game. Revenues began to fall, too. The derby against City generated £4123 in gate receipts in November 1920, but only £3682 a year later. With the finances beginning to look a little shaky, Davies agreed to suspend taking his share of the gate receipts for a while.

And some of the fall in attendances may have been due to United's decline on the pitch. At the end of October 1921, 67-year-old John Robson stepped down as manager due to ill health, staying on temporarily as assistant. He bequeathed to his successor a club that was struggling in the league, but far from doomed. John Chapman came with a fine reputation, based on his achievements in Scotland. The team he had helped build, Airdrieonians, would go on to finish second in the Scottish league for four successive seasons. He was therefore able to command a reported four-figure salary, plus a house, from United – exceptionally generous terms for that time (Matt Busby would get less in 1945).

United, with eleven points from their first twelve games, were about to find that things could get worse, as United won just one of Chapman's first fourteen league games in charge. Just before Christmas the club had to dismiss Robson for 'misconduct' –

seemingly arising from an FA investigation into overpayment of a particular player earlier in the year. Within another month Robson was dead of pneumonia, and the club donated £105 to a testimonial fund for his widow and children.

The Reds duly finished the season bottom of the table, eight points from safety. Their defence was leaking goals at an alarming rate, and without the inspirational Meredith or anyone else to create them, goals were not going in at the other end either. Reports of dressing-room splits between the Scots and English in the squad did little to help.

Once relegated, United were unable to bounce straight back to the top division. Somewhat surprisingly, season ticket prices remained unchanged, and United even managed to persuade their caterers to increase their fee for exclusive rights at Old Trafford from £75 per season to £110. With the inaugural Wembley final the prize for the winners, Old Trafford was once again the host of an FA Cup semifinal on 24 March 1923. Bolton took on Sheffield United, and perhaps the lure of Wembley had an impact on the gate that day, as a new record crowd of 73,000 made their way through the turnstiles, which had to be shut with an hour to go. Even so, in the crush, particularly on the Popular Side (the north side), many fans fainted or were passed to the front of the terracing, so they ended up on the edge of the pitch.

Meanwhile, the United fans grew restless, and there were demands that one of their number be appointed to the board; this idea was inevitably rejected. Instead, the board decided to open the ground to the All Blacks for a match against Lancashire during their tour of 1924–25 in return for a 20 per cent share of the gate receipts. As well as the Americans' wartime baseball, hockey and athletics had already been staged at Old Trafford. But this was the first time the ground had been used for rugby, and it was the beginning of an association with both codes of the game that continues to this day.

It was only in 1924–25 that United finally amassed enough points to be promoted. The outcome was essentially guaranteed at

Old Trafford in the Reds' penultimate game of the season. A crowd of 33,500 saw United beat Port Vale 4–0, one of their biggest wins of the season, and no one left until the Tannoy announcement came through to say that promotion rivals Derby County had been held by Coventry. The relief and joy were unconfined, as the band played 'Auld Lang Syne' to celebrate.

By now John Chapman's methods had finally begun to bear fruit. His focus on defence meant that United conceded only six league goals at home all season. Frank Barson, one of the most intimidating defenders ever to don the United shirt, was a key figure in United's parsimony. He had joined the club three seasons before from Aston Villa, signed for £5000, a huge amount at the time. A former blacksmith, he tackled as hard as a hammer, and wasn't too worried whether he got the ball or the man. A straight-talking Yorkshireman, he was even known to warn the referee that he was seeking retribution if he believed an opponent had fouled one of his team-mates. Unsurprisingly, his disciplinary record bore little resemblance to that of Stanley Matthews.

United's fifty-seven goals scored, however, contrasted wildly with Division Two champions Leicester City's ninety. Their main goal threat came from Joe Spence, who had played in the Reds' first post-war game and was a regular with United all the way to the end of 1932–33. He would eventually score 168 goals for the club, often cutting in from the wing to do so, and more often than not during this period was the man most likely to get the crowd going. In truth, the team was hard to beat, but hard to love.

United remained in Division One until 1931, when they were relegated with just twenty-two points, bottom of the table by nine points and conceding 115 goals in the process. Their best season in this six-year spell at the top was their first, when they finished ninth and reached the FA Cup semifinal for the only time between the wars. Over 41,000 turned up to Old Trafford to see United back in Division One, and a 3–0 victory over Aston Villa suggested that the good times might be returning, but that was to be the biggest league crowd of the season apart from the Manchester derby, when 48,657 saw United humiliated 6–1 by City – their worst ever defeat to their local rivals.

The Cup run was another matter. Having beaten Port Vale away, and then drawn against Tottenham, Old Trafford hosted the fourth-round replay, when goals from Clatworthy 'Charlie' Rennox and Spence saw United through to the next round, where they faced Sunderland. Having held them in a gripping 3–3 draw at Roker Park, 58,661 fans turned up to see the replay in Manchester. A 2–1 victory meant they were through to the quarterfinal, but this didn't guarantee that the fans were there to stay, for United's next home match, against perennial rivals Liverpool, drew a crowd of just 9214 – the midweek scheduling keeping most people away. When United beat Fulham away, they set up a semifinal encounter against Manchester City who, despite their recent victory over the Reds, were battling against relegation. Wembley beckoned for the first time, but City won comfortably in a poor game to stop that happening. United would have to wait another twenty-two years for their next chance.

A further sign that Old Trafford was back in the big time came on 17 April 1926 when the ground hosted its first international. In those days, even after the completion of Wembley in 1923, England's matches were held at various stadiums around the country – it wasn't until the 1950s that the London venue became England's 'home'. It was arguably the biggest game in the international calendar of the time that came to Manchester: the Home International against Scotland. A crowd of some 49,000, including 10,000 Scots (many of whom invaded the pitch before the kickoff), turned out to see Scotland ease home 1–0 winners on their way to taking the championship. No United players were selected for either side on that occasion.

If United supporters thought all this was going to be the beginning of a revival, they were to be frustrated. Early the following season, John Chapman was suspended as manager by the FA 'for improper conduct in his position as Secretary-Manager' for the rest of the campaign. What was behind this decision remains unclear to this day. Whatever the case, the United board were effectively forced to fire him, and brought in United's first and only player-manager, Clarence Hilditch, to run things for the rest of the season. Hilditch had joined the club during the war and would continue playing for United until 1932. He did what was required of him, and not only kept United up but also balanced the books.

In fact, during that season, the United board took up the option to buy the freehold of Old Trafford, which was costing the club £1300 a year in rent and rates. A deal was concluded with the Manchester Brewery Company in March 1927 whereby the club would pay the brewery £21,350 for the freehold and unpaid rent. To pay for it, United took out a mortgage. A few months later, Davies died. The man who had saved United in the past, and whose money and vision had been so crucial to the building of Old Trafford, was gone. He may have been more of a background figure in recent years, but his passing, just after United had taken on this huge commitment, could not have been timed worse. The new chairman of the club was George Harry Lawton.

On the playing side, the new man who took charge in 1927–28 was Herbert Bamlett, a former referee, but also an experienced manager who was used to working to a tight budget with struggling clubs – and that was just what United had now become. In one of the most extraordinary seasons ever, when just seven points separated Derby County in fourth place from bottom-placed Middlesbrough, United achieved the great escape, winning their last three games to stay up, one point clear of the drop zone. In their last game, United took on Liverpool in front of more than 30,000 at Old Trafford and trounced them 6–1, their biggest ever win against the Merseysiders, with the ever-reliable Joe Spence scoring a hat-trick to round off his best season for the club with twenty-four goals.

With the decline of the cotton industry hitting the Manchester economy increasingly hard, crowds were falling year on year at Old Trafford, down now by 10 per cent on the first season back at the top. Things were about to get even worse, as 1929 would see the Wall Street Crash and the beginning of the Great Depression; the previous years soon seemed like a golden era. Attendances tumbled from an average of over 25,000 in 1927–28 to just 11,685 in 1930–31 when the team was relegated, the worst attendances for United since 1902–03 and the worst of all time at Old Trafford.

In 1928–29 United again flirted with relegation; after 27 games they had just 17 points and were looking certainties for relegation, but the last 15 matches brought 24 points – a run that was title-winning form. Scottish forward Tom Reid scored thirteen goals in that period, while local lad Jimmy Hanson scored nine. One key to this remarkable revival was that, apart from a few changes at full-back, where duties were shared between three players, there were only two changes in personnel in these games, whereas previously the side had been more unsettled.

Things didn't improve the next season, and so began United's worst ever campaign in the top level. In the autumn of 1930, the Reds lost the first twelve games of the season – the worst start any team has ever made to a top-flight season – conceding a horrendous forty-nine goals in the process. When their luck finally changed, and Birmingham City were beaten 2–0 at Old Trafford at the beginning of November, there were just 11,479 hardy souls there to see the match.

The fans hadn't given up on the players, but they knew that changes were required at the top level on the board and with the manager; they understood that new players had to be signed. A Manchester United Supporters' Club was formed, and George H. Greenhough, a shareholder in the club, was elected its secretary. He was hardly a troublemaker: his club would regularly help out with small maintenance tasks, or cleaning the terraces. He claimed that the board's accounts did not give a full picture, and that it was unclear where the money was going. The supporters noted that the club was spending money on building a new road on the Popular Side of the ground when it was the team that urgently needed money spending on it, rather than the surroundings that drew in fewer and fewer people.

The Supporters' Club put forward a five-point plan to the board, but chairman Lawton refused even to meet them, claiming they did not speak for the vast majority of fans. Given that perhaps 3000 of them (roughly a quarter of Old Trafford's attendance at that time) gathered at Hulme Town Hall in mid-October 1930 to discuss what their next step might be, after they had been snubbed, this was a dubious debating point. The motion to boycott the following evening's fixture against Arsenal was carried by a huge majority, despite a call from former captain Charlie Roberts for everyone to get behind the players.

The following day, heavy rain fell and the visit of champions-to-be Arsenal drew a crowd of over 23,000, the second highest of the season after the derby, but expectations had been that the crowd could have been double that. Whether it was the rain or the boycott that prevented more from turning up, we will never know. The United board received letters of support from other clubs' boards, and the press was largely supportive of them against the fans. At this time, the club and its players really did 'belong' to the board to do with as they pleased. Whatever the truth of the matter, United lost again.

The picture of a board out of touch with the realities of the situation is hard to avoid. None of this controversy makes its way into the board minutes of the time. Indeed, the minutes become increasingly terse. Mention is made of the BBC requesting permission to broadcast commentaries of the second half of two games from the ground (delaying the broadcast until then to ensure everyone who might have gone to the game was securely in the ground); the directors turned them down. A week later, Allied Newspapers wanted to interview the manager and the board, giving them a great opportunity, perhaps, to explain their side of things and to issue a rallying cry to fans; the directors turned them down as well.

The downward spiral continued and, towards the end of the

season as United's relegation was confirmed, attendances twice dipped below 4000. No one needed a call for a boycott to persuade them not to go and watch their team lose again. After all, they had conceded 115 goals in the campaign while their 22 points was a record low.

To no one's surprise, Herbert Bamlett was sacked before the season ended, but United's board decided to ask club secretary Walter Crickmer, assisted by Louis Rocca, to run the team. These two stalwarts of the club could obviously be relied upon for their loyalty, but neither was exactly what was needed to bring about a recovery. That autumn, paralysis seemed to have afflicted the board; each week the minutes record some new creditor emerging to demand payment. Occasionally they responded by asking them to hold fire, so mortgage repayments were postponed even though they were £442 behind. When the taxman came asking for unpaid income tax, the board merely decided to 'delay consideration to the next meeting'. When that meeting came, they postponed discussion until the next time. It couldn't go on like this for much longer.

The debts kept on rising, with the overdraft at the bank growing by about £500 a month, and the board was now desperately searching for ways to save money, even asking the fans to help out with the players' laundry. In these circumstances, there was little chance of United bouncing straight back up to Division One, and so perhaps drawing in new support. Indeed, a mid-table position in 1931–32 was a pretty decent effort in the circumstances; crowds were even up slightly on the year before, though not significantly enough to prevent further day-to-day losses.

With the banks owed £30,000 in mortgages and overdrafts, and the gas cut off because of non-payment of bills, the players were in danger of not being paid. One of the players, Jimmy Hanson, had to call in a solicitor to sue for unpaid benefit money. As bankruptcy loomed, George Lawton called for new investors to come in. Just as had happened thirty years previously, when John Henry Davies had stepped forward, this time United had their Christmas saviour in James William Gibson, the owner of a Collyhurst-based clothing company that specialised in producing uniforms. The board minutes of 21 December 1931 record that he offered to 'be responsible for the liabilities of the club' until 9 January. Hanson was paid, but Gibson wanted the entire board to resign.

Like Davies before him, he wasn't a football man, but saw a key Manchester institution threatened and wanted to help as the Great Depression reached its nadir. His first investment of £2000 at least ensured that the immediate day-to-day expenses could be met. In early January, he took over the mortgage liabilities, and announced he would make a press appeal for investors to raise £20,000; ideally he wanted ten backers, each providing a further £2000. At this stage, he was formally appointed to the board, and became club chairman when the old board resigned on 19 January; the new board included George Westcott, Matthew Newton and Albert Thomson. Gibson also wanted the fans to back him, and they responded enthusiastically to a man who at least provided some sort of vision and drive. He even met George Greenhough, who immediately backed the new regime, and the Supporters' Club became an official part of the United set-up (as long as they didn't embarrass the board). They were allowed to put up a hut on the Popular Side for the comfort of the club's members.

Recognising United were in a relegation fight, the new board bought Ernest Vincent from Southport for £1575, Leslie Lievesley and John Moody from Doncaster for £1000, Louis Page from Burnley for £1050 and Arthur Fitton from West Brom for £1000 in the first two months. Three more signings would follow during the next month, costing almost £4000 between them. Press rumours that the club was considering leaving Old Trafford were swiftly denied, and land between the railway line and the Stretford End was made available as a practice ground. As the last game of the season took place at Southampton, Gibson decided to let the players stay over in Bournemouth. He also paid for a dinner to celebrate the fact that they had, in the end, comfortably avoided relegation, largely due to a run of eight games from 30 January when they took fifteen points. New players, fans reassured, new directors, and even the bank was happy for United to run up an overdraft of £10,478 by the end of April – the club had a long way to go, but at least there was now some stability.

The temporary arrangement with Crickmer and Rocca finished after the end of the season. Clearly, if progress was to be made, a permanent manager was required. So for the start of the 1932–33 season, another Scot, Scott Duncan, was appointed manager with a two-year contract on a salary of £800 per year, with a bonus of £100 if he got United into the top four of the Second Division, and a further £100 if they were promoted. The top-price season ticket was set at £3 3s for good seats, while ground entrance season tickets were £1. Duncan declared that he wasn't looking for star names, but wanted to build a team. This cautious approach may not have set the pulse racing, but it was a realistic one given the circumstances. United needed stability more than anything else while the new board tried to revive the club's organisation. One of his first signings was Tommy Frame, who came in from Cowdenbeath for £1300, and whose shirt can still be seen in the Old Trafford museum. More Scots arrived that season, including Stewart Chalmers from Hearts, William Stewart from Cowdenbeath for a relatively hefty £2350, and Neil Dewar from Third Lanark for the huge sum of £5000. By this stage, including match fees, players were earning a maximum of £8 per week.

That season, crowds again increased to a level last seen four years before and the team ended up sixth, but a long way off the pace of the promoted sides. Early on in the campaign, the board agreed to build a roof over much of the Popular Terrace and carry out various other improvements at a cost of almost £36,000; it was the first major rebuilding works since Old Trafford had been built. It was an ambitious plan at a time when attendances were still not great and the overdraft continued to rise. Meanwhile, the Supporters' Club was causing trouble, as their hut was being used by all and sundry, much to the disgust of the official supplier of cups of tea, who had paid for the exclusive rights and now found his customers deserting him.

Gibson continued to ensure everyone was supporting the new board's efforts. Before the new season started, he entertained the local sports editors to lunch at Queens Hotel to help keep them onside. Any hopes that this was the beginning of a revival on the pitch looked doubtful when United failed to win any of the first five games in 1933–34, and as the season progressed it soon became clear they were in another relegation battle. The club's finances continued to be tricky: because of arrears on its payments to the Manchester Brewery, it was agreed they would take a £100 cut from each home game; the overdraft continued to rise, reaching over £18,000 by early January.

Even the board was clearly not a happy place: two of the three members Gibson had brought in resigned, Westcott through ill health, but Thomson left saying, 'I cannot work under your chairmanship with that harmony which is necessary.' Lawyer Harold Hardman, who had been part of the old board, returned, while a Dr McLean also joined. Gibson told them he could not continue to guarantee all of United's debts with no security. He agreed to guarantee an overdraft of up to £30,000, but only if he had a charge over Old Trafford and the club's assets. Effectively, United's assets were now owned by the Manchester Brewery Company and James Gibson.

The unthinkable, that United might become a Division Three side, was a real possibility. Duncan chopped and changed his side with bewildering regularity, using thirty-eight players all told, but this was no modern-style rotation strategy, this was panic and confusion. New players were signed in a desperate attempt to save the season. When United drew their last home game, against Swansea City, the players left Old Trafford knowing that only victory at relegation rivals Millwall would keep them up; a draw and Millwall would survive. United won 2–0 and the returning players were greeted as heroes by large crowds in Manchester. In truth, this was hardly cause for celebration. Things had to improve.

And they did. The key summer signing of George Mutch from Arbroath for £900 provided much-needed firepower up front, and although it would take him a few games to break his duck, once he did he became a regular on the score-sheet, scoring more than forty times over the following two seasons. The club was once more making a profit, albeit a small one of £4490 in 1934–35. One of the most significant developments that would have far-reaching benefits came when Gibson persuaded Cheshire Lines, who ran the railway line that passed by Old Trafford, to build a station by the ground and to run special match-day trains, costing tuppence each way. Now fans could get directly to the ground even if they lived outside the city. As many would have previously had to come by foot, this immediately helped raise attendances. Gibson's business acumen meant he could persuade others of the benefits they would receive from such ideas, while ensuring that the real winner was Manchester United. It seems staggering that it had taken all this time for the railway company finally to agree to something Archibald Leitch had suggested before the ground was even built.

The next season, United won promotion back to Division One, going unbeaten from early January to the end of the campaign. They went up as champions just a point clear of Charlton Athletic, but it wasn't clear cut that this would be the case when they played their final game at Old Trafford, with two away fixtures to come. As it turned out, they still needed a point from their last match at Hull City, which was what they duly achieved. Manager Duncan received a bonus of £300 for his achievements. During the summer, much work was done to improve Old Trafford, which had not seen top-division football for more than five years.

A crowd of over 42,000 turned out to see United take on Wolves in the first home game of the season in the expectation that Fortress Old Trafford would still be working, as it had done in Division Two. A 1–1 draw showed United would be hard to beat, and so it proved with the Reds losing just four times all season at home. But their away form was awful, as they had to wait until after Christmas for their first win on the road and

United ended up going straight back down. But at least the crowds were back: an average home league attendance of 32,332 was the biggest since the post-war boom year of 1920–21, and the club made a healthy profit of £10,486.

Back in Division Two, United did not immediately look like promotion candidates. Scott Duncan's days were numbered, but before he left he made two signings that would have a vital impact in the years to come: Johnny Carey was spotted by Louis Rocca in Ireland and quickly snapped up, while Jack Rowley was brought in from Bournemouth for £3000 in mid-October. It was part of a new focus the club was giving to youth and improving its scouting arrangements. If United couldn't spend big sums to bring in the best talent from other clubs, it made sense to discover that talent in the first place. Backed by Gibson's money, Walter Crickmer and Louis Rocca set up the Manchester United Junior Athletic Club (MUJAC) in 1938 to help give this youth policy a proper focus. Assisted by three teachers – Maurice Williams, his brother and John Bill – Rocca's team became a familiar sight around the playing fields of Manchester. Rocca, a stocky man whose family sold ice cream, was tenacious in getting the best for United, even if his methods were sometimes a little unorthodox – he once donated four freezers of his family's ice cream to Stockport in return for them releasing a player to United.

Duncan was not around to see the results from the first two products of this policy, as he moved to Ipswich (his wife had been advised to move away from polluted Manchester to the country because of her poor health). Crickmer was once again put in charge, and almost immediately results picked up. As they'd done two years before, United went on a strong run in the second half of the season. While Aston Villa were always the likeliest winners, there was a hard-fought battle for the second promotion spot between United, Sheffield United and Coventry City. A crowd of 53,604, the biggest of the season, came to cheer on the Reds in their home fixture against Bury, knowing a win would see them through. Goals from Bill McKay and Jack Smith were enough to record a 2–0 victory; Smith had been signed from Newcastle in February for the large sum of £6500, but that goal certainly helped to justify some of the fee. United were back at the top, and this time they were going to stay there.

The return to the First Division brought about more invest-ment in the stadium. Some £35,000 was spent on roofing the quadrants at either end of the Main Stand, redecorating the changing rooms and a new treatment room. The 1938–39 season saw United finish safely but unspectacularly in fourteenth place – it was actually the club's best position in a decade. This time the club was getting more ambitious. The board minutes of September note that they put in an inquiry to sign Stanley Matthews from Blackpool. Nothing came of it, but it signified a real change in attitude.

The work done by the club on upgrading the stadium meant it was once again chosen as a venue for the FA Cup semifinal, and on 25 March Grimsby took on Wolves for the honour of going to Wembley. Surprisingly, of all the matches that have ever been played at Old Trafford, including many semifinals, it was this one that created the all-time record attendance: 76,962 saw Wolves thrash Grimsby 5–0. With gate receipts that day of £8193, it helped ensure the club made a profit for the fifth successive season, this time of £5993.

James Gibson had a vision that United would be a club that could give local pride to the city that had been through such a dif-ficult period. The economy was getting stronger, and so was United. In the summer, the club signed a 21-year lease on the Cliff, United's new training ground, at an annual rent of £136.

Unfortunately, all this progress was about to come to a shud-dering halt as war broke out in September 1939 and all football was immediately suspended.

Fans who recall those pre-war days remember having a remark-able freedom to move around the ground. Of course, with the vast majority of fans standing, rather than being seated, this was easier. Wilf Sudlow was at the derby match against City in September

1936, one of 68,796 in the crowd that day to see a 3–2 United victory. His main memory of the day was being passed down over the heads of the fans to a whitewashed wall at the front, after getting squashed among the crowds higher up in the stands and getting soaked in the Manchester drizzle. On more normal match-days, with the crowds perhaps half as big, Bob Tinker recalls being able to wander among the crowd collecting cigarette cards. For Laurence Cassidy, 'people were always friendly . . . dressed decently for the game'. Stan Orme was almost the archetypal fan, coming from Sale, an area that had always backed United since the club moved out to Old Trafford. He saw it as his local club, just as James Gibson hoped would be the case. There were, Orme noted, 'virtually no women at games then', but despite this there were no fears about going either.

5

Rebuilding United and Old Trafford

When the nation went to war against Hitler's Germany, attempts were made to maintain some sort of normality at home. Churchill believed that giving fans the opportunity to watch football was good for morale. So, after Old Trafford had been briefly requisitioned as a depot for the army, the sport continued in a series of wartime leagues and cups, often with surprising players guesting for teams, because they happened to be stationed in the vicinity. For them it was a way of earning a little extra on top of their military wage. Clubs continued to recruit players, after a fashion, in the hope that the war would soon come to an end and their new signings would benefit them in the longer term.

But at United, things suddenly became very much more complicated eighteen months into the war. John Henry Davies's visionary decision to locate the ground in the Trafford Park area of Manchester, close to the Ship Canal and the attendant docks, railway lines, factories and other essential industrial facilities, meant that Old Trafford was in the middle of a prime target for the *Luftwaffe*. Trafford Park was hit on 22 December 1940, with Old Trafford taking some minor damage.

The directors and staff of Manchester United pose in their new stadium. John Henry Davies is standing in the centre, wearing a top-pocket handkerchief, J.J. Bentley is next to him holding a cigar, and Louis Rocca is seated, wearing a pale overcoat.
(Manchester United)

'Rocca's Brigade', some wearing red and white suits, sitting in the Main Stand, ready for Old Trafford's first game, against Liverpool, on 19 February 1910.
(Manchester United)

A celebration meal to mark the opening of Old Trafford. The architect, Archibald Leitch, is second from the right.
(Manchester United)

The United team line-up for 1911-12. In the club's first full season, they had won the league title. Secretary-manager Ernest Mangnall is standing on the left, star winger Billy Meredith is seated in the middle row next to him, and captain Charlie Roberts is two along, next to the trophy. *(David Stacey)*

Sandy Turnbull, scorer of Old Trafford's first goal and a victim of the First World War, takes guard while Enoch West is ready to catch anything. *(Getty Images)*

An early aerial shot of Old Trafford reveals just how open to the elements most of the 80,000 capacity were. *(Getty Images)*

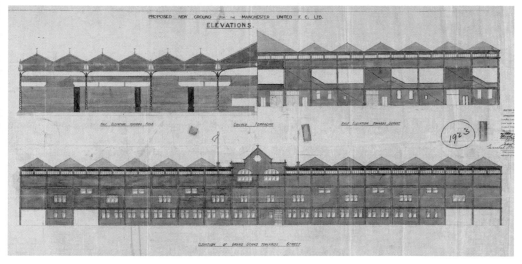

One of the original drawings of the outside of the stadium produced by Archibald Leitch, in association with local firm Brameld and Smith. *(Trafford Borough Council)*

Action from United's October 1913 clash with Tottenham. In the background, you can see the huge entrance tunnel for the fans in the middle of the stand, one of the features of Archibald Leitch's design.
(Getty Images)

The Khaki Cup final, 24 April 1915, was the only time in the twentieth century that a venue outside London was originally chosen to host the event. The captains of Chelsea and Sheffield United shake hands before kickoff on the muddy pitch.
(Getty Images)

Even before the famous 'White Horse' final of 1923, police had to call in animal reinforcements to bring the crowd under control for the semi-final at Old Trafford when a then-record crowd of 73,000 came to see Bolton take on Sheffield United. *(Getty Images)*

While United's crowds dwindled to 4000 in 1930-31, the magic of the FA Cup could still attract packed crowds to Old Trafford for the semi-final between West Brom and Everton. *(Getty Images)*

Walter Crickmer (left) and Scott Duncan in November 1935, during United's promotion campaign. Between them, these two managed the team from 1931 to 1945. *(Mirrorpix)*

Old Trafford shows the devastation caused by the bombs that hit the stadium on the night of 11 March 1941. The club wasn't even allowed to clear up the mess until late in 1945. *(Mirrorpix)*

The Main Stand as it looked in December 1948, when government inspectors finally gave United a licence for rebuilding work to commence. *(Mirrorpix)*

Back in action at Old Trafford, United beat Bolton Wanderers 3-0 on 24 August 1949 in front of a crowd of 41,478. This picture is taken from high up on the uncovered Main Stand, with the covered quadrant at the Scoreboard End just visible on the right. *(Mirrorpix)*

Johnny Carey leads United off the pitch after their 6-1 win over Arsenal to secure the league title on 26 April 1952. The patched-up roof on the Popular Side is visible in the background. *(Mirrorpix)*

Seventeen-year-old Duncan Edwards trains on an incredibly heavy Old Trafford pitch in January 1954. He was the personification of Busby's faith in his young players. *(Press Association)*

Busby watches over Jackie Blanchflower, another of his 'Babes', as he takes on the crossword in the players' lounge before a match early in 1955. *(Mirrorpix)*

Then as now, just ahead of the European Cup semi-final against Real Madrid in April 1957, the sprinklers get to work on the Old Trafford pitch. *(Mirrorpix)*

Action from the game – the first European tie to be played at Old Trafford. Here United attack in their silky red shirts, but the final score of 2-2 was not good enough to take them through to the final. *(Press Association)*

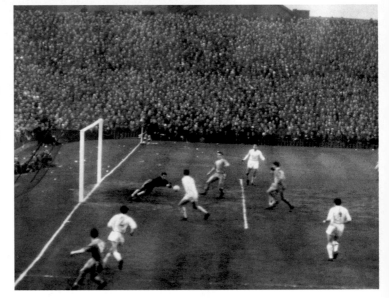

Harry Gregg makes a save in United's last home game before Munich, against Ipswich Town on 25 January 1958. In the background is one of the new floodlight pylons, built the year before. *(Press Association)*

On 11 March 1941, the stadium was hit by two bombs, one of which all but destroyed the Main Stand, dressing rooms and offices, while the other damaged the north end of the terracing on the Popular Side and its roof, and the pitch was hit by incendiaries. The club's offices were moved to a nearby building owned by James Gibson, and from there United put in their application for compensation for war damage. However, there were too many other higher priorities in wartime Britain (not least factories and homes) for Old Trafford to be repaired just so that football could be played on its pitch, so the stadium began to crumble. Despite this, Gibson continued to lobby the government for funds for rebuilding work to start. It wasn't until November 1944 that he received a licence to demolish what was left of the damaged stand, with the War Commission concluding that the stadium wasn't 'a total loss'.

In the circumstances, people pulled together, and so Manchester City offered United the use of their Maine Road ground until Old Trafford was rebuilt in order that they could continue to fulfil their wartime fixtures. Unlike Davies's offer to City a generation before, this support did not come for free. After the war, the club was charged £5000 a year to use Maine Road, with City being granted free usage of Old Trafford for its Central League (reserve) games, where United also played its reserve side.

Unsurprisingly, the club struggled financially during the war, even though there were only two full-time employees: secretary Walter Crickmer and his young assistant, Les Olive. Olive was responsible for sending out postcards to players, with details of meet times, travel instructions and so on (most players at the time did not have phones, so this was the most efficient way of contacting them). He was also responsible for paying the two gatemen, one for adults and one for juniors, who manned the two turnstiles that were open during the reserve team's matches. At one stage, late in 1943, the mortgage interest payments could not be made without taking United beyond its overdraft limit. Gibson agreed to make an interest-free loan to the club to tide it over.

Meanwhile, as the war drew to a close in early 1945, United were looking for a new manager. Louis Rocca knew just the man he wanted, and began writing him a series of letters trying to enthuse his target with the exciting opportunities ahead. He must have been some salesman, for United was not the most appealing prospect at that time. The club had failed to win a trophy since the new man, now aged thirty-five, was a toddler and since then it had flirted with relegation to the Third Division and with bankruptcy, its stadium was in ruins with no clear idea as to how or when it would be repaired, and there hadn't even been a permanent manager since Scott Duncan in 1937. A new team would have to be put together as well, although the MUJACs scheme would help smooth this process.

Happily, Company Sergeant Major Instructor Matt Busby liked a challenge, and the blank canvas United offered him meant he could create a football club in the image he wanted. Busby had played for several years for Manchester City as a half-back, signing for them in 1928, before moving to Liverpool in 1936 until the war effectively ended his playing career. Liverpool had offered him the position of coach, working with manager George Kay, but the appeal of returning to Manchester, combined with the opportunity to be in charge, was too strong. United had its man, and Busby immediately made it clear that he was going to be in sole charge of team matters; there would be no say for the directors on playing issues.

On 19 February 1945, Matt Busby joined United on a salary of £750 a year for four years, although he would not take up the role until October that year after he was demobilised; it was the bargain of the century. A month before he arrived, the club bought him a house at 33 Coleridge Road, Old Trafford, for £1200, reducing his salary to £675 per annum accordingly. His son, Sandy, recalls the sight that greeted them at the stadium and how 'the offices, dressing rooms – all down one side of the ground – they were demolished. The football pitch itself was full of . . . shrapnel and glass. Wooden planks had been thrown onto the ground.' Harold Riley was a young lad when he was one of many given some extra pocket money to help tidy up the pitch, and he remembers: 'Just after the war, we were asked to go and collect glass from the ground . . . By the time we got to the middle, our buckets were full of glass, which was shattered glass from the bombs.' Meanwhile, things were no better in the stands: 'I looked into the Main Stand and there was a tree growing; it was five or six feet high . . . It was a renewal of the place.'

The Salford-born painter could be forgiven some artistic licence in his viewpoint, but for others it must have seemed a mountainous challenge. Busby knew the man he wanted by his side to help rebuild the team: Jimmy Murphy, who had impressed him with his organisational skills during the war. He was the archetypal sergeant-major type, with the language to match. Harry Gregg, who would play under Busby much later, described him as 'football's first diplomat', while Murphy would 'laugh with you, fight with you and cry with you'. Their contrasting personae proved a perfect combination.

The two men worked together throughout Busby's entire career as manager of United, the most enduring partnership in the club's history, with Murphy stepping up from coach to assistant manager in 1955. And, unlike pre-war managers, Busby was with his assistant on the training ground at the Cliff, the first of the so-called 'tracksuit' managers. He wanted to know everything that went on; more to the point, he wanted his players to know that he knew everything that went on as well. Busby and Murphy wanted to ensure they were fit, and that they knew their roles in certain situations, such as defending corners. The preparation involved was far more detailed than the norm at that time. It even extended off the field, where Busby ensured that players were well looked after. In October 1946, Busby persuaded the board that the team should be allowed to go and play golf as part of their preparation, ensuring they got free membership at his club, Davyhulme.

In some senses, rebuilding the team was the easy part for Busby, as most other clubs were in a similar position after the war.

However, Busby had to change the level of expectation at the club. It was no longer going to be a case of hoping to stay in the First Division; he wanted to make the club winners again. In the 1945–46 season, the last before official Football League fixtures resumed, United finished fourth in the North Division, but were knocked out of the FA Cup in the two-legged fourth round. The board had seen enough to award Busby a bonus of £250.

For the 1946–47 season only Johnny Carey, Jimmy Hanlon, Jack Rowley and Jack Warner had played significant roles in United's last pre-war campaign. But the efforts of Walter Crickmer and his squad of scouts to bring in the best young players before the war to play for MUJAC had borne fruit as well, with the likes of John Anderson, John Aston, Allenby Chilton, Charlie Mitten, Johnny Morris and Stan Pearson all still on the books, even if they had little or no experience of the Football League. Many of these players would go on to form the nucleus of Busby's first great team.

It was just as well that the nucleus was there, for there was relatively little money for transfers before the season started. Instead, Busby was able to find new roles in the team for players, with Johnny Aston, Henry Cockburn and Johnny Carey all benefiting from positional changes soon after Busby took over, after he had seen what they could (and could not) do on the training ground.

Rebuilding the ground was proving less straightforward. Attlee's post-war Labour government had set aside funds to help businesses rebuild their facilities if they had suffered bomb damage, but getting access to those funds was not easy. United got a grant of £4800 in August 1945 to clear the rubbish and shrapnel from the ground. Fortunately, then as now, there was political capital to be gained for MPs who were seen to help their football clubs. So, in November 1946, United received another small grant of £1430 to help with the costs of demolishing the remains of the Main Stand, although much of this work had already been done.

Progress remained slow. Some 300 tons of soil and turf were laid on the pitch to bring that back into a fit state to play on, though until the stands were ready the ground would be used only for training and for reserve-team fixtures. The groundsman at the time, a Mr A. Powell, received £4 10s per week for looking after it. Finding the required building materials was the real problem, as they remained in short supply with so much rebuilding under way in the aftermath of the war. For now, Maine Road continued to be the first team's 'home' ground.

In the end, James Gibson persuaded the Stoke MP, Ellis Smith, to get the subject debated in the House of Commons, for United was one of a handful of clubs whose stadiums had been bombed. The club held a meeting (set up by Smith) in December 1947 with the Minister of Works, who explained that as fans were not in any danger while watching from the undamaged areas of Old Trafford, it was not a priority. However, it was added, if the club could find its own materials and use voluntary labour for the rebuilding work, then a licence could be granted. For Gibson, getting this meeting was his final major achievement for United, as he suffered a stroke just before it took place. After 2 December 1947, he was not well enough to attend another board meeting for almost two years, and Harold Hardman stepped in as acting chairman. Gibson's son, Alan, joined the board in February 1948 to look after the family's interests. Finally, in March 1948, the War Damage Commission gave United a grant of £17,478 to help with the reconstruction, and once the necessary steel permits had also been granted, work on rebuilding could begin.

In one of the tightest title races of all time, United just missed out on winning the league that first season of 1946–47, ending up in second place with 56 points, a point behind Liverpool, with Wolverhampton also on 56 points and Stoke City a further point back. With the crowds flocking to football matches in relief that the long years of war were over, the club was finally making some serious profits. Having started the season with an overdraft of £11,000, United ended it with more than £16,000 in the bank. This meant that the second charge on Old Trafford, held by Gibson, was no longer necessary – the document was returned to

United and his guarantee was cancelled in November 1946. The next month, Busby received a pay rise, taking him up to £1000 per year, and at the end of the season he got a bonus of £400, while Murphy's bonus was just £15.

The following season, United again finished runners-up, comfortably behind Arsenal, but went on a great FA Cup run that took them all the way to the final, where they beat Blackpool 4–2 in one of the best Wembley matches. Before the players went on their celebration parade around Manchester, however, they stopped off to visit chairman Gibson in Hale; the man who had saved the club had not recovered sufficiently to go to Wembley, so the FA Cup was brought to him instead. It was a great gesture, and nothing less than he deserved after his work for United. Busby had already received another pay rise earlier in the season, taking him up to £1750 per annum, and now he was granted a bonus of £1750, while the team as a whole received £550 to share for their FA Cup success and £440 for the league performance.

Jack Crompton, United's post-war goalkeeper, recalls those years: 'We were a team. Any one of us could speak for the rest. We were all on the same money, unlike today, and we all got the same bus tickets. Coming from the war helped: we'd all known hard times and the roughness of the war period, and it felt great to be playing the game. They were great pals.' This combination of shared experience and team spirit was not unique to United, but when alloyed to the excellent preparation they received it ensured the Reds would be challenging for honours. The team was also honest with each other, ready to highlight their own shortcomings and look at how to improve things.

By the start of 1948–49, United were still struggling to gain the licences to rebuild the Main Stand, and City had already given notice that not only was the rent to be increased to £6500 for the forthcoming campaign, this was to be the last time United could use Maine Road. United's requests for an extension were repeatedly turned down. A member of the City board was subsequently quoted as grumbling that 'eight years is ample time for a football club to put its house in order'. United's failure to rebuild Old Trafford during the war when the bombs were still falling, or after it when they couldn't gain access to any building materials, was clearly part of some cunning Red ploy that the Blue half of Manchester was not going to fall for any more.

Fortunately, in December local inspectors viewed Old Trafford, stating that a decision on whether work could begin would be taken before the year was out, although it was not until 24 January 1949 that a licence was finally granted. The next month, George Wimpey's quote of £21,726 to build a concrete retaining wall, temporary terracing and toilets in the Main Stand was confirmed, with the War Damage Commission agreeing to reimburse United. Because a separate licence was required (and was turned down in April) to rebuild the roof, the board decided to furnish the stand with slatted seats to ensure they dried as quickly as possible after any rain. Goodalls supplied 3600 seats for two shillings each, and a further nine pence installation fee per chair.

The team continued to challenge for honours, finishing runners-up in the league for the third successive season, and losing out in a replayed semifinal in the FA Cup. But for a falling-out between Busby and Johnny Morris, who was sold to Derby County as a result, it might have been an even better season. Busby was not going to let a player make demands on him – even if he was one of the team's key stars. Intriguingly, despite his firm line on players' demands, in April Busby's salary was again increased to £3250 for three years. Despite the cost of playing at Maine Road, attendances had been so good, averaging 53,624 in the league in 1947–48, that United continued to make good profits, and by December 1949 the club had over £65,000 deposited in the bank. Some of the money was invested in buying property for use by the players. For example, Jimmy Delaney got to live in a house at 177 Kings Road, Stretford, on the far side of the cricket ground from Old Trafford. Bought for £1350, he paid 25s per week to the club in rent.

The race to have Old Trafford ready for the start of the new season was touch and go. The board again contacted City to see if United could play there for a game or two at the start of 1949–50 if work overran, but were once again rejected. Entrance to the ground for the new season was set at 1s 3d, while the covered terrace was 3s 6d. Season tickets for the uncovered enclosure were £5 5s. Fortunately, everything was ready just in time, even if the facilities were somewhat basic.

Although the temporary Main Stand had incorporated toilets, according to Wilf Sudlow, quoted in *Red Voices*, the terraces at that time were not a great place to be: 'Sometimes when the crowd was so great you couldn't get to the toilet and you'd have to pee where you stood . . . There'd be puddles everywhere.' Despite this, fans had their regular places on the terraces, where they would meet up each game, often holding sweepstakes among themselves for who would score the first goal. For many fans, the Beswick Prize Band, who provided half-time entertainment, were a memorable feature of the games. The band received five pounds per match during the 1950–51 season.

The players were getting to know Old Trafford, even before they finally stepped out to play Bolton Wanderers in an evening kickoff on 24 August 1949, just two days under ten years since the previous league game had been played there, as part of the team's training took place there. Jack Crompton recalls how 'we would train there and then go into Manchester to the gym' afterwards. Many of these training sessions took place not on the pitch but between the Main Stand and the railway line, where in the five-a-sides the opponents were the least of a player's worries – the tarmac surface was badly potholed and the passenger barriers from the railway jutted out into the playing area. Players would also do laps around the pitch, or around the stadium; for variation, they might run up and down the terracing. Of course, some had played Central League games there, too.

For Crompton and the players, being back at Old Trafford didn't have quite the significance it did for the fans: 'We were used to the pitch because we'd practised on it, but we'd not played an actual game on it. The crowd was pleased to be "back home". It didn't mean as much to us.' Certainly, there was no improvement in performance that season. Despite christening the ground with a 3–0 victory, Charlie Mitten having the honour of scoring the first goal back in front of a crowd of 41,748, United slipped to fourth in the closely fought title race.

Around the edge of the pitch was a white picket fence. Wilf McGuinness, who joined the club in June 1953, remembers being one of many youngsters who was helped to the front of the stand to watch the game, standing just behind the fence. He even won five shillings once, when his face was picked out from the crowd by the local paper. Like many football-mad kids in Manchester, he would go to games at both City and United, though he did favour United if the two were playing each other. Being helped to the front did have one disadvantage, though, because in those days the pitch was not only raised (as now), but was much more heavily cambered than is the case today, to improve the drainage. This meant that when play was on the near side, one could often see only the players' legs, while if the action was on the far side then the ball disappeared from view. Whatever was done to improve the drainage and the grass, by winter most of the central portion of the ground was mud, with grass clinging on only by the touchline.

Old Trafford may have been ready for action again, but more work was required to bring it back to the state it had been in previously. The Main Stand was still uncovered, with roofing only at the quadrants at either end of the stand, the Stretford and Old Trafford Paddocks, as well as the central part of the Popular Side. An application in May 1950 to rebuild this whole stand was turned down, as was a suggestion to put up temporary roofing. Unfortunately, while what roofing there may have been helped keep the spectators dry, there was danger from another aerial source, as it proved a good roosting place for pigeons. One member of the board was up to the challenge of solving the problem – or at least his chauffeur was. He set about shooting the pigeons, but a consequence was holes in the roof where the bullets had penetrated! Still, given a choice between Manchester rain and pigeon droppings . . . Happily, the wait to put a roof over the Main Stand did not continue for much longer, and in August 1950 a licence was granted. Later that year, permission for further restoration was obtained.

Over the next three years, the Main Stand was completely rebuilt, with modern facilities including a gymnasium and a proper medical room, the latter on the insistence of Dr McLean, one of the board. United's last remaining mortgage debt to the Manchester Brewery and Mrs Davies from the original construction and purchase of Old Trafford was finally paid off in March 1951; United at last possessed the deeds to the land on which Old Trafford was built.

By now, the post-war United side was beginning to change: Charlie Mitten headed out to Colombia for the fortunes seemingly on offer there, £40 a week (the maximum wage in England increased from just £12 to £14 in June 1951); some, like Jack Crompton, were gradually replaced; others, such as Johnny Morris, had been pushed out.

Behind the scenes there were changes, too. On 28 March 1950, Matthew Newton, one of the directors brought in by Gibson in 1932, died. Soon after, on 13 June, the long-serving Louis Rocca, who had been with United quite literally since its birth, also passed away. More recently Rocca had been Busby's chief scout. Later that month, Gibson would attend a board meeting at Old Trafford for the last time. It was in many ways the end of an era.

However, even as one era finished, Busby was looking to the future. He thought the club could further improve its scouting network and youth development, partly because he had seen the success already achieved (more than half of the 1948 FA Cup-winning side were local lads). Joe Armstrong, an old friend from Busby's days at Manchester City, headed up the new scouting system, and the focus was no longer simply on finding the best players in Manchester – now the club scoured the country for the best prospects. Even by the end of the 1960s, there were just eight scouts in the set-up, but plenty of people were willing to tip them off if they thought they'd found someone special. More importantly, Busby said he wanted to bring in young players and train them up 'with a feeling for the club, character-wise, loyalty-wise'. If they owed everything to the manager, they were perhaps less likely to rebel, as Mitten and Morris had done.

The youngsters didn't begin to come through during the 1950–51 season, when United finished runners-up for the fourth time in five attempts, but during the following campaign Busby began to try out one or two of his young starlets. The junior teams often played against open-age sides, so when players graduated to the top team, they were used to playing against men. On 24 November 1951, after United had drawn 0–0 at Anfield, Tom Jackson's *Manchester Evening News* report, noting the presence of debutants Jackie Blanchflower and Roger Byrne in the side, was headlined 'United's "Babes" Cool, Confident'. The term stuck, especially as both men settled into the first team without fear, though only the latter kept a regular place in the side that season.

Sadly, James Gibson, who had supported the original MUJAC set-up before the war, did not live to see the birth of the 'Babes', as he suffered another stroke and died on 11 September 1951. Harold Hardman succeeded him as chairman, paying fulsome tribute to the man who had saved the club: 'By his unbounded enthusiasm, personal help and guidance, he has been the driving force' of Manchester United.

Hardman was appropriately named. Jack Crompton, when he returned to the club in a coaching capacity, recalls his chairman's thoughts on the much-debated topic of substitutes: 'Bloody substitutions. If they can't stand up for ninety minutes they shouldn't be playing the bloody game.' But this wasn't just the view of someone with no knowledge of the game. Hardman had been an FA Cup winner with Everton and an England international before the war – the First World War, that is – and had played briefly for United, making four appearances in 1908. He lived in an equally down-to-earth manner. When Jimmy Murphy once saw him standing at a bus stop in the pouring rain, he suggested that his chairman could take a taxi, 'but all he said was that . . . the bus was good enough' and if one didn't come, he would walk home, a distance of four or five miles.

That season, 1951–52, United finally won the elusive league title. By the final Saturday, Busby's team were all but guaranteed to be champions – only visitors Arsenal could overhaul them, and they needed to win by seven clear goals at Old Trafford. A crowd of 53,651, the biggest of the season except for the Manchester derby, came along to ensure the unthinkable didn't happen. Jack Rowley settled any nerves, scoring after eight minutes from a long ball from Johnny Carey, before an injury to Arsenal centre-half Arthur Shaw reduced Arsenal to ten men midway through the first half. Thereafter, it was all United, with Rowley going on to complete his fourth hat-trick of the season, Stan Pearson scoring twice and Roger Byrne (playing on the wing) adding another: 6–1 the final score. As the players came off the pitch, the fans poured onto it, climbing over the picket fence to celebrate United's first title in forty-one years. This was what Old Trafford had been built for, and what it had missed for so long.

The good times hadn't arrived just for Manchester United. The period of post-war austerity was beginning to come to an end, with rationing increasingly limited to fewer and fewer items. After the inter-war depression, followed by the horrors of the Second World War, there seemed to be a new calm and stability in the country. Unemployment was at historically low levels, especially in Trafford Park and the Manchester docks, and the new welfare state gave everyone something to fall back on if ever hard times should strike. But the city was still a grim, polluted place devoted to industry, with factory chimneys puffing out smoke; smog was a regular feature of people's lives.

Somewhat surprisingly, however, during the first few seasons of the rebuilt Old Trafford, attendances for United's home matches were lower than their average away crowds; it wasn't until 1955–56 that this changed, with the first title success of the Busby

Babes. Thereafter, in only one season (1961–62) would United ever attract more fans away than at home. Busby's United hadn't yet entirely captured the imagination of their home city.

But one who had been excited by United was Wilf McGuinness, for very personal reasons. He'd already been the England Under-14 captain, and as such was courted by many clubs. He was among a 21,000 crowd that went to watch United's youngsters in action in the 1953 Youth Cup final, a midweek tournament that began that season: 'When I saw the youth team play for United, Duncan Edwards was left-half and the right-half was Eddie Colman, and they beat Wolves seven–one. I saw what they'd done for Eddie – and he wasn't even playing for England – so I wondered what were they going to do for me?'

Edwards had been signed in June the previous year at the age of fifteen. Plenty of scouts had been monitoring his development at Dudley Boys, but he wanted to join United, and when Matt Busby went to see him in action the deal was quickly concluded. He made his debut for United before the season was over. But it was an injury to Henry Cockburn that gave him his first sustained run in the team and, as he told *Charles Buchan's Football Monthly*, Cockburn would 'give me tips about my opponent. Those tips usually proved invaluable to me.' Soon, opponents would need tips on how to deal with Edwards.

With John Doherty, Bill Foulkes, Eddie Lewis, David Pegg, Jack Scott, Tommy Taylor and Dennis Viollet all also making their debuts in 1952–53, and all of them twenty-one or under, youth was certainly being given its chance. Only Taylor had been signed from another club, struggling Barnsley, for the then astonishing fee of £29,999, just short of the British record at the time. In his short career, he was already averaging roughly two goals every three games, a phenomenal rate he maintained at United. Busby, who had previously been quoted as saying, 'I do not believe you can buy success,' knew there would always be exceptions to that rule, especially when the club was now making handsome profits. That season also saw not only United's first Charity Shield match at Old Trafford, but also the first to be broadcast live on BBC television, with United beating Newcastle 4–2 in a thrilling game.

With youth and glamour on the United books, it was time for one more of the old guard to step away. Johnny Carey looked like someone from a bygone era, and when he commented in his statement on retiring that 'I don't feel capable of playing the United brand of soccer for another season', one suspects he also felt it when he looked round the changing room and saw the fashionable haircuts of the younger players. His replacement as captain was Roger Byrne, just twenty-four but one of the more experienced characters in the side.

No wonder that a different sort of crowd was beginning to come to Old Trafford. As McGuinness recalls: 'There were a lot of girls, groupies if you like. We noticed them as we ran out, but our minds were focused on the game. But we used to think, there's the girls cheering us on, because they stayed there every week. It was unbelievable. And they still do, some of them. Some of them are there from when we were young lads, which is wonderful.' In this period, admission to the ground was 2s, the covered terrace was 3s 6d, and good seats cost 6s 5d, or £6 10s for a season ticket. As had been the case before the war, some fans still changed positions at half-time, so they were always watching from the end United were attacking.

United's emphasis on youth proved to be in the vanguard of the cult of the teen that developed throughout the 1950s. Rock and roll formally announced itself in 1955 with Bill Haley's 'Rock Around The Clock'; James Dean and Marlon Brando would provide a Hollywood version of youthful rebellion; then Elvis would get the world onto the dance floor. The Western hemisphere had finished with looking back at the sombre events of the war; now it wanted to look forward with those who had not been caught up and scarred by it all. As so often before, developments at Old Trafford reflected those in the wider world. The new United again reflected a change in the city. In 1956, Granada began transmitting from its Quay Street base; part of the ITV network, it was the fresh voice of television compared to the BBC, and gave the city a media buzz – even if its most famous programme, *Coronation Street*, which started airing in 1960, hardly reflected the glamorous side of Manchester.

Today, when people talk about a star's 'boy next door' appeal, they mean that he seems ordinary and down-to-earth, and that one might conceivably imagine them living next door to one of their fans. Of course, they never do. But United's young players were just that. After all, on a basic wage of £15 per week, plus appearance and win bonuses, they could hardly afford to be anything else. They mostly lived in digs close to Old Trafford or the Cliff, they rode bicycles or went on the bus to go to training, and afterwards they'd head into Manchester to go shopping or to a dance hall. They were very much around, and if you wanted to meet one of your footballing heroes, it was easy enough to do so. Tom Clare recalled how he waited for Edwards before a game: 'The big man would suddenly appear on the forecourt on his bicycle, which he would proceed to tie to a lamppost beside the ticket office with a piece of string.' Similarly, many would wait outside the players' dressing rooms after a game so they could get on the same bus as their idols. But if you didn't follow the game, it would have been difficult to tell them apart from other young men of the time. No wonder Manchester would become increasingly united by them.

The summer of 1953 saw the arrival of two new recruits who are still familiar figures around Old Trafford today, Bobby Charlton and Wilf McGuinness. Both England Boys internationals, they signed for the club in Coronation Week. The latter recalls how even as part of the youth set-up, Old Trafford became a familiar home: 'When I signed professional, we trained most of the time at the Cliff, but when we trained at Old Trafford we usually had a practice game on a Tuesday where everybody wanted to play well. There was the Stretford Paddock where the top layer was made out of wood and it was easy on our feet and limbs because the wood was very springy. We did a lot of work inside, lapping round the ground four times, and then went in the gym and did exercises. The gym was only small.'

The season that followed found United still some way short of title-winning form, as Busby built from a pragmatic base. The Reds' defence was the second best in the land, conceding just two goals more than champions Wolves, while their attack scored 'only' seventy-three goals, just five more than bottom-placed Liverpool. Home attendances slipped to under 34,000. The benefits of all the changes hadn't yet come through, and the fans were still to be per-suaded that Old Trafford was an essential destination.

The year after, United became more adventurous, the third highest scorers in the league, with Dennis Viollet and Tommy Taylor each scoring twenty goals. But results swung wildly: one week they were losing 5–0 at home to City, a few weeks later they were beating Sheffield United 5–0. Sometimes the thrilling attack and the careless defending combined in one fixture, as when United beat eventual champions Chelsea 6–5 at Stamford Bridge in October 1954. In a sense, this inconsistency is what you might expect of a side packed with youthful exuberance.

But Busby certainly was convinced he was right to put his trust in the new blood, comforted by the fact that United won the Youth Cup again in 1954, once more beating Wolves in the final. Bobby Charlton and Wilf McGuinness had joined the likes of Eddie Colman, Duncan Edwards, David Pegg and Albert Scanlon in the line-up. In 1955, against West Brom, Shay Brennan became the latest to join the production line as United completed a hat-trick of Youth Cup triumphs. With the pressure from below, competition for places remained high; senior players such as Henry Cockburn were sold on to allow Edwards and his team-mates their space; the transfer market was left to others to recruit from.

Finally, all that had been hoped for from this new generation came together during the 1955–56 season. Not only the team had improved, so had the stadium, with an extra 3000 seats provided and new bars. The team also benefited from the work that had been done over the summer, as the home and away dressing rooms had been redeveloped and redecorated, each with its own communal bath that could accommodate the whole team, plus hot and cold showers. The medical room had, according to Busby, 'some of the most modern electrical equipment available for treatment of various types of soccer injury'. Above these facilities were the boardroom, the manager's office, the players' lounge with its billiards and table tennis tables, and a refreshment room where the final scores from matches around the country were displayed.

The signs were there early on that season when United took on Wolves at Old Trafford in October. If any side could be said to have rivalled United during the 1950s, it was Wolverhampton, who had finished in the top three in each of the previous three seasons and would do so again this time. It was a real top-of-the-table clash, so Busby threw in a debutant against them, Wilf McGuinness, who recalls the occasion: 'We scored a last-minute goal to win the game [4–3] – we did it even then. I remember the crowd being a full house cheering you on; if you made a mistake, they lifted you as though it didn't matter and you carried on. It was absolutely brilliant.'

It wasn't immediately plain sailing, but in the last third of the season from the start of February, United would go undefeated and ended up romping home to the league title by a huge margin of eleven points. The average age of the side was just twenty-two, but they had plenty of experience already: the eleven most regular members of the team had over 1100 league appearances for United between them by the end of the season. Of the regular eleven, only Eddie Colman made his debut that campaign, and he'd been part of the Youth Cup side since 1953 so knew all about playing the United way.

The title was confirmed when United beat runners-up Blackpool 2–1 at Old Trafford on 7 April 1956 in front of a post-war record crowd of 62,277. Busby was away that day at a funeral in Scotland, but his young team, with only Roger Byrne and Johnny Berry left from the championship side of 1952, were not to be denied. Berry scored the equaliser from the penalty spot as

United came back from behind, and almost inevitably Tommy Taylor got the winner with a tap-in, his twenty-fifth league goal of the season. As the reporter from the *Sunday Dispatch* noted: 'United could stay on top for some time to come for most of their players are at the start of their careers.' In case there was any doubt about the potency of the club, the Youth Cup came back to Old Trafford again, despite the best efforts of a young Gordon Banks in the Chesterfield goal to keep out Bobby Charlton et al.

The man from the *Sunday Dispatch* was not proved wrong the following campaign, as United stormed away, amassing sixty-four points, a total that had been bettered only by Arsenal back in 1930–31. The crowds streamed in to watch the most charismatic side England had produced. Old Trafford's gates averaged an impressive 45,393 for league fixtures, up more than 16 per cent on the previous season; for the first time since the war United was the best-supported club in the country. The Red Devils, as they'd recently been nicknamed, were an irresistible force, scoring 103 league goals, and they could turn it on just as well away as at home (in fact, their record was identical home and away). The championship trophy was presented to the team at Old Trafford on 21 April where 58,725 watched a 4–0 romp against Sunderland. United now had the chance of a unique Treble of league, FA Cup and, for the first time, the European Cup.

All of this came as something of a surprise to Alan Hardaker of the Football League, who had thought United could never give their all to the league because of this new continental distraction. But he had been outmanoeuvred by Matt Busby. The previous year had seen the inaugural European Cup take place, which in its first year was an 'invitation' competition between the best teams from all over Europe. Well, not quite all, for Chelsea, who had been English champions in 1955, had been refused permission by the Football League to take up their invitation.

Busby had noted how England had performed modestly in the 1950 and 1954 World Cups, and how Hungary had torn England apart in 1953. His United side had played a friendly against Red

Star Belgrade as early as May 1951 as part of the Festival of Britain celebrations; they were the first European team to visit Old Trafford, and 41,000 had turned out to see the 1–1 draw, with United lucky to achieve even that. He realised that good football was played abroad, and that English sides might actually learn something from the continent. He had already entered United's youth side in various international tournaments to give them a different experience, while the senior team had also played many friendlies in Europe and North America. Given the opportunity to test his first team against the best Europe had to offer, he was never going to turn down the chance.

Hardaker feared any English team entering the European Cup would be distracted from the real domestic business, and that his own competition would be devalued. Busby thought his players could cope with a few extra midweek games and the travelling they would involve. He believed the players would benefit from the excitement of a different challenge, and that the club would win financially. United's chairman, Harold Hardman, saw the financial arguments, and believed this would help fund improvements to the stadium, enabling the club to provide more seats and to cover more of the stands. Once convinced, he was nothing if not robust in the face of a challenge to what he thought was best for the club. United persuaded Stanley Rous at the Football Association to give his permission. Rous's decision might have upset Hardaker, but for Rous that was almost an added bonus. Once the FA's approval was secured, United were heading off into Europe whatever anyone else had to say on the matter.

But this wasn't immediately to be the start of the great tradition of European match nights at Old Trafford; it was the beginning of the much briefer tradition of European Cup nights at Maine Road. The former home of Manchester City played host to four European Cup games in its history, but three of them featured United, who had not yet installed floodlights at Old Trafford when they began their odyssey. However, as early as September 1956, new floodlights were being planned.

The Reds began their campaign against Anderlecht with a 2–0 win at the home of the Belgian champions. It suggested that the return leg in Manchester should be a relatively comfortable affair, but European football was new to everyone, so some tension remained. It needn't have done, as on a wet night Anderlecht were annihilated 10–0 in United's biggest ever victory, with Viollet scoring four, Taylor three, Whelan two and Berry one. Busby thought it 'the finest exhibition of teamwork I had ever seen'. Next, German champions Borussia Dortmund were beaten 3–2 on aggregate and then United took on Athletic Bilbao.

Beaten 5–3 in Spain in vile weather more appropriate to Manchester, United won 3–0 at Maine Road as they began another European tradition, scoring two late goals. As one journalist wrote, 'The whole country is proud of you.' McGuinness recalled: 'I've never known such passion; that was the game of my life . . . That was the game I most remember.' Indeed, United's pioneering role as the English team that could take on foreign sides and destroy them 10–0, or show backs-to-the-wall grit as against Dortmund, or never-say-die attacking skills as against Bilbao, meant they *had* become England's favourite team. Already, European nights had something special about them, according to Albert Thorpe: 'The atmosphere was much better against the European teams . . . because these teams came with such a reputation . . . It was an outing, a social evening with the lights on.'

The victory over Bilbao meant United had booked their place in the semifinals against the reigning European champions, Real Madrid. For any who still doubted the impact of European football, the quarterfinal was the second time in United's European campaign that 70,000 or more had turned up to watch. Amazingly, the Bilbao game, which was played four days after the derby at Maine Road, attracted more than 6000 extra fans.

Old Trafford was ready to welcome the greatest side in Europe, but before Real Madrid arrived, the floodlights were given a trial run-out in a league fixture against Bolton Wanderers a fortnight or so beforehand. Built by the General Electric Company, the floodlights were part of a whole range of improvements that the club made to the ground during the 1950s, with increasing parts of the stadium now under cover, though most were still open to the elements. Costing £38,000 to build, the pylons on each corner were 160 feet high, and each one had 54 floodlights in it. Ken Ramsden, who would be one of the club's greatest servants in years to come, recalls the excitement he felt at the time. His mother worked at the ground and told him they were going to try out the lights: 'I went to stand on Canal Bridge in the evening a few days before, just to see the time they were switched on for the first time.'

McGuinness was part of the team that lined up for that first match under lights. Strangely, given that there were floodlights at the Cliff and at various other grounds, the match was treated almost as some kind of unusual experiment, but he recalls the special atmosphere created by night-time games. 'We played in shiny satin, silk red shirts to reflect the light, as we thought. We had seen [what it was like] under lights because we'd played at Maine Road, and the Cliff had lights, and the ball was white. Under lights you can't see the crowd. It could be half-empty, but if they make a lot of noise it sounds like it's a full house. I don't know anybody who preferred playing day games to night games – the white ball seemed to ping a bit more, everything seemed more intense. I loved it.'

In fact, it was far from half-empty; a crowd of 60,862 packed in to Old Trafford that night, with the gates closed half an hour before kickoff, and thousands locked outside. But it wasn't an auspicious start as they watched United lose 2–0 to Bolton. Harold Riley was one of them, and he recalls: 'They dimmed the floodlights at half-time to save electricity, but it was like Blackpool illuminations as everyone lit up. You had all these red spots like red stars everywhere.'

Even more turned up to see Real Madrid. The nation was captivated by United's European adventure, and Granada secured the rights to broadcast the whole game live. Having lost 3–1 in the first leg at the Bernabeu, after holding out for an hour against Di Stefano, Gento and the rest of them (Charlton, watching from the stands that night, called Di Stefano 'mesmerising'), United hoped they could once again overturn a two-goal deficit on home soil against a Spanish side. The British press ensured that everyone was behind United for the return leg, with the *Daily Herald*, under the heading 'Murder in Madrid', complaining that Real had 'hacked, slashed, kicked and wrestled' their way to victory. Another theme that would run for many years in media reports of European encounters, 'cheating foreigners', was thus established.

Ken Ramsden recalls how the fans responded to Madrid's antics at Old Trafford: 'The Spanish players were going down, feigning injury, and Duncan Edwards was having none of this. He and another player picked up this Spanish, ankles and arms, and lifted him off the pitch. It was hilarious.' The same newspaper that had complained about the Spanish side's behaviour in the first leg now decided that it was United's turn to be criticised, Edwards' behaviour five minutes from the end being something he 'would rather forget', while the fans' support was a 'squalid show of one-eyed partisanship'. Even in those days, the media could change their tune at the drop of a hat. For Charlton, the noise from the supporters was something special: 'Did the Stretford End just suck the ball down to this end?' he wondered.

Bobby Charlton was given his European debut that night, deputising for Dennis Viollet, as Busby once again showed his willingness to thrust inexperienced players into the biggest of games. Charlton responded with a goal, United's second of the night, but as Madrid had taken a 2–0 lead, it was too little too late. United still emerged with great credit, and a bond between the two clubs was formed during the two matches. Busby and everyone at Old Trafford knew they would be back the following year to try again.

Defeat left United having to settle for an attempt at the Double. In today's football, such events are relatively regular occurrences, but in 1957 no team had managed this achievement all century.

En route to the Wembley final, United played at home only once, beating Everton 1–0 in the fifth round, thanks to the only goal Duncan Edwards ever scored in the tournament. But the final didn't go to plan when early in the game Aston Villa's Peter McParland charged goalkeeper Ray Wood as he prepared to kick the ball upfield. Today, he would have been sent off; in 1957, Wood was carried off with a broken cheekbone and the ten men of United lost 2–1, with centre-half Jackie Blanchflower taking over in goal; to rub salt into the wounds, McParland scored both Villa goals.

Champions two years on the run, backed by ever-increasing and passionate crowds, United had fallen just short of winning a unique Treble. In 1957–58, their young side would be more experienced and surely would be able to go the extra distance to win even more trophies. The club had not only achieved success on the pitch and spent money on improvements, it had also managed to turn in a profit of just under £40,000, enabling the board to announce in September 1957 plans to expand the capacity of the ground to 100,000, and to build further roofing on the rest of the Popular Side. Busby, with his newly gained European experience, would have felt sure that the best was yet to come for Old Trafford and for the team that drew so many to the stadium.

6

Munich and Its Aftermath

United got off to a flying start in the 1957–58 season, taking 11 points out of 12 and scoring 22 goals in the process, but the next 15 games brought just 14 points, leaving United off the pace in the title hunt, well behind Wolves and Preston. So Busby made a rare foray into the transfer market, bringing in Harry Gregg from Doncaster Rovers for a record fee for a goalkeeper of about £23,000. At twenty-five, he was relatively young for a keeper, but one of the older members of the team and he found himself welcomed into the set-up immediately. A man who liked to dominate his penalty area, he brought an immediate resolve to the defence, and United's form began to improve.

Gregg, who was one of only five players on United's books that had been signed from another club (the others were Tommy Taylor, Johnny Berry, Colin Webster and Ray Wood), had not played at Old Trafford before. He had, however, visited once, when he came over the Pennines to watch a former Doncaster team-mate, Bill Paterson, in action for Newcastle United soon after he transferred to them in 1955. He paid for a ticket and stood on the Stretford End to watch the match – 'an unbelievable pleasure' – little thinking he would join the club not long after. His other United connection had come when he had the chance to see himself on the Movietone news early in 1956, when he'd had a good game in the FA Cup against Bristol Rovers – but the only reason their match against Doncaster was being covered at all was because Bristol had beaten United 4–0 in the third round.

Gregg joined the club after some cloak-and-dagger stuff in Doncaster, hiding under a rug in the back of an estate car before meeting Busby and Murphy. He was struck instantly by the fact that Busby 'had that aura about him' that demanded instant respect, rather as one would show to a clergyman or a policeman in those days. Busby immediately made it clear that if he wanted to join United, he had to understand there would be 'no money' in it for him; in other words, no little extras as some clubs tended to offer. The next day, Gregg was on the train to Manchester and was greeted at Piccadilly station by the manager and his assistant, as well as Jackie Blanchflower and his wife. Blanchflower was a former schoolboy team-mate of Gregg's and so the most familiar and welcoming face. Busby may not have done much in the transfer market in those days, but he knew how to make someone immediately feel welcome; Gregg felt this was 'very important'.

The training in those last days of the Babes was, according to Gregg, a 'doddle' – not because Busby and Murphy were in any sense lax but because, with the team being in action so frequently, they understood that players needed time to recover and recharge their batteries without being worn out with excessive running. Training on the pitch at Old Trafford was almost self-regulating. Gregg recalls how the squad would see coach Tom Curry coming out of the tunnel in the middle of the pitch and abandon their exercises, bursting into a spontaneous rendition of the 'Folies Bergère'; Curry would shake his head and wander back inside Old Trafford, and the players would resume their training.

With the title almost inevitably lost, United could concentrate on the two trophies they had so narrowly missed out on the year before. They had already reached the European Cup quarterfinals, having beaten Shamrock Rovers and Dukla Prague. Their next opponents were Red Star Belgrade, who had played United back in 1951. Over a period of eleven days in January, the Old Trafford faithful saw United in action in three different competitions. First up was Red Star, and after United went behind, Bobby Charlton and Eddie Colman hit back to give the Reds a narrow 2–1 lead to take to Yugoslavia. Four days later, Bolton were hammered 7–2, with Charlton scoring a hat-trick. The following week, Ipswich Town were beaten 2–0 in the fourth round of the FA Cup in front of a crowd of 53,550, Charlton scoring both goals. Television images of the pitch show the field was heavily sanded, which must have made the going extremely heavy work. There was one more game before United flew out to Belgrade, a topsy-turvy breath-taking match at Highbury, which ended 5–4 to United. Then it was off to secure a place in the semifinals of the European Cup; a draw would be sufficient. Having gone 3–0 up by half-time, in the end United were left hanging on at 3–3, through to the next round.

The story of United's trip back, and the tragedy of Munich, has been told many times over. A book about Old Trafford is not the place to go into detail about those horrific events, suffice to say that among the twenty-three people who eventually died as a result of the crash on 6 February 1958 were eight players: Geoff Bent, Roger Byrne, Eddie Colman, Duncan Edwards, Mark Jones, David Pegg, Tommy Taylor and Billy Whelan. Club secretary Walter Crickmer, who had been at United since 1919, trainer Tom Curry and coach Bert Whalley also perished in the accident. Manager Matt Busby was on life support, and had the last rites read twice, before making a remarkable recovery. Nine players survived: Johnny Berry, Jackie Blanchflower, Bobby Charlton, Bill Foulkes, Harry Gregg, Kenny Morgans, Albert Scanlon, Dennis Viollet and Ray Wood, but Berry and Blanchflower never played again.

Jimmy Murphy had not travelled with the team because of his commitments as manager of Wales, who had been in action that same evening. He did not even know about the accident until he returned to the club on that cold, sleety afternoon the next day. Alma George, Crickmer's secretary, was the first to hear, having been contacted with the news by the airline BEA. When Murphy heard, he recalled in his memoirs, 'The numbing horror of that moment will live with me till I die.' Murphy was left in charge of team matters and, after a quick trip to Munich to see the survivors in hospital and arrange the return of the bodies, that meant finding eleven players to turn out for the next game. Two of them took the train home with him, Bill Foulkes and Harry Gregg, but where would he find the other nine?

Les Olive was promoted to acting secretary of the club, having to deal with the mountain of correspondence that poured into the ground. He could barely get hold of a typewriter to respond to them all. The ground committee and stewards came in to open the post and sort it out. The Lord Mayor sent his secretary to help reply to all the letters of condolence. Olive's wife went round to the houses of the families who lived nearby to tell them the terrible news. Harold Hardman's stoical, resolute qualities were never given a stronger challenge, but even at the age of seventy-five he rose to it. It was he who would pen the famous message in the programme for United's first game after the disaster: 'United Will Go On.'

In all that was to follow, it was in some ways the response to the tragedy almost as much as the tragedy itself that helped change Manchester United from a Manchester football club into a worldwide sporting institution. Hardman wanted things to return to normal as quickly as possible as 'the best way of paying tribute to everyone concerned in this tragedy'. The fact that on the surface things did return to normal helped build the legend, but for those who had to continue as though nothing had changed, the personal cost must have been high.

The club was able to get its first game postponed, but there was no delaying things indefinitely; Hardman wouldn't have it that way, even if United had been allowed to do so. Everyone was sympathetic to United's plight, but football could not be put on permanent hold. Murphy decided that the best thing to do was to take the players away from it all. As Jack Crompton, who was brought back from Luton to be the coach, recalls: 'After Munich, Jimmy Murphy decided the atmosphere wasn't right and took the whole squad out to Blackpool to train for a month to get away from it.' The squad stayed at the Norbreck Hydro in the week leading up to the FA Cup game, their first since the tragedy.

It was hardly surprising that they'd wanted to get away, given that the gymnasium at Old Trafford had been used as an impromptu resting place as some of the players' coffins were flown back and laid to rest there. An estimated 100,000 people lined the route as the funeral cortège set off from the airport at 11.15 on the evening of 10 February, not reaching its destination at Old Trafford until well after midnight. For days, outside the stadium, fans milled about wanting to hear the latest news, particularly as Busby and Edwards battled to stay alive.

Murphy then had to go to a succession of funerals, burying the young men who had been his charges, who he had seen grow up and helped develop into the players they had become. For a man who had enjoyed being the power behind the throne, he was suddenly thrust into the limelight at the most difficult time imaginable to be the face of Manchester United. His own emotions would have to wait, for Busby had told him from his bed in Munich, 'You have got to keep it going, Jimmy . . . The club must go on.' He was accompanied by someone from the board in each case, a board that added Louis Edwards to its number the day after Munich, following the death of board member George Whittaker earlier that year.

All around the city, people were in shock, hoping and praying to hear good news. My mother, who was growing up in Cheetham Hill at the time, remembers how at her school the boys would be excused from class to run down the street to phone for the latest news about the survivors. Colin Shindler, in his compelling memoir *Manchester United Ruined My Life*, wrote of how his disciplinarian teacher asked everyone to keep a diary recording their response to Munich, for once 'making no attempt to correct anything'. Shindler, a City fan, comments: 'The day Duncan Edwards died, I could scarcely write for tears.' For the whole of Manchester, who, as we have seen, had grown used to seeing the players about the city, 'it was a death in the immediate family'. All around Manchester, those who were there recall the eerie quiet that descended on the city.

It was agreed that United would return to action on Wednesday 19 February, to play Sheffield Wednesday in the fifth round of the FA Cup, the match having been postponed from the previous Saturday. Tickets were due to go on sale on the morning of 16 February at ten o'clock, but huge queues began to form the night before and so the ticket office opened early to cope with the demand. Within hours they were all sold, as so many people wanted to be there to show their respects. Touts made huge profits on the tickets. Famously, the match programme for that evening had eleven blank spaces where the United team should have been listed. Murphy was still scrambling to put together a side for the game.

Murphy was still working on filling the team sheet as teatime approached. Tom Finney, one of the game's most respected players, was whisked to a Manchester hotel to help persuade Aston Villa's Stan Crowther to join United. He agreed, the FA waived the fact that he was cup-tied, and within an hour of putting pen to paper he was putting on the red shirt of United. Ernie Taylor, an experienced forward at Blackpool, also signed for United ahead of the game. As well as the two Munich survivors, the other seven players were lifted from the ranks of the youth team and reserves. Gregg recalls how, apart from Foulkes, he'd barely met most of his new team-mates before they appeared in the dressing room that day.

All those who were there that night agree that Sheffield Wednesday had no chance. On a wave of emotion, a crowd of 59,848 ensured United won the match. The ground was packed full long before kickoff. Shay Brennan said: 'Everyone was just lost in his own thoughts in the dressing room' before the match. Jack Crompton recalls: 'I felt sorry for Sheffield Wednesday; the crowd would have lynched them if they'd won . . . It was emotional, tense that night, and some of the fans didn't know if it was right to cheer when we scored.' Bobby Charlton hadn't recovered sufficiently from his injuries to play, but he was there that night and also sympathised with United's opponents. 'They had no chance because the crowd just lifted [United] every time. Every time a player got the ball, it was knocking on the Sheffield Wednesday goal.' Denis Law, then playing for Huddersfield, paid eight times the ticket price to visit Old Trafford for the first time. Even if you weren't a United fan, you wanted to be there.

If the fans were feeling it, it is hard to imagine what the players must have been going through. For a few, they were playing to continue the work of their fallen team-mates; for the rest, it was a case of stepping into the shoes of the lost heroes and trying to live up to their legacy. It would have been hard enough to follow Duncan Edwards if he'd been transferred to another club; but imagine the pressure on Stan Crowther, knowing that Edwards was still fighting for his life in a Munich hospital. After the match, the newsreel cameras went into the dressing room to film the players having a 'victory toast', but the faces of Foulkes and Gregg don't show any joy; their jaws are clenched, their eyes sad and looking anywhere but at the camera. If this was a good moment, imagine what every other time must have felt like.

Jim White, in his excellent book *Manchester United – The Biography*, questions how much understanding there was about the pressures on their new players as they tried to put the horrific events of Munich behind them. Yet Gregg, one of the heroes of Munich for his actions in helping to rescue team-mates and other passengers, looks at it in a slightly different way. Before Munich, 'after a game, we were full of euphoria of the occasion, delighted, proud as can be, wonderful'. But the first game afterwards was 'just another game. Get it over with. Go home.' For training as well, the normal release wasn't the same, either. Despite this, however, he still feels: 'If I hadn't have had football to turn to; if I'd have had to sit in the house, instead of getting down to Old Trafford and kicking lumps out of each other, I think I would have gone mad. Football was a safety valve.'

Full-back Brennan made his debut that evening, on the left wing, a position he'd never played before, and scored the first two goals in the 3–0 victory, including one direct from a corner. According to *Charles Buchan's Football Monthly*, 'In the great grandstand, a woman crossed herself and said: "Perhaps one of them gave it a push."' Brennan played another 358 times for United, but scored just four more goals in that time. It was that sort of night. Michael Parkinson made the pilgrimage: 'I couldn't get in the ground, because there were thousands outside the ground. So I stayed outside and wrote a colour piece about it . . . It made it impossible not to be a Manchester United fan for the rest of my life.' Indeed, so great was the crush outside, with perhaps more locked out than got in, that a policeman trying to control the crowd broke his back, not through any trouble but just sheer weight of numbers. At kickoff, according to Pat McDonald, 'There started a shriek. I have never heard a noise like it, before or since. It was like a shrill, animal cry.'

Two days later, Duncan Edwards finally lost his battle to survive, as his kidneys failed. For many, this was the final blow. It is hard for football fans today to know where he should stand in the pantheon of greats. Modern stars can be seen every week on TV, their flaws and errors highlighted from a dozen different camera angles. With Edwards there is little footage to go by. Instead, we have the testimonies of those who watched him or played alongside him. Jimmy Murphy said: 'Whenever I heard Muhammad Ali on television say he was the greatest, I had to smile. There was only ever one greatest and that was Duncan Edwards.' Wilf McGuinness has this to say: 'If it had happened to any other player at the age of twenty-one that you'd ever thought of, they wouldn't be remembered like we talk about Duncan Edwards. He was that special.' Bobby Charlton says: 'He was the only player that made me feel inferior.'

Gregg, who had seen the players in their hospital beds, and heard the prognosis for each of them from the doctors, didn't hear the news immediately. Having finally moved into his club house, he was at home while the decorators were in. Sitting there, the enormity of what he'd been through began to hit him, so he tried to distract himself by reading the papers, but he couldn't find them anywhere. Eventually, he discovered them. They'd been hidden away, for the headline revealed that Edwards had died. That was when he finally broke down.

Twenty-four hours later, United returned to league action, against Nottingham Forest, and a post-war record crowd of 66,123 saw them draw 1–1 in a game they deserved to win. Before the match kicked off, there was a brief service held on the pitch before the players came out. After that, it was the FA Cup quarterfinal against West Brom, when thousands travelled to the Hawthorns to see United earn a replay. Once more tens of thousands were locked out of Old Trafford, but this time some attempted to force their way into the ground after the gates had been locked, with the police moving in to prevent things getting seriously out of hand. Bobby Charlton was back in action at Old Trafford, but Colin Webster scored the winning goal as United rode the tide of emotion that washed away all who would deny them their destiny. But for Gregg, the results didn't really matter: 'It was a case of getting there, doing your bit and getting the hell out of there.'

West Brom were back three days later in a league match, and before the game started a recording of Busby was played, introducing the surgeons, doctors and nurses who had worked so hard to save the lives of the players and help their recovery. As the German healthcare workers walked onto the pitch, a huge cheer rang out. Professor Maurer, who led the Rechts der Isar hospital staff in their efforts, made a brief comment to the fans, concluding: 'Manchester United leads every time.' Perhaps the emotion of it all was too much for the players, as this time United lost 4–0.

United won through a replayed semifinal against Fulham before meeting Bolton Wanderers in an emotional FA Cup final, made even more poignant by the return of Busby for the first time. He wasn't strong enough to lead the side out onto the pitch, that honour rightly going to Murphy. Throughout the Cup run, everything had been done to honour the memories of those who had died; it seemed as though United's opponents felt it would be sacrilege to deny them. But Bolton weren't going to give up their chance of glory, even if there would be a horrible echo of the year before, when Nat Lofthouse bundled Gregg and the ball into the goal to score Wanderers' second and decisive goal.

Despite this, the crowds still turned out to cheer the team when they returned to Manchester. The club may have become popular everywhere else, but the passion for them in their home city was always more intense. Partly this was due to the fact that footballers of the day remained very much ordinary people, the club still a family affair. Gregg recalls how he and other players would nip down to the laundry rooms, run by Ken Ramsden's mother Irene and his Aunt Joan, who were nicknamed Omo and Daz. The walls there were plastered with pictures of the players from the past, though the Munich boys became the ones that were the most prominently displayed after the tragedy. Indeed, as Gregg points out, of how many other football clubs could it be said that the eventual club secretary (from 2007 to 2010) would be the son of the team's laundrywoman and rise to the top from being an office boy? Ramsden's family lived on the same street as Les Olive, which was how he got the job initially. At first, he helped out in the cash office, handing out the players' weekly wages in cash every Thursday morning, and on one occasion he even had to work one of the turnstiles.

One last task remained that season: the European Cup semifinal against AC Milan. Incredibly, United won the home leg 2–1 despite the absence of Charlton, who had been selected to win his

second cap for England in a pre-World Cup friendly (there being
no club postponements for international matches in those days),
but the emotionally, mentally and physically exhausted players
could not summon up one last big effort in the San Siro and succumbed 4–0 to bring an end to a season that would never be
forgotten – for all the worst reasons.

Amazingly, in 1958–59 United would drag itself forward again
and somehow manage to finish the league campaign in the
runners-up position, scoring 103 goals in the process to equal the
best the Babes ever achieved. With sympathy for United's suffering continuing, the crowds at Old Trafford reached an average of
over 53,000.

Busby was now back in charge of the club, but the accident had
aged him; he now appeared an old man. Physically he was still
frail; Crompton recalls in his autobiography how as 'he reached
the narrow corridor, which led to his office, he would . . . negotiate the corridor by steadying himself with one hand on each wall,
forcing himself to walk to the office door without assistance'. Had
it not been for the support and encouragement of his wife, Jean,
he might have decided to pack it in, but she persuaded him that
he could best honour the victims of Munich by following through
on the work he had begun. Hard work would be the way forward.

Busby's first major signing on his return was Albert Quixall
from Sheffield Wednesday for a record fee of £45,000. His partnership at inside-forward with Charlton worked well, allowing
Bobby to score a career-best twenty-nine goals that campaign,
while Quixall managed just four goals for himself. When United
beat league leaders Wolves at Old Trafford in February, they not
only went joint top of the table with their beaten opponents, they
had dropped only one point in twelve games. But a defeat at third-
placed Arsenal in the next fixture damaged their momentum, and
Wolves ended up winning the title by six clear points.

The links between Old Trafford and rugby league received one
of their first boosts at this time, when Salford played Leeds under
the floodlights. In future years, this would become a much more

regular arrangement for the sport. The plans to redevelop Old Trafford had been somewhat amended after Munich. However, the growing number of young fans meant that extra turnstiles had to be built for them at the Stretford End.

Among the new following was someone who had made his first visit to Old Trafford that season, Cliff Butler. He would go on to be the club's historian, official photographer and much else besides in years to come. Now United's official statistician, he remembers that in those days, many of his friends supported both Manchester teams, and his father said it was up to him which way he should lean. He can't recall if Munich was behind his decision, but recognises that it was likely to have been a factor, especially as he remembers his father's tears on hearing of the disaster.

In any case, on Boxing Day 1958, Butler was one of 63,098 in Old Trafford that day: 'I was nine. They played Aston Villa [winning 2–1]; my dad had already taken my sister. We lived on the east side of Manchester and I pestered him to take me, so it was a Christmas treat. The journey in was like travelling to Australia for me as a little kid; it was the bus into the city and then the train out to the Warwick Road station, as it was then. Old Trafford looked vast, and I remember we stood on the very wall, the back steps of the Stretford End Paddock looking into the stadium, and the atmosphere – it went dark as the game went on, and in those days people smoked a lot and that brought in the atmosphere. It was like going to a rock concert almost. In those days, there were steam trains, so towards the end of the game the trains parked up outside the ground, their smoke bellowed in to the ground. The whole scene and the crowd had a bigger impression on me than the actual match. The size of everything, and that was it: from day one I was hooked; you were part of the event.'

But that first post-Munich season was something of a false dawn, rather like the one United would experience nearly thirty years later, the season after Alex Ferguson joined the club. In both cases, the runners-up position actually concealed the fact that all was not quite right. For a period, many new players would be signed, and there would be some disciplinary issues that the manager had to resolve. Then, eventually, the team would win its first trophy in a while, the FA Cup, while narrowly avoiding relegation. The following season the club would give a debut to a good-looking dark-haired winger who would augur the start of something truly spectacular.

During the following season, on 25 February 1960, the Munich memorial was unveiled, close to the main entrance. Busby made a brief speech to those who had been invited to the occasion, and saw the plaque that had been built by a local firm, Jaconello, to a design by M.I. Vipond. A memorial to the sports writers who had died was also unveiled. The Munich memorial clock was put up at the Warwick Road end of the ground.

There were many problems as the 1960s dawned. First, Busby was no longer a 'tracksuit' manager and so his presence wasn't as prominent on the training ground, which meant that some newcomers found the whole situation surprisingly lax and unfocused. Busby's belief in letting the players play and express themselves might have worked when you had the best footballers in the country; but United could not claim that now, and this freedom contrasted with the increasing tactical awareness of other managers, who would practise set-piece situations to ensure their teams were fully prepared. However, some found a logic in this. Gregg remembers that after a game in which he had slightly mishandled, he went to practise on his own, 'kicking a ball up the back of the Stretford End, maybe sixty feet in the air against the wall, and running underneath it hopefully to catch the ball over my head. Jimmy Murphy came out and said: "What the hell are you doing?" I said: "Well, my handling . . ." He replied: "You get the hell out of here. I'll tell you when you need to do this." What a lift for people! Wonderful man management!'

Second, as Gregg's story illustrates, the training facilities themselves remained poor: neither the Cliff nor Old Trafford had a proper gym – Crompton was reduced to hanging footballs from the stands so players could practise their heading. The terracing and the seats in the ground were all used as obstacles in fitness and running exercises. In the end, Crompton resorted to taking the players to the YMCA in Manchester where there was proper gym equipment and a good pool.

Third, team spirit was poor. Captain Bill Foulkes – always loyal to the United cause and never willing to accept second-best from anyone – was not the most popular man in the changing room, and there were splits within the team, with arguments increasingly common. Gregg remembers one such row between Foulkes and another player provoking Busby into raising his voice – something that was almost unheard of in his time at the club: 'Busby came in to the dressing room and told them to be quiet; the player continued; Busby said, "I've told you, that's enough." He still wasn't ready to be quiet, so Busby shouted: "How in the name of God I ever signed you, I don't know. Don't say another word."' The impact was instant, but this wasn't the usual Busby way of doing things.

Fourth, the players were weighed down with expectation. Any lapse in behaviour on or off the pitch brought forth criticisms, from the media in particular, that players were letting down the memory of Munich; if they didn't perform well, they weren't as good as the Babes who went before. In short, the demands on them were so high that they could only ever fail to live up to them. As the years went by, time eased this pressure and enabled players to be judged on their own merits. But for now, even if Munich was barely mentioned around Old Trafford, it hung over everyone.

Indeed, some of his players from that time have commented on how Busby seemed to be out of step with the times, old-fashioned even. This problem was about to get worse when the £20 maximum wage was finally abolished in 1961. Johnny Haynes of Fulham famously became the first £100-a-week player soon after; United raised their top wage to £25. Money was behind Busby's decision to let go Dennis Viollet, the forward who had recovered from Munich and in 1959–60 scored a record thirty-two league goals.

If things weren't quite right on the pitch, at least they were getting better in the stands. In 1959, United finally built a roof over the Stretford End to cover the 22,000 fans who could fit in there, as part of a programme of development that would ensure that Old Trafford would become one of the smartest grounds in the country by the end of the 1960s. During the following summer there were repairs carried out to the Paddock, too. After all the work, the capacity of the ground was now 66,500, with admission starting at three shillings. The United Road area was re-roofed in the summer of 1961.

Because of these costs, United began to look for new ways of raising funds, especially as these improvements had coincided with a rapid decline in attendances. By the end of 1961–62 an average of just over 33,000 came to Old Trafford games – 20,000 fewer than three years previously. However, in 1961 the club set up the Manchester United Development Association, which began as a football pools business in August under Bill Burke, specifically enabling fans who contributed to know that the profits they generated would go towards improvements to the ground. The following year MUDA was able to contribute handsomely to the 1678 seats that were added at the back of the Stretford End, known as Stand E, which were used for the first time in a friendly against Benfica, a team that was to loom large in United's story in the 1960s.

Covering building costs in this way was especially important because, unusually, Busby sought solace in the transfer market. The production line of great players from the youth side had almost dried up, Nobby Stiles being a rare exception, and the team needed new blood. Following McGuinness's career-ending injury in 1959, the man who had been Duncan Edwards' understudy was replaced at a cost of £30,000 in January 1960 by West Brom's tough-tackling Maurice Setters. Full-back Noel Cantwell joined from West Ham for a similar sum in November of that year. Then, in July 1961, the hard-shooting forward David Herd arrived from Arsenal for £40,000.

All of them were to prove good, solid buys, delivering all that could have been expected of them. But none of them was a true crowd-pleaser, guaranteed to get the turnstiles ticking over; nor could any of them transform United's fortunes on the pitch. By the end of 1961–62, United were in fifteenth place in the table, their lowest finish to a campaign since 1938. So that summer, Busby went back into the transfer market, spending more on the son of an Aberdeen trawlerman than he had on the other three put together. Breaking the British transfer record to do so, paying £115,000 to Torino, he brought in the best young inside-forward around.

His name: Denis Law.

7

The Best Times

Although Busby now had a team that looked as though it could compete at the highest levels, 1962–63 found United in an unthinkable relegation battle. The defence leaked more goals than at any time since the war, despite the presence of Harry Gregg, Bill Foulkes, Tony Dunne, Nobby Stiles and Noel Cantwell. Up front, the goals dried up even though Denis Law, Bobby Charlton and David Herd could all manage twenty a season. Add to that list Johnny Giles, who would become one of the most influential players of the 1960s (albeit not for United – he was transferred out to Leeds after an argument with Busby over being played out of position), as well as the mid-season signing of Pat Crerand as both a creator and a midfield enforcer, one might have expected United to be challenging Everton for the title, not battling to avoid the drop.

In the end, there was a crucial derby match against City on 15 May at Maine Road that was almost a relegation decider. A draw, thanks to an Albert Quixall equalising penalty after Law had been fouled, was just about enough to guarantee safety for United. John Aston, who would be part of the Reds' European Cup-winning side five years later, was living in Clayton at the time and recalls how his City-supporting friends still came out to play in the street the next day: 'I thought they must have been devastated. I would-n't have dared to show my face.' Perhaps it was a sign that the old era of Mancunians happily supporting both clubs was beginning to break down. United still weren't definitely safe, and the visit of relegated Leyton Orient for the last game of the season at Old Trafford gave the Reds the chance to stay up. United fell behind to an early goal as the crowd grew uneasy. Fortunately, an own goal by Orient and the news that City were losing meant the players could relax and eventually secure the vital victory.

Law had seemed to be the man who would transform United. Although just twenty-two years old and slightly built (the *Daily Mirror* worked out that he was worth about £48 per ounce), he was tough, fiery and a natural goal-scorer. That first season, he scored twenty-nine goals in all competitions, starting with one on his debut at Old Trafford against West Brom, to begin a mutual love affair with the Stretford End that continues to this day, almost fifty years on. As Bobby Charlton has commented: 'Denis Law was ruthless as a forward.' His on-field persona, which contrasted completely with his quiet, home-loving life away from it, marked the dawn of the 1960s at United. He was a rebel and he had atti-tude; his arrival coincided with the age of satire and the breakdown of deference, typified by the Profumo Scandal. On top of that, he gave his all to the cause, taking the kicks from the opposition defenders, coming back for more – and even on occa-sion getting some of his own back. Above all, he could score goals. Lots of them. No wonder they loved him.

In his memoir, *The King*, Law also gives some insight into how new players were looked after by Busby, and also by his wife Jean. Within a few months of joining the club, Law married Di, an arrangement Busby always encouraged, because he felt married players would be more settled and less likely to fall prey to the dis-tractions offered by Manchester. Married players didn't have to live in digs, so when Law was looking for his new house, it was Jean

Busby who came with him to help. Law would have picked somewhere near the club, but she suggested an alternative near some
shops and a school so that Di would be able to bring up their
family more easily. As Law says: 'Matt and his wife were good at
making sure the family was settled, because he believed that was as
important as your performance on the field.'

Despite slipping down the table, the Old Trafford crowds had
started to rise again, and in the FA Cup they had a run to make
people feel things really were beginning to turn round for United.
It had been one of the coldest winters on record, which meant
United played only one competitive game in the whole of January
and February. During that period, United trained indoors most of
the time, with the corridors of Old Trafford often being used.
There were three trips to Ireland for friendly matches, as that
country wasn't as badly affected by the weather. With United's
still-basic facilities, it was a battle for the players to remain fit.

Once the FA Cup finally got started, the Reds went from the
third round to qualifying for the last eight in twelve March days,
beating Huddersfield, Aston Villa and Chelsea in Manchester. Law
scored a hat-trick against his first club Huddersfield, but United
may have been helped on the way to their 5–0 victory by the fact
they had been given a new design of boot to try out to help them
combat the icy conditions. It certainly seemed to do the trick, and
also showed that sports manufacturers were well aware of the mar-
keting power of the men from Old Trafford.

In fact, Villa were the only First Division side United met until
they faced Leicester City in the final at Wembley. The East
Midlanders were clear favourites to win the cup, and looked in
charge of the game until Law scored a superb goal that turned
the match in United's favour and set the Reds not only on their
way to a 3–1 triumph, but towards the good times once more. It
was United's first trophy since Munich; the new team had their
own achievements to boast of, rather than their predecessors' to
live up to.

If Law had been the harbinger of the 1960s at United, the next season saw the arrival of the man who personified it – and not just for United but for all of football in England: George Best. Best had come over from Belfast as a shy, homesick fifteen-year-old. Spotted by Bob Bishop, United's man in Northern Ireland, he was touted as a genius. When he decided he couldn't cope with life in Manchester, Busby made sure he came back. Already he had begun to show what he could do in training at the Cliff or 'round the back' at Old Trafford. His ability to dribble the ball, ride scything tackles from hardened pros (who didn't like being shown up by a boy the club was almost having to force-feed to bulk him up) and score goals was already all too apparent.

Best's debut at the age of seventeen, on 14 September 1963 against West Brom, earned him his first headline in the *Manchester Evening News*: 'Boy Best Flashes in Red Attack'. Yet it was another teenager, David Sadler, just three months older than Best, who scored the only goal of the match in front of the 50,453 fans who can say 'I was there'. Best had a difficult debut, up against Welsh international Graham Williams, who tackled 'with power and accuracy' according to the *Daily Telegraph*, but Williams was merely the first of many defenders who would find out just how hard it was to stop Best coming back for more. There would be many more headlines in the years that followed and, initially at least, they would focus on his football. It was perhaps no coincidence, in the light of all that was to follow, that a few weeks after Best's debut, United should unveil the Unitedettes, a short-lived experiment in having cheerleaders parade around the pitch before kickoff.

Best and Sadler were joined that season by an even younger debutant, Willie Anderson, who was a month short of his seventeenth birthday when he played his first game. Busby might have been spending the cash, but he still kept on giving opportunities to his youngsters, which was certainly one reason why so many of them chose United over other teams when their scouts came to call. Sadler, for example, had been spotted by Joe Armstrong's team of scouts, even though he was living in Kent. Armstrong then spoke to him, and finally Jimmy Murphy appeared to close the deal with Sadler's father. Sadler recalls how 'everyone felt something for United, because of [Munich]'. Armstrong was always very clear when approaching a family to sign up their son: 'I pay most attention to the mother! . . . It is usually Mum who makes the final decision. This is chiefly because she . . . has an eye . . . on his happiness.' He made sure the family knew their son would have nice digs, be well looked after and shown about life beyond football.

Murphy's youth side was the best he'd had since the days of the Babes. The club's vigorous scouting system secured players not just from under the noses of City, but anywhere in the country. Despite this, the club nearly lost out on the signature of John Aston Jr, even though his father had been a part of United's great post-war side and was on the coaching staff. It was only when Everton made him an offer that United decided to do so themselves. United offered opportunity and also a safe environment (thanks to Busby's emphasis on providing pastoral care and family digs) for young teenagers who'd rarely stayed away from home. Interestingly, the youth team was also made to feel very much part of the United set-up, their match-day routine the same as the first team, even down to the pre-match game of golf at Busby's club in Davyhulme.

The Youth Cup was back on Busby's agenda. For those who wonder about players' crowded schedules these days, they might like to take a look at George Best's run in the four weeks from 18 March to 15 April 1964. On 18 March, he played in Lisbon in the European Cup-Winners' Cup quarterfinal, then he had six games in the First Division, before turning out in the Youth Cup semifinal against Manchester City, another league game and then he made his international debut against Wales in Swansea – ten games in all for the seventeen-year-old, including an overseas trip and his first cap. That the Youth Cup semifinal was also a derby meant that it was a big occasion, drawing 29,706 fans to Old Trafford. Earlier in the week, on the Monday, the first team had beaten Aston Villa 1–0 in front of just 25,848 fans – it was that big an occasion. With more than half the players on show born in Greater Manchester, it was always going to be a passionate occasion, arguably too passionate according to the newspaper reports of the time. United won 4–1, took the second leg 4–3 and went on to beat Swindon 5–2 on aggregate in the final. United's youngsters were champions again.

But their seniors fell just short of emulating them, ending as runners-up to Liverpool. In a year, they'd gone from relegation candidates to title contenders. There was also a significant moment on 25 January when Best, Law and Charlton lined up together for the first time at Old Trafford, beating Bristol Rovers 4–1 in the FA Cup, with Law scoring a hat-trick. United also fell just short in the FA Cup, too, losing out to West Ham in the semi-final on a boggy Hillsborough pitch.

In fact, United had challenged on three fronts, being back in Europe thanks to their FA Cup success the previous year. On the way to the quarterfinal, United met Spurs and had to overcome a 2–0 deficit from the away leg when the Londoners came to Old Trafford. Pat Crerand remembers that it was 'a great match', while Denis Law's main recollection was of the horrendous collision early in the game between Noel Cantwell and Spurs' Dave Mackay that resulted in the latter being carried off with a double fracture of his leg. It was a case of two of the game's toughest customers going for a challenge that neither was going to pull out of. The injury helped tip the balance in United's favour, roared on by a passionate Old Trafford crowd. David Herd had already scored United's first with a header from close in, before adding another close-range effort. Jimmy Greaves pulled one back, but then Charlton stepped up with two from the right-hand corner of the six-yard box.

Law was in inspirational form that season, scoring thirty league goals, an incredible ten in the FA Cup and six in the Cup-Winners' Cup – a record forty-six in all – that helped make him the European Footballer of the Year, the first United player ever to win the award. United weren't quite the finished article yet, as their failure to hold on to a 4–1 lead against Sporting Lisbon in the return leg of the Cup-Winners' Cup in Portugal showed. United's 5–0 defeat was their worst ever in Europe, and provoked a rare outburst from Matt Busby, who, according to Crerand, said 'our performance was an insult to the people of Manchester'.

Busby's comments are notable, not just because it was so rare for him to lose his temper, but also because he saw United as representing Manchester. Nowadays, with a worldwide fan base of 333 million, although United still remains a Manchester institution, there is no chance that the same words would be used. And while the process of creating a global support, or at least a national one, had arguably been set in motion by the Babes and Munich, the next season saw an innovation begin that would eventually bring United's stars into everyone's living rooms: *Match of the Day*. From small beginnings in August 1964, this programme, and its subsequent ITV equivalent *The Big Match*, ensured that players could become nationally famous for the first time. And United had some of the greatest stars in British football in their team.

Change was in the air in many other ways. Not only were there social and political changes afoot (Harold Wilson's Labour party came to power in October 1964), things were getting a bit naughtier, on the pitch and off it. But only a bit. There is a picture of Law leaving the pitch after being sent off against Aston Villa in November 1963, something the country's most expensive player ought not to do, according to most of the press at the time. However, in the background of the picture, children at the front look up in awe, with one boy giving him the thumbs-up; a couple of fans, wearing ties, look as though they may be shouting something at him, but otherwise there is calm.

In music, the 'clean-cut' Beatles had a new rival band in the Rolling Stones, and famously one wouldn't have wanted one's daughter to marry one of the band. Furthermore, there was trouble on the terraces involving Manchester United. The first time it was noticed was at an away match against Burnley on Boxing Day 1963. Burnley's chairman, Bob Lord, had been less than sympathetic to United's suffering after Munich, and some fans had decided it was time for a bit of payback. The result, a 6–1 defeat for United, probably played its part, too, in the fans venting their anger. The growth in violence and obscene chanting was a trend that was to affect many clubs over the next generation, and it would leave old-style managers like Busby and Bill Nicholson of Spurs baffled and horrified.

Cliff Butler has one explanation for why the problem arose around this time: 'Trouble began to develop in grounds when mass movement became easier: motorways were starting to be built; train travel was a lot easier. When I was a young kid, people still went to away games, but the access wasn't easy. I used to get the train to London, but it took seven hours and you had to get the midnight train on the Friday night. The length of time it took to travel meant you couldn't go to a midweek game because you couldn't get the time off work – that was unheard of to go to a football match. That accelerated what became a major problem in football.

'I can remember going to the Clock End at Highbury and it would be full of United supporters, primarily from Manchester, but from other parts of the country too. And the same thing happened at Old Trafford, too, and I think that's where the tribal part of it came in: they came en masse to a ground and they would congregate in one spot. The Kop was probably the first. We had our Stretford End and it was territorial, and it was defending the territory.'

If the arrival of terrace violence was a change for the worse, there were other ways in which things were getting better: Old Trafford was getting a facelift ahead of the World Cup. Having been chosen in 1963 as one of the venues for the 1966 World Cup, United began a three-year programme to upgrade its stadium, helped by a grant of £40,000 for improvements. This time, it wasn't just a case of providing some cover from the weather for the fans. The entire Popular Side (now the North Stand) was rebuilt at a cost of £350,000, with a new cantilever roof to a design by local architects Mather and Nutter. Work began in the summer of 1964; the new stand when it was completed was 660 feet long and the terracing 48 feet high, with the roof suspended from concrete yokes 30 feet above the stand. Much of the funding came from the Manchester United Development Association, but Busby was also happy that he had the strength in his squad not to require much in the way of extra signings, as the Old Trafford coffers were seriously depleted by all this work.

'You knew there'd be no pillars or obstructions to your view,' says Ken Ramsden, who remembers it being built. It was the beginning of the construction of the modern bowl arena of Old Trafford. The new stand, completed for the start of 1965–66, found space for 20,000 fans, half seated and half standing. The tip-up chairs were specially designed, with curved backs and seats. It also included a special feature: fifty-five executive boxes, each holding six people, the first in any football ground in England. Busby had been entertained in the private boxes at Manchester racecourse, and understood that wealthy locals could be tempted to the club if there was something a bit special made available to them. As Les Olive described it in one magazine, it was 'a sort of Soccer-Ascot'. The heated boxes had waiter service, a private lift to take spectators there and high-class refreshment bars.

Sir Bobby Charlton states: 'The private boxes were Matt Busby's idea. He'd been in America and he'd seen things there that he thought had to be here. He persuaded the directors to clamber to the back of the terraces, as they were being built, to a narrow deck and put some kitchen chairs there, and said: "Look, gentlemen. This is what a box would be like, and look at the view here."'

The directors were won over and went for it. Crerand recalls how 'a pal of mine, Paddy McGrath, got the first box at Old Trafford, right on the halfway line . . . and he paid for the season exactly four hundred quid. Those boxes now must be forty or fifty grand.'

Elsewhere in the stadium, the corner paddocks were rebuilt. In the Main Stand, extra space was created for the press box to accommodate up to 400 journalists. All these pressmen were also provided with the back-up facilities required: 300 phone lines, interview rooms, camera platforms for TV, as well as 'working and rest rooms'.

In the meantime, United got on with the task of going one better in the league. Winger John Connelly was signed from Burnley, but otherwise the side was pretty much the same (Connelly would become United's first ever substitute at Old Trafford, coming on for John Aston on 6 November 1965). In the 1964–65 season, their main rivals were not champions Liverpool or Spurs, but newly promoted Leeds United, who were just beginning a period of a decade where they would be perennial challengers for trophies. Don Revie's men may have played in white, but they were no angels; they did manage to provoke the devil in the Reds, however. The FA Cup semifinal between the two sides that season was a battleground – Leeds being the victors – with the violence on the pitch leading to violence off it. However, United won the April league encounter between them, as part of a run of seven successive victories that brought the title back to Manchester for the first time in eight years.

The decisive moment came on Monday 26 April, when 51,625 saw United beat Arsenal 3–1 at Old Trafford, thanks to two goals from Law, who played despite having six stitches in his knee after a clash with Liverpool's Ron Yeats in a game two days before. Best scored the other. United still had one more game to play, at Aston Villa, but if Leeds failed to win their Monday game at Birmingham, that had kicked off at the same time, United could go to the Midlands as champions.

During the match against Arsenal, the stadium announcer kept the crowd updated with the score from St Andrews, and by the middle of the second half Leeds were 3–0 down. News filtered through that Leeds had pulled a goal back, then another, and another. With United's game over, it was merely a question of waiting to see if Leeds had completed a stunning comeback to win. But happily for all concerned, they had drawn and United were champions again. The fans invaded the pitch to celebrate their return to the top.

Three and a half weeks later, on 19 May, the team were presented with their trophy before the Fairs Cup quarterfinal second leg against Strasbourg. Each player emerged from the tunnel to receive his medal, with Best the last to appear, before Busby. Law then received his award as European Footballer of the Year.

United could point to the silky skills of Best, Law and Charlton as setting them apart from Leeds, and the fluidity of the Reds' formation gave them a tactical edge few opponents could fathom. As Law explains: 'If I was not getting any joy up front, I would just go to the right side and let somebody else come in. Bestie could always play through the middle.' More than thirty years later, the combination of Berbatov, Ronaldo, Rooney and Tevez displayed a similar tactical flexibility. However, it was the solidity of United's defence that truly made the difference, as they conceded just thirty-nine goals, the fewest by any side since 1949–50.

There was one other factor: United played 60 matches that season (starting on 22 August and finishing on 16 June) in all competitions and seven players appeared in 59 or 60 of them, three more played in 55 or more; Law was a relative slouch, playing just 52 games (and most of those he missed were due to disciplinary reasons). Has there ever been a more settled line-up than Pat Dunne, Brennan, Tony Dunne, Crerand, Foulkes, Stiles, Connelly, Charlton, Herd, Law, Best? They might not have been as young as the Babes, but they would all be around for some time to come, and there were some more good young players coming through the ranks. Busby's third great team was up and running. What was more, they were back in the European Cup, the trophy Busby wanted more than any other.

He moved into the new campaign with a new chairman, for Harold Hardman died on 9 June 1965. Hardman had been born in Manchester, taking his first breath less than four years after the club that became United first kicked a ball. Having briefly played for United in the pre-Old Trafford days, he knew the club as well as anyone. His replacement was Louis Edwards, who had been on the board for seven years. He had long been a Busby ally, even before he joined the board, and had been one of those who had most encouraged the manager during his spending spree in the aftermath of the Munich tragedy.

Work continued on the new cantilever stand over the summer, but it wasn't quite finished in time for the start of the season as there had been complications in the construction, so the Warwick Road end of the stand wasn't completed until October. The nature of the crowd was continuing to change during this period, too. Chanting and singing by the fans was getting louder, more passionate; in some cases, the behaviour went too far for Busby and the board. The final match of the previous season, the semifinal of the Fairs Cup against Ferencvaros, had seen various objects thrown onto the pitch. Mostly it was nothing more dangerous than rolls of toilet paper, but it would get worse.

Equally, the chanting wasn't as polite as Busby wanted. The manager may have been able to stop his assistant Jimmy Murphy from swearing in his presence, but in taking on the crowd he was hoping for too much. The programme noted when youths were banned from the ground for obscene chanting, in the hope that this would dissuade others from following their example. But this was to be one battle that Busby could not win. Society was changing, and what had previously been unacceptable was now a part of everyday life for most United fans. One programme concluded its plea as follows: 'So what about it you Stretford Enders? Cut out the obscenities and let us hear some comedy' in your chants. It didn't have any effect.

United's campaign in the season before the World Cup didn't quite go to plan. At the smart new Old Trafford, United were almost unbeatable, losing only to Leicester City in the league. But away from home, they conceded as many goals as they had in all forty-two games the previous season and lost eight games (including every game played after a European Cup away fixture). It was an example of what United – along with other successful English sides – have had to put up with ever since. As Brian McClair comments on his later experience of playing for United: 'Every game you went to was a big game' for United's opponents; everyone upped their efforts when Busby's men were in town. The Reds finished in fourth place, ten points adrift of champions Liverpool. The visit of the Merseysiders in October proved to be another instance where there was trouble on the terraces, with missiles then thrown through the windows of the boardroom after the match. If Liverpool fans were to blame for that incident, then the finger of accusation could point only to the home supporters when the coach carrying Blackburn Rovers players was stoned.

In the FA Cup, United reached a fifth successive semifinal, only to lose at that stage again. However, the real focus was on one thing: the European Cup. United began against the Finnish amateurs of Helsinki HJK, before taking on the East German army side ASK Vorwaerts from East Berlin. Both were easily beaten in low-key matches that had little 'big European night' glamour, to take United through to the quarterfinals. Now there was a much more daunting prospect lined up against them in Benfica, four times finalists (and twice winners) in the previous five seasons. Like United, the Portuguese champions had never lost in Europe on home soil, so this was a real challenge.

A crowd of 64,035 turned up at Old Trafford that February evening and saw a marvellous spectacle of a game. United may have had Best, Law and Charlton, the latter on particularly good form, but Benfica had Eusebio, Simoes and Torres. The crowd applauded both sides off at half-time and at the end of the match with United 3–2 victors, knowing they had seen two excellent teams playing at their peak of their skills. Or so they thought. A month later, the return leg in Portugal proved that United, and Best in particular, had another level to reach.

In a tense changing room beforehand, Busby told everyone to

keep things tight to start with. Crerand shattered the changing-room mirror, and the bad omen made everyone even more nervous. Best ignored it all, scoring two and setting up a third in the first fifteen minutes. The Reds destroyed Benfica 5–1 on their own turf with a performance that suggested Busby's long wait for European glory was about to come to an end. It was a decision by Best to don a huge sombrero stepping off the plane after the flight home that created the legend of 'El Beatle', as the *Daily Mirror* christened him, and finally catapulted the shy, young Belfast teenager into superstardom, where the distractions away from the game quickly began to mount up.

Best was now central to everything United did. Despite cartilage problems, he was sent out to play in the first leg of the semifinal in Belgrade against Partizan, but even Best couldn't perform if he couldn't run properly. United lost 2–0, and Best had played his last game of the season, as the club bowed to the inevitable and sent him off for an operation. The return leg drew 62,500 to Old Trafford, but United could not find the intensity they had shown in Lisbon, though Crerand discovered it in one way, getting sent off along with one of his opponents. Stiles scored a late goal, but the Reds could not find the vital second they needed. Both Busby and the players knew they had missed a golden opportunity to win the European Cup. United had to go and win the league again before they would have another chance to compete for the biggest trophy of them all.

Before they could do so, Old Trafford had a role to play in that summer's World Cup. Along with Goodison Park, it was chosen as one of the venues to host three games in Group 3. Tickets to watch all three games started from £1 2s 6d and rose to maximum of £6 6s for the best seats. On the evening of 13 July, Portugal beat Hungary 3–1 in front of a crowd of 37,000. Three days later, an even smaller crowd of just 26,000 saw Portugal ensure qualification for the next round with a 3–0 victory over Bulgaria, with a familiar face on the score-sheet: Eusebio. The final match in the group saw Hungary overcome Bulgaria 3–1, but only 22,000 came along to see the former side qualify.

There was a major surprise in the group, as Brazil failed to progress, with Pelé notoriously the target of some gratuitous tactics to kick him out of the tournament. Old Trafford wasn't used as one of the venues for the later stages of the competition, and it could hardly be said (after all the work that had been done on the stadium) that the Manchester crowds had got behind the tournament in a major way. Perhaps the price of the tickets was set too high. But then, this was a very different era: London's White City was used for one of the matches in England's Group 1 when Wembley refused to rearrange a greyhound meeting to accommodate the tournament! After 30 July, when England won the World Cup, the role of football became more central to people's minds, but for now the World Cup could take its place behind some dogs chasing after a fake rabbit.

That summer Denis Law found himself on the transfer list, after he wrote a letter asking for a pay rise of ten pounds a week, saying that he would leave if he didn't get it. Busby went public, insisting, 'No player will hold this club to ransom.' Law duly apologised (Busby had his apology ready to be signed in his desk), and the rest of the players were given another lesson in the importance of not asking the Boss for a rise. Some things in football still hadn't changed.

But there were other changes afoot. Alex Stepney was signed as the new United goalkeeper in September 1966, bringing an end to a period where the team had alternated between three goalkeepers. He immediately noticed 'a seriousness and a hardness' about his new team-mates. They could play, but they weren't anyone's pushovers. England World Cup squad member John Connelly was on his way out, replaced by John Aston. And the problem of violence on the terraces continued to get worse. Cliff Butler recalls: 'The major watershed was when Everton came here in 1966 early in the season and they decided they were going to go in the Stretford End. They were on the lower terraces and we were above, and there was just one hell of a battle – it really went off. The Stretford End became the province of United, and only United. It became a mission among some fans to go to an away game and infiltrate their end.' As a result, extra barriers were built on the Stretford End and it was made easier for the police to have access to any problems there.

Pride and passion in the club were growing all the time. Increasing numbers of people travelled from all around the country to Old Trafford. In Law and Charlton, they had two of the three most recent European Footballers of the Year, Charlton having received the honour in 1966. And in Best they had the man who was every fan's hero, arguably the greatest player ever to come out of the British Isles. No wonder the stadium was packed full almost every game, with average attendances just short of 54,000. Best had his own fan club, and by 1967 he was receiving a thousand letters a week, sent from all around the world.

It was also the last season when the 'holy trinity' of Best, Law and Charlton operated at anything like full strength, missing just six league games between them. Thereafter, Law's damaged knee, Best's off-field distractions and Charlton's age all gradually began to tell, and so the number of games they missed increased. But for now, as Wilf McGuinness recalls, the three had plenty to offer: 'They all had something great about them. George was the film star, pop star type; he was the first of the pop-star footballers. They kept the Busby Babe thing going, because two of them started here. George was the young one, and as soon as he'd finished he was off into town; Denis went home for sure, and Bobby was pretty much the same. Bobby was more quietly spoken, but Denis was a home bird and he enjoyed his family life. Denis was very fiery [on the pitch].'

After a relatively slow start to the campaign, United upped their performances and did not lose in the league after Boxing Day. At Old Trafford they were even more invincible, going unbeaten for a record thirty-seven home league matches between 27 April 1966 and 20 January 1968. In March 1967, in another first for the ground, United's game at Arsenal was shown on a big screen at Old Trafford, with more than 28,000 watching the 1–1 draw.

Later that month, David Herd's leg was badly broken, effectively ending the Old Trafford career of a man who had scored twenty-plus goals in each of the previous four seasons, but it did not slow United's momentum. They secured the title with a 6–1 victory at West Ham (Moore, Hurst, Peters and all) that had even Busby purring with delight at his team's performance: 'You have a sense that your players can do anything.' The trophy was presented to the team before the next fixture, against Stoke at home, and after the match there was a largely good-natured pitch invasion, though increasingly the police were becoming concerned about such events, whereas even two years before this had not really been the case.

This time, there was a feeling that winning the title was the start of something bigger, that the European Cup awaited. However, if you had mentioned to anyone that evening that it was to be United's last domestic trophy for a decade, and they would not be champions again for another twenty-six years, few would have believed you. After all, United had won five titles and been runners-up six times in the last twenty-two seasons.

More work was done on the stadium, by the forecourt, creating room for a club shop early the following season. It began as little more than a wooden hut, but after a year it moved into the offices of the Development Association because of its immediate success. Martin Edwards recalls how the boardroom moved from the quadrant between the East and South Stands, to an area above the new shop. Run by Frank Gidley and his family, it sold a range of the usual sorts of merchandise, such as scarves, badges and so on.

Embarking on his twenty-third season as United manager, Matt Busby felt his squad was strong enough for the challenges ahead. As ever, new blood was coming up through the ranks, this time local boy Brian Kidd. The season began with the Charity Shield at Old Trafford against Spurs, which would be remembered above all for two goals. One, by Pat Jennings, was from a long punt down-field that sailed down the pitch and bounced over Alex Stepney's head into the goal. The other was one of Charlton's best: Law picked up the ball in the left-back position and sprinted down the touchline, laying it off to Kidd. The debutant crossed the ball to Charlton, twenty-five yards out on the edge of the D, who unleashed a fierce shot that flew into the top of the net. Charlton recalls, 'It wasn't the shot, it was the whole build-up. It was almost an unstoppable goal.' Kidd modestly remembers that his pass was mishit – the sort of mishit we'd all love to make.

It proved to be one of the most intriguing title races in years, with both big teams from Manchester and Liverpool in the mix, along with Leeds. The crowds flocked to see the matches in ever-increasing numbers: by the second half of the season it was rare for fewer than 60,000 to come to Old Trafford. Football was the fashionable sport, and not just because Best was opening boutiques and hanging out in nightclubs. More than 15 million spectators went to First Division matches that season – the only time since 1955 that figure has been exceeded for the top tier. Home and away, fans wanted to see United, who drew incredible crowds averaging just short of 46,000 away from home, a figure beaten only once in the club's history. The title race went to the final day, when United surprisingly lost 2–1 at home to fifteenth-placed Sunderland while Manchester City beat Newcastle away. Busby graciously congratulated City manager Joe Mercer on his achievement live on *Match of the Day*, but perhaps his mind was already elsewhere.

For the league was always secondary to the main event: Europe. Ten years on from Munich, with the final due to take place at Wembley, and after Celtic had become the first British side to win the trophy the previous season, everything seemed set up to bring closure to the agonies of a decade ago. Hibernians of Malta were the first to try their luck at Old Trafford, and lost 4–0 in the first leg of the first round, before a goalless draw in the return leg. Yugoslav champions Sarajevo had proved stubborn battlers (in every sense) on their home pitch, where they'd also held on for a 0–0 draw and left Busby 'so angry about the way they'd played', according to Stepney. So there was everything to play for in

Manchester in the return leg. The keeper recalled how the team still took a lot from the game, however: they might not have been able to display their skills, but they'd shown their own resolve and professionalism in the face of great provocation.

There was more of that to come in front of almost 63,000 fans crammed into Old Trafford. United took an early lead through Aston. But in the second half, Best responded angrily when the goalkeeper tried the oldest trick in the book: digging his nails into him as he helped up the Ulsterman. Prljaca went in search of revenge so blatantly that he was sent off; Best had an even better riposte, scoring United's second. The ten men of Sarajevo were not done, and pulled back a goal, but the Reds held on and even won the fight in the tunnel as the players left the pitch, thanks to Crerand.

Polish side Gornik Zabrze were United's opponents in the quarterfinals, and somehow an extra few hundred fans squeezed into the ground to see a Best shot deflected in for an own goal, before Kidd added a second late in the game. This time when the players reached the tunnel to leave the pitch, they applauded rather than thumped each other. In Poland, on a pitch of compacted snow in blizzard conditions and in the face of a hostile crowd of 105,000, United held out until twenty minutes from the end, but there were few alarms afterwards as they won 2–1 on aggregate.

Benfica, Juventus and Real Madrid remained with United in the tournament, and it was the Spanish side that came to Old Trafford on 24 April for the first leg of the semifinal. They had been United's conquerors in their first European campaign, but the two clubs had developed a healthy respect for each other and the way each side looked to play the game, as Real had been hugely supportive of United in the aftermath of Munich. Although there had been no official games between the two sides since 1957, they had met frequently in the interim. Jack Crompton recalls in his memoir how, in one friendly, Alfredo di Stefano had deliberately missed a penalty that had been dubiously awarded, and how the match officials were banned from the post-match dinner by the club's president, who did not want to win by underhand means.

The game in Manchester was one of high skill in front of another full house, but the only goal of the game was a left-foot volley by Best from an Aston cross from the left. Against a team such as Real, with all their European experience, it didn't seem enough to take to the Bernabeu. And when United went in at half-time 3–1 down, the doubters seemed right, but Busby reminded them that the aggregate score was 3–2, and one more goal would put them level (this would have resulted in a replay, since away goals didn't count double then). Real seemed not to have done the same maths, as they appeared to think the tie was won. Having pulled a goal back, United took the aggregate lead with fifteen minutes remaining, thanks to the only man who had been on the pitch that fateful day in Belgrade, Bill Foulkes. He scored just his second goal in Europe and was as surprised as anyone when he found himself in the right position to score from Best's pass. Given that United had just lost the league title four days before this match, it was a performance of enormous character.

In between the two legs, Old Trafford had played host to its first post-war FA Cup semifinal, between Everton and Leeds. A packed crowd paid record receipts of £51,000 to see the Merseysiders through to the final, which they eventually lost to West Brom.

After beating Real Madrid, everyone felt confident about the final at Wembley against Benfica: surely it was United's and Busby's destiny to win the European Cup? Even without the injured Law, the players felt their name was on the cup. Busby ensured the players were in the right frame of mind on the day of the final, as some went to Mass first before all headed off to race-horse owner Robert Sangster's house to watch the Derby, cheering on Lester Piggott's horse to victory. Relaxed and composed, with Wembley thronged with optimistic United fans who monopolised the stadium, the blue-shirted United ran out on a very warm night to seize what was theirs. For a long while, the game did not settle, but then another Munich survivor, Charlton, scored. After Benfica equalised, they had a chance to seal the game in the final moments, but Eusebio blasted the ball at Stepney, who saved it. In extra time, Best came into his own, as the other players tired and he scored the second. Kidd (on his nineteenth birthday) and Charlton added the extras and United had won 4–1. After the final whistle blew, the players all headed to Busby, who said of the triumph: 'It cleansed me . . . It was my justification.'

At last, United were champions of Europe. Busby's decision all those years ago to start on the continental campaign trail was finally vindicated, and the trophy United had never won seemed as though it was coming to its rightful home at Old Trafford. What more could this team and this manager go on to achieve? Sir Bobby Charlton had the answer: the European Cup had come 'in the nick of time . . . the 1968 team was probably no longer at its best . . . and a lot of us were past our peak'. No one thought that on that glorious late May night in 1968, but Charlton was right: United had reached the top, and the only way now was down. What was surprising was how far down United went before they began the long road back to the top.

8

The Decline and Fall
of the Red Empire

Champions of Europe, legendary manager Matt Busby knighted, star player George Best the third Red to win the European Footballer of the Year award in four years, United were seemingly set for further domination in 1968–69 and beyond. But after all the emotions of finally reaching the European summit, everything that the club had been striving after for so long had been achieved. The energy that had driven the club onwards slowly dissipated. Sir Matt turned sixty just after the end of the season, and he now seemed unable to put things right on the field when United struggled.

Some major rebuilding of the team was necessary, as a few players neared the end of their careers; while Best, still just twenty-two that season, was living in a world that a man who had fought in the Second World War could not begin to comprehend. Signing Willie Morgan from Burnley for £105,000 early in the campaign to replace the injured John Aston gave United new options out wide and another heart-throb, but more was clearly needed. There were some young players coming through, including such names as John Fitzpatrick, Alan

Gowling, Steve James, Frank Kopel, Jim Ryan and Carlo Sartori – but they weren't going to make too many opponents quake in fear.

Did Busby have the will to rebuild or re-motivate his team? Denis Law has argued that it was merely the latter that was required, as United's decline that season was more due to a series of injuries to key personnel, rather than their age: although Bobby Charlton ended the season aged thirty-one, Law was still (just) in his twenties, Pat Crerand had just turned thirty, Nobby Stiles was twenty-seven. Only Bill Foulkes was genuinely nearing the end of his career. Certainly, the team needed a major over-haul during the next five years, but it could be a gradual process. However, once the press narrative was that the side was an ageing one, that became the accepted wisdom and the aura around the players was diminished. Any dip in form or mistake was put down to age rather than normal human fallibility.

There were still highlights in 1968–69: on 19 March, United beat QPR 8–1 at Old Trafford to record their biggest league win of the Busby era, with new boy Morgan scoring his only hat-trick for the club, but it was seen by the lowest home crowd of the season, just 36,638. Old Trafford remained a stronghold, with just three defeats in the league, but away from home United registered a paltry two victories. In the FA Cup, even home advantage wasn't enough when United finally met First Division opposition in the quarterfinals in Everton.

By then, Busby had already announced that he would retire, following three straight league defeats. The press conference at Old Trafford came on 14 January, and secretary Les Olive read out a short statement in which it was explained that Busby would take on the role of 'general manager' after the season ended, Louis Edwards and the board having failed to persuade him to carry on. He would remain in charge until then, while a suitable replacement was found. If the news was supposed to spur on the players to one last effort for the Boss, it didn't work as United picked up just one league win in the next six games.

Busby was also feeling baffled by the club's supporters. He couldn't comprehend the behaviour of some of the Stretford Enders, or their willingness to cause the club embarrassment. Early in the season, the club had written to all visiting teams, advising them to warm up at the Scoreboard End, so as not to provoke the United fans at the opposite end. In October, when United took on Arsenal, the referee had an announcement made over the loudspeaker that if any more objects were thrown onto the pitch, he would have to abandon the game. Bob Wilson, in the Gunners' goal, was suffering under a terrifying barrage of objects. When Busby or chairman Louis Edwards wrote in the match programme to ask for calm or positive support, they were ignored. Respect for elders and authority figures just did not feature in the minds of the lads on the terraces. As Cliff Butler comments: 'The sixties was an era when you could do as you bloody well liked. Promiscuity became a popular word, free love, flower power, and all that: the war had finished now and the youth had grown out of [deference].'

There was still the magic of international competition to enjoy, though in the case of the World Club Championship against Estudiantes of Argentina it proved to be a very black kind of magic. The first leg in Buenos Aires was a battleground. After the violence of the first encounter, which United somehow managed to lose by only 1–0, the return leg at Old Trafford was hardly any better. A full house of 63,500 saw the Argentineans take an early lead and then do everything to disrupt the Reds for the rest of the game. Some of it was legal, but most of it wasn't, and the Old Trafford faithful were not going to let their opponents off lightly, taunting Estudiantes with animal chants. United equalised late on, and then the ball was en route to the back of the net when the referee blew the final whistle to spare all concerned a deciding third leg.

So just the European Cup remained. As the cliché goes: winning a trophy is difficult, retaining it is even harder. While

United had been used to being the team everyone lifted their game for in domestic football, in Europe they had been something of the plucky underdog, yet to match the likes of Real Madrid, Benfica and Internazionale as regular winners and finalists. Now they had become the team to beat in Europe as well; their campaign to hold on to the trophy would be the hardest yet, even though there were no serious domestic distractions.

United's fans had perhaps grown a little complacent, too. Against Waterford, a sporadic burst of slow hand-clapping broke out shortly before United took a 37th-minute lead. That opened the flood-gates, with the Reds eventually running out 7–1 victors.

In the next round, United faced Anderlecht and a moderate crowd turned up, perhaps remembering the one-way traffic of the teams' previous encounter back in 1956. A 3–0 victory seemed enough, but United made hard work of the away leg and ended up winning through to the quarterfinals just 4–3 on aggregate. Rapid Vienna stood in the way of United reaching yet another European Cup semifinal, something they had achieved every previous time they had contested the tournament. This time Old Trafford was packed; it was serious now. United's glamour boys, Best and Morgan, shared three goals between them, to make the job easy for the return leg in Austria.

AC Milan, who had just beaten Jock Stein's Celtic, barred the way to the final. They had beaten United at the same stage in 1958 in the aftermath of Munich, and had won the trophy back in 1963, so they were serious foes. The first leg took place in the San Siro on 23 April 1969, but a crowd of almost 23,000 turned up to stand on the Stretford End to watch the first ever live screening of a European Cup match at a football ground on a giant screen. The passionate fans cheered on their team, but saw them beaten 2–0.

The United faithful believed they could overturn the deficit, despite the fact that Milan's goalkeeper Cudicini (father of

Fans gather outside the offices at Old Trafford to find out the latest news after the team's plane bringing them home from their European Cup tie in Belgrade crashed in Munich. Twenty-three people, including eight from the team, died in the disaster of 6 February 1958. *(Press Association)*

Bill Foulkes tosses the coin as United prepare for their first game after Munich, against Sheffield Wednesday on 19 February. Suddenly, Old Trafford was at the centre of media attention. *(Press Association)*

Harold Hardman, chairman and the man who insisted 'United will go on'. Here he thanks Professor Maurer, who led the team at the Rechts der Isar hospital that looked after the injured players, for all his work. *(Press Association)*

Bobby Charlton is thwarted in United's game against West Ham, October 1963. Behind him is the roof over the Stretford End, which had been built at the end of the 1950s. *(Mirrorpix)*

Local boy Barry Fry, who never made it as a United player, practises outside Old Trafford in 1964. For a long time after the war, much of the team's training took place 'round the back'. *(Mirrorpix)*

United fans swarm onto the pitch to celebrate a 3-1 win over Arsenal on 26 April 1965, ensuring the title was coming back to Old Trafford. In the background, the new cantilever stand on the Popular Side is seen under construction ahead of the World Cup. *(Mirrorpix)*

Action from the World Cup, as the Portuguese defence holds out against the Bulgarian attack. The new cantilever stand, with its executive boxes, is in the background. A crowd of just 26,000 turned up. *(Press Association)*

George Best, scorer of the only goal, attacks the Real Madrid defence in the 1968 European Cup semi-final on a dramatic night at Old Trafford. *(Mirrorpix)*

A dream achieved: Matt Busby with the European Cup trophy. *(Getty Images)*

After Milan keeper Cudicini was apparently hit by a missile thrown from the crowd in the 1969 European Cup semi-final at Old Trafford, his team-mates begin to clear up some of the mess – it was one of the most intimidating nights at the ground that anyone can remember. *(Press Association)*

Above: New manager Wilf McGuinness in the dugout (centre), with a pensive Jack Crompton to his left. *(Press Association)*

Right: After a record TV audience saw Chelsea win the 1970 FA Cup final at Old Trafford, the players celebrated with their very own form of bubble bath – facilities nowadays for the United team are somewhat better. *(Getty Images)*

Below: George Best outside the club shop at Old Trafford in 1970. Shay Brennan and Willie Morgan (signing an autograph) keep him company. *(Mirrorpix)*

Frank O'Farrell sits in the stands at Old Trafford, September 1971. The cantilever roof had now been extended round to cover the Scoreboard End. *(Press Association)*

New manager Tommy Docherty joins Denis Law and David Sadler (right) in the United changing room after the draw against Leeds on 23 December 1972. *(Mirrorpix)*

The notorious pitch invasion of 27 April 1974, when relegation was confirmed at the end of the derby match against Manchester City. It has to be said that many of them look less like hooligans than kids having a party on the turf. *(Getty Images)*

The United fans find themselves behind fences at the start of their Second Division campaign in 1974, after a series of worrying incidents at Old Trafford. *(Mirrorpix)*

Dave Sexton signs Joe Jordan for a then record fee for United of £388,888, while club chairman Louis Edwards looks on. *(Mirrorpix)*

A different way of doing things: Bryan Robson signs for United on the pitch at Old Trafford, watched not just by Ron Atkinson, Les Olive and Martin Edwards, but also by 46,837 fans. *(Getty Images)*

Carlo) had not conceded more than two goals in a game for over two seasons. Italian sides had long known how to defend, and how to take the sting out of their opponents, slowing things down with feigned injuries, taking time over every restart, frustrating their foes. But the 63,103 in Old Trafford were not having any of it, and it became one of the most memorable nights in the ground's history. 'The atmosphere was electric,' says Crerand. Cliff Butler, who was watching on in the stands, recalls:

'The [game] that stands out more than any is the European Cup semifinal against AC Milan in 1969. It's almost indescribable; it was just incredible the noise. Old Trafford was four-fifths terrace then, and though Milan had one or two people there, it was as though the crowd were picking up the team and throwing them at the goal, wave after wave of attacking. It was a different thing in those days because you didn't see the famous players all the time; it was a different culture and so they had all the little dirty tricks: spitting and the pinching and that was going on all through the game . . . United were capable of nasty little tricks as well, but the crowd would react to what Milan did.

'United scored with about twenty minutes to go and for that last twenty minutes it was just staggering the noise. Everybody was shouting and roaring, and it was just constant. I was absolutely knackered after that game, emotionally and physically drained; I don't think I had a voice for about three days after that game. I also think that probably ninety per cent of that crowd was from Manchester; it wasn't about United, it was about the city as well.'

Charlton scored the goal after a brilliant run from Best, and during the last period of the game Law thought he had scored the aggregate equaliser, but an Italian leg reached out to clear it. Had it crossed the line? The referee said no, but Willie Morgan, who was closest to it, said yes; television pictures seemed to suggest that Morgan was right. Many supporters felt it wasn't the only decision the referee got wrong that night, and some fans had already shown their displeasure by hurling missiles onto the pitch, one of which hit Cudicini. Rather than putting off the Italians, it was United who lost their momentum after the disturbances, as the force wasn't quite with them any more. Milan went through and then took the European Cup, while United had seen the last of this tournament until 1993.

The problem of terrace violence was now so serious and frequent that the board began to consider various options to control things. As a result of this incident, the central section of the Stretford End was closed at the start of the following season. It reflected the changing culture of the times, an era when Bank Holiday violence at seaside resorts between rival gangs became commonplace. The terraces were populated with adrenalin-fuelled young men, high on excitement and ready to take on any who tried to stop them doing what they wanted.

But the problems were nothing compared to what they would become within a few years. A reporter for *Charles Buchan's Football Monthly* went along to the Stretford End in January 1969 to record what it was like there, and to check up on the big issue of the day. In truth, he found little to worry about. He commented: 'This is the spot for the cheerleaders, the singers, the chanters and the punch-up youths, all caught up in hysterical non-stop adulation.' He reckoned that about 70 per cent of the fans in that part of the ground were teenagers, but there was actually little trouble that day. The sum total of it all was two lads fighting, and they were escorted out of the ground by three policemen, bowing to the crowd as they left. In some ways, the fact that a couple of idiots felt proud of their behaviour was the really significant change, not so much what they had actually done.

Before the season ended, Busby had persuaded the board that his successor should not be a famous outsider, but instead should come from within the club, to preserve continuity and the United way of doing things (or more particularly the Busby way of doing things, for that *was* the United way). It was a ploy that has subsequently been seen to work, as would be shown a few years later when Bob Paisley emerged from the Anfield boot room to replace Bill Shankly. But, more often than not in football history, the ploy hasn't worked. And the man Busby wanted, it was announced on 9 April, was Wilf McGuinness.

McGuinness was just thirty-one when he stepped up to the manager's role, except he wasn't even given the title; instead he was 'head coach'. Already an experienced coach, he had been at United since 1953 and on the coaching staff for most of the 1960s. He'd even worked alongside Alf Ramsey with England during their successful World Cup campaign. Immediately he had a problem, though, because the man who had ruled the club for more than a generation was still there, in charge of key aspects of the playing side, such as transfers and so on. McGuinness may have been running things on the training ground, but everyone knew that Sir Matt was pulling the strings. His opinions were unlikely to be overruled by a rookie boss in his first campaign. The new man himself looks back positively on Busby's reasoning: 'Busby was a great man and I think he wanted continuity, and that's why nobody from outside had his job – he was loyal to his staff.' An outsider, of course, might have brought in his own people to replace those who had served the club so well.

In fact, United did better in the league in 1969–70 than they had done the previous season, finishing eighth, and they reached the semifinals of both the FA Cup and the League Cup. All this would have been solid enough, if United hadn't been European champions less than two years previously. McGuinness struggled to impose himself, despite taking brave decisions to 'rest' senior players, who often did not expect to be 'rested'. They felt he was trying too hard to show who was boss.

It didn't help that United faced local rivals City (who had gone on a similarly precipitous decline in form since 1968) five times that season, and won only once – 3–0 in the FA Cup fourth round at Old Trafford. This time it was Best who was out of the side for disciplinary reasons. But by then they'd already been humiliated 4–0 at Maine Road and lost the two-legged League Cup semifinal against them. It was even worse news when United lost out in the FA Cup semifinal second replay to Leeds United: 0–0, 0–0 and 0–1 showed the tension of the three ties, but neither the result nor the style of the games was what people expected from the Reds.

Leeds were in the process of going the long way round with everything. After two replays to overcome United, they drew 2–2 with Chelsea in the final on a dodgy Wembley pitch. Two and a half weeks later, the replayed FA Cup final took place at Old Trafford. Amazingly, it was the first time a replay had been required since before the First World War and the first time in the Wembley era that the trophy was decided away from North London. Indeed, the last time the final had been held outside London was back in 1915, when Old Trafford had played host to the Khaki Cup final.

The two sides were closely matched, having finished second and third in the league. Between them, they also had some of the toughest players in the game: Ron 'Chopper' Harris and Norman 'Bites Yer Legs' Hunter had earned their nicknames. Early on, Harris caught Eddie Gray on the back of the knee to slow down the man who had given them so much trouble in the first contest. Punches were thrown and head-butts traded as players went looking for retribution. With England due to fly out for the World Cup soon after, some were lucky to make it onto the plane in one piece. Just occasionally a game of football broke out, with Leeds dominating for much of the time. Mick Jones scored for Leeds to give them a deserved lead, before Peter Osgood equalised for Chelsea, and then in extra time David Webb forced home the winner to give the West London side its first ever FA Cup trophy. A crowd of 62,078 saw the drama and violence, paying record receipts of £88,000, while a record FA Cup UK television audience of 28 million saw the X-rated match unfold.

For United, McGuinness was finally given the title of team manager for the start of the following season, but was then demoted to trainer of the Central League side over the Christmas period of 1970 after United's form continued to decline and they were in eighteenth place. He quit the club a couple of months later. Losing the two-leg League Cup semifinal to Third Division Aston Villa with Best, Law, Charlton, Kidd, Crerand and Morgan in the line-up was essentially the final straw. Busby returned to ensure United did not have to endure the ordeal of a relegation battle and they finished in eighth place again, as Best and Law knocked in twenty goals in the nineteen league matches that remained, with the latter scoring his final hat-trick for United at Crystal Palace in April.

Best was coming towards the end of his time at United by now. There were flashes of brilliance, of course, such as the game against Tottenham in February that season. A clearance fell to him on the edge of the box, he controlled it on his chest and then lobbed it over the defenders and the keeper under the cross-bar in front of the joyous Stretford End, who knew they had just witnessed one of the best goals they would ever see. His father, watching in the stands, was up and celebrating before he'd even hit it; he knew what was coming. However, Best began to miss training sessions, and Busby could not ignore his lack of team spirit. Best had his excuses, claiming that the club were not making the signings that would help to share the load, but the balance had begun to tip. Previously, he had worked hard on the pitch and in training and played hard away from it; now the partying was beginning to take precedence over the football.

On his return, Busby not only had the on-field issue of dealing with Best to worry about, he also had to deal with the fans again. The objects being thrown onto the pitch were no longer just toilet rolls, but included much more dangerous items such as coins, with Bob Wilson requiring a stitch in a wound when he was once again targeted. As a result, the area of the Stretford End behind the goal was again kept empty all the way up to the tunnel. In his programme notes, Busby wrote of his regret that spectators had brought 'such action upon themselves and such disgrace upon our club'. Within a couple of months, during a match against Newcastle United, a knife was thrown onto the pitch. This time it wasn't going to be a matter for United – the FA Disciplinary Committee was called in, much to Busby's intense embarrassment.

Busby's return was only ever meant to be a temporary one, and so for the second time in two years the search was on for a man who could replace him. In June 1971, the board and Sir Matt went for 42-year-old Frank O'Farrell, who had just guided Leicester City to promotion to the top division, having previously been at Torquay. Although Busby was involved in the negotiations, made the announcement and was with O'Farrell for the photo call, it was also stated that he was now moving onto the main board and was not going to have any more managerial input. O'Farrell's teams had always played attacking football the United way, whereas there had been much criticism over the defensive approach of McGuinness, so he was a popular choice.

O'Farrell had to start his United career by playing his first six games away from Old Trafford, as the club had been ordered to play its first two 'home' fixtures at neutral venues following the knife-throwing incident, and had also been fined £7000. To make matters worse, there was more trouble at the first of these 'home' games, held at Anfield. When United finally started playing at Old Trafford, the capacity was reduced to 54,000, as the club had decided to extend the cantilever stand all the way round to the Scoreboard End. This new project added 5500 more seats to the stadium and a further 25 boxes. However, in the interim, there was occasionally chaos outside the ground as too many fans tried to get in. In the end, it made sense to make the games all-ticket. A new scoreboard was also built, and the floodlights were upgraded so that colour television pictures would be of sufficient quality.

However sympathetic O'Farrell's methods were to United's style, this was an enormous step up, as he was to find out after he once dropped Charlton: 'The letters I got! They came from all over the world! And all telling me I was wrong.' O'Farrell's conclusion was: 'The interest is ridiculous.' But it wasn't; it simply came with the territory. The side might have slipped into mid-table of late, but they were still the second-best supported team in the land (behind Liverpool) after four years at the top of those rankings; they were the only club in England ever to have won the European Cup; and they had the only footballer in the country whose activities could regularly propel him onto the front pages of the newspapers. Could the new man cope?

For the first time since 1968–69, he got more than fifty goals (thirty-six by the New Year) in the season in all competitions out of Best, Charlton and Law, with the first two missing just two games each in 1971–72; even Law's creaking knees got him onto the pitch more than forty times. Up until Christmas, all went well, with United top of the table again. He found in Sammy McIlroy one of the best young players to emerge from United's scouting system in several years. After six months in the job, his first buy was an inspired one: central defender Martin Buchan joined from Aberdeen for a fee of £125,000, a record transfer from a Scottish club. Buchan soon became United captain and would eventually give more than a decade of service to the club.

But the reason United had to buy a defender was that they had lost seven league games in succession from the start of 1972, and the club finished the season in eighth position again. The resurgence in form in the first half of the season had not been sustained. The Reds needed replays in the cups to beat lesser opposition, such as Burnley, Southampton and Middlesbrough, and O'Farrell's other signings were expensive – Ted MacDougall, Wyn Davies and Ian Storey-Moore – and all fell short of what was expected of them, though the latter was lost to injury problems.

As McGuinness had found before him, there was still someone

above O'Farrell that players could turn to when they didn't like his decisions. In December 1972, he finally lost patience with Best, whose behaviour was now out of control, and placed him on the transfer list. Best went to see Sir Matt, who announced, without telling the manager, that Best would come off the transfer list. The fans obviously sided with their hero; the players may have had enough of Best's antics, but didn't particularly care for O'Farrell either. After a 5–0 thrashing at bottom-placed Crystal Palace, the board moved: on 19 December 1972, O'Farrell and his assistant Malcolm Musgrove were sacked – and so was Best.

Busby had already sounded out the man he thought should follow on from O'Farrell during the debacle at Palace. He and chairman Edwards had the briefest of conversations with Tommy Docherty, who had been there to watch one of Palace's Scottish players. The new manager couldn't have been more of a contrast with his predecessor. In the photo call to announce O'Farrell's appointment, he had looked a younger version of Busby: sensible haircut that probably hadn't changed for a decade, sober tie, smart suit, quiet, sombre demeanour – this clearly wasn't the man to 'get' George Best, or to understand the emotions of the lads on the terraces, supporting the most fashionable club in the country.

The new man, Docherty, was finally appointed on 30 December. Currently the manager of Scotland, where he had worked with Buchan, Law and Morgan, he had already had a stormy career, both as a player and a manager. He was charismatic and sparky, bringing with him a sense of fun and passion; he was the complete opposite of O'Farrell. He developed an instant rapport with the Stretford End; he knew what they wanted and he was going to bring it to them. The swagger, style and excitement of United were back on the agenda, and the fans were welcome to come along for the ride. Busby recommended Pat Crerand as his assistant, and Docherty willingly agreed. Whereas his two predecessors appeared daunted by Busby, the

Doc seemed happy to have him around: 'I've got the greatest manager in the world in an office down the corridor. Of course I'll talk to him. You'd be mad not to.' Jimmy Murphy and Jack Crompton were also brought back to the back-room team.

If Busby's men were useful to have around behind the scenes, on the pitch Docherty wanted to move them on: a clearout was required, he believed. Law, who had spoken to Busby about Docherty after Scotland's summer tour of Brazil, where he'd been impressed by his tactical knowledge and flexibility (when the players said it was too hot to train, he moved the session to a cooler time in the day), and had reiterated his praises when the vacancy came up, was one of the first to go. He was unhappy at the way he was let go, as he had been told he would have a job at the club when the time came to retire. Instead, he was surprised to be given a free transfer at the end of the season, so he had no chance to say goodbye to the fans who loved 'the King' as one of their own and would have wanted to celebrate one more time with the man who had raised an iconic finger in celebration at scoring 237 times for United.

Tony Dunne, who made his debut back in 1960, was also given a free transfer, having been eased out of the side. Charlton also decided it was the right moment to call time on his Old Trafford career at the end of the 1972–73 season. He was the leading goal-scorer in his final campaign, but his seven goals were the lowest tally of his entire career at United. Although the legs were still willing and more than able, Charlton did not want to be a part of a side battling to avoid relegation and his enthusiasm for the game finally appeared to be waning. He was given an emotional farewell by the Old Trafford faithful on 23 April against Sheffield United. A crowd of 57,280 were there that day, but the team could not give him the send-off he'd have wanted, losing 2–1. It was his 757th appearance for United, and his club record 249 goals still stands today. He still had one more game to play, away to Chelsea, but that also ended in defeat. That summer of 1973 it was as if Giggs, Neville and

Scholes all left the club at the same time. The old guard had gone, taking with them a combined total of 1697 appearances and 488 goals.

In their place had come, well, half of Scotland, it appeared. In Docherty's first month, he signed Scottish full-back Alex Forsyth, Scottish midfielder George Graham, Scottish striker Lou Macari (a spectacular move, from under the noses of Liverpool), Scottish central defender Jim Holton and Mick Martin from Ireland (he didn't stay long). All of them arrived in time for Burns Night, but United had spent about £500,000 in bringing them there. Where his predecessors had sometimes struggled to sign their targets, Docherty had the backing of both Busby and Edwards to get who he wanted. Results picked up, including an eight-game unbeaten run in March and April, but the Reds still finished in eighteenth place. At least the Old Trafford crowds were up, with two of the three biggest attendances that season coming in the last two games.

The first of them, the Manchester derby, saw United draw 0–0 to secure safety in the First Division. At the end of the match, some of the near-62,000 crowd ran onto the pitch to celebrate the fact that the Reds had retained their top-flight status for another year. It was perhaps an odd thing to be celebrating five years after being European champions.

Hopes for a new dawn the following season were quickly scuppered, as United could not get going. By Christmas 1973, one of the joint top scorers was Alex Stepney, who was United's penalty-taker, with two goals. The fact that none of the ten men in front of him was deemed to be a better option shows how bleak things were. Best was even brought back briefly, in the hope he would rediscover his old magic. But he remained true to form and went AWOL instead.

As the season wore on, another of the old guard was eased out, David Sadler leaving in November 1973. Docherty signed more players: Stewart Houston, another Scottish full-back, and Jim McCalliog, a Scottish forward brought in later in the season to provide some added goal threat. But Docherty wasn't simply going to spend his way to a new team: youth was given its chance, too, in the old United style. McIlroy had recovered from a car crash and was back, Brian Greenhoff was given his opportunity, and nineteen-year-old Gerry Daly was snapped up from Bohemians, after scoring against United in a friendly. Some of it worked – the back five of Stepney in goal, full-backs Forsyth and Houston and centre-backs Buchan and Holton were solid enough to give United the best defensive record they'd had since winning the league in 1967. But Macari and McIlroy were the joint leading goal-scorers with just six each in the league and cup all season.

Towards the end of the season, there was a brief rally as United picked up ten points from six games to give them a chance of survival. Docherty, who had been sending out his team to play cautiously beforehand, decided to go out positively, urged on by Busby. Hopes rose, and the crowds began to return to Old Trafford, hoping for a miracle. But the last of these matches was an away draw against relegation rivals Southampton, when a win was vital. Next came Everton at Goodison and a 1–0 defeat. For the final home game of the season, the visitors were Manchester City and in a tense derby United attacked but could not score. Then the final, fatal blow was dealt by Denis Law, the man Docherty had discarded, the man who could always score, with a natural finisher's touch: a clever back-heel past Stepney. Law, evidently still with divided loyalties, trudged off without celebrating and was substituted straight afterwards – the goal was his last kick in domestic football.

Because of results elsewhere, United would have been relegated anyway, but for City fans they had the joy of claiming to have sent down their local rivals, thanks to a goal scored by one of United's greatest heroes. It was too much for United fans to bear, and from the Scoreboard End in particular they invaded the pitch, hoping, perhaps, for the game to be abandoned and the result nullified. Or maybe it was just to express their frustration that a club who had been champions of Europe just six years before was now heading for the Second Division. Busby and Docherty pleaded for the fans to go back so the match could continue; the referee made one last attempt to restart the game and then abandoned it. Edwards tried to excuse their behaviour, saying it was a case of 'excitable youngsters' causing the problem. However, some of the City players had not managed to get down the tunnel before the fans arrived, and were lucky to escape largely unscathed, albeit terrified.

But this was not the first, or even the worst, example of hooliganism at Old Trafford that season. A friendly against Rangers in March saw the Glaswegian fans invade the pitch before kickoff, provoking an angry response from United supporters in the Stretford End. In total, seventy-seven fans were arrested in what the *Manchester Evening News* called 'the worst outbreak of hooliganism the city has ever seen'. As United's performances slumped, so many fans decided to make their own 'entertainment' and cause trouble.

There wasn't usually a lot of trouble between rival supporters at Old Trafford, because there were so many United fans there and few opponents were willing to take on the 'Red Army'. But even so, the decision was taken to try to prevent such incidents happening again: for the next season, United fans would have to watch the game behind nine-feet-high spiked fences at either end of Old Trafford, with safety gates in case of emergencies. The FA, who had been horrified by all the trouble at United, accepted what the club had done, and stated that as long as the fencing was in place, games could be held there. It was a sign of a troubled era that had spread throughout the sport, and would take almost a generation to quell.

So, with United relegated, Docherty felt sure he would be sacked: he had spent a lot of money on rebuilding the team, and this was the result. Instead, Busby gave him a crate of champagne and told him to make sure United bounced straight back to the First Division. It was a key moment, because it meant that once more everyone at Old Trafford could start to look forward, rather than looking back to the glory days of the Busby Babes or the European Cup triumph. Now all Docherty had to do was win promotion.

9

The March of the Red Army

The last visitors to Old Trafford to play a game against United in the Second Division had been Bury, way back on 7 May 1938. Now, on 24 August 1974, it was Millwall's turn, and a crowd of 44,756 saw Gerry Daly score a hat-trick in the Reds' 4–0 summer stroll. Impressively, the attendance was bigger than United's average the previous campaign – and the crowds were going to get even larger as the season wore on. Reds are not fair-weather supporters. Less impressively, as well as the barriers that had gone up around the ground, United had decided it needed to employ cameramen to spot troublemakers in the crowd. The club was doing what it could to make Old Trafford safe for the vast majority who came to the ground to cheer on their team. On this particular occasion, given the reputation of the opposition, it helped that United fans had forced many of the Millwall supporters who'd come up by train to go straight back on the next one south.

Making his Old Trafford debut that day was centre-forward Stuart Pearson, bought during the summer for £222,222 from Hull City, who also found the net and would go on to be United's leading scorer in the league for each of his first three seasons at the club. To help pay for him, Brian Kidd, another of the Busby generation, was sold for £110,000. Pearson, at least, had experience at this lower level, which some thought might prove crucial at a club that was used to higher things. Fortunately, United took to the Second Division with a style and verve that outsmarted most opponents, and didn't lose until their tenth league match of the season.

Soon after that came an opportunity in the League Cup to gain revenge on Manchester City. The blue side of Manchester had celebrated long and hard at United's demotion; now was the chance for the Red Army to show that their team was on the way back to the top. Making his debut that day was Arthur Albiston, in front of 55,169 fans creating one of the all-time special Old Trafford occasions. At just seventeen, he made several key interventions, including a late run down the left flank to start a move that ended in a penalty, which Daly converted. It seemed a measure of payback for the pain caused a few months before.

Despite relegation, the United board continued to develop Old Trafford to ensure it remained the best club ground in the country. Rebuilding work was carried out in the Main Stand, as a new cantilever roof was added to the central part of it. Inside, there were improvements to the hospitality facilities, including two new restaurants, as well as heated seats for the lucky few. An Executive Suite opened the following season, with a strictly limited membership, at a cost of £135 per season, but it proved hugely popular from the outset – United continued to be innovators in providing the widest and best range of match-day experiences (the facilities were also available for hire on non-match-days). Disabled access was enhanced, and the television gantry moved to a better position. The club was doing all it could to ensure that everyone's experience of Old Trafford was as good as possible – even those who could only watch United on television.

With victories almost expected from the team, up to 20,000 fans would sometimes travel to away matches, while Old Trafford regularly had up the 'house full' signs. This pattern began at the first match of the season, away at Orient, when the crowd was almost 18,000, as opposed to their average that season of 7605. For fifteen of United's twenty-one away games, the home club had their biggest crowd of the season. (Sadly, as began to happen with many teams in the 1970s, a minority of these 'supporters' were more intent on making their own dubious form of entertainment when they travelled away.)

A wobble at the start of 1975, when United lost four games out of seven in the league, saw Tommy Docherty go back into the transfer market, picking up undergraduate Steve Coppell from Tranmere Rovers, thanks to a surprise recommendation from Bill Shankly (after Liverpool decided against signing him). The Reds did not lose another game after he made his debut in the 4–0 home win against Cardiff on 1 March. Wearing boots he'd borrowed from Pearson, Coppell's first touch set up the former to score. Both men clearly knew how to make an instant impact in front of the Old Trafford crowd.

With two wingers, Coppell and Willie Morgan, supplying width and crosses, United went on to win the Second Division title in style, and in a way that has remained popular at the club ever since – wide men usually having a key role. Furthermore, United were again a young side, so this team had the opportunity to develop together. Amazingly, United were the best-supported club in the country that season, surely the only time a second-tier side has boasted that honour. The team had got back into the habit of winning and regained confidence, but no player should ever join United and be happy to win a Second Division title medal. There was more serious business ahead, back in the First Division. But the question was whether or not this young, vibrant side would get found out by the classier opposition to be confronted in the top league.

United began the new season in excellent form, picking up eleven points out of twelve, and continued to play in a style that made this team one of the most fondly remembered sides of all for United fans. They were also one of the best behaved – they went through the entire league campaign without anyone being sent off. Gordon Hill, on the left wing, was signed from Millwall for £80,000 as a replacement for Morgan, who had been offloaded to Burnley by Docherty. Hill soon became a cult hero on the Stretford End. He made his debut in November 1975, and was the only major new recruit that season from the side that had dominated the Second Division. With Coppell on the right, the Reds terrorised defences as wing-play roared back into fashion once again. By early April, United were threatening to achieve the Double, having just beaten reigning league champions Derby County in the FA Cup semifinal and lying one point behind league leaders Queens Park Rangers, with a game in hand. With Second Division Southampton awaiting them in the final, it was the three-way battle for league honours with QPR and Liverpool that occupied the team's thoughts first.

For the fans, it was a campaign that began with cautious optimism about United's prospects, but sheer joy and enthusiasm at being back in the top flight. The crowds piled into Old Trafford well over an hour before kickoff to sing and chant; they were ready to do their bit to inspire the players. However, after the strong start, attitudes on the terraces soon changed into genuine belief that here was a team that could take on anyone, and provide all the excitement and drama one could wish for, with a series of thrilling late winners. The 3–2 win against Wolves in the FA Cup sixth-round replay was a classic example, as United came back from 2–0 down to win in extra time. No wonder the crowds at Old Trafford averaged 54,750, the best since the European Cup-winning campaign. And, for the second successive season, their fanatical support helped ensure that only one game was lost at home.

In 1975–76, United had a very settled side, with only one change to the team in the entire FA Cup run that took the side back to Wembley for the first time since the European Cup final eight years previously. And it was that fact that perhaps meant they ran out of steam during the run-in, losing three of their last six league fixtures (including four games in seven days at one stage), before slumping to a 1–0 defeat in a poor FA Cup final. Hugh McIlvanney, writing in the *Sunday Times*, lamented that United had 'nothing tangible to show for all those months of inspired and adventurous football, for a long string of performances that represented the most exhilarating flourish of the English season'.

The fact that a crowd of more than 100,000 welcomed the side back to Manchester after they lost the final showed just how well the public had responded to this thrilling young team. They had been taken to the hearts of the fans, and the expectation was that they could clearly go on to even greater things. Docherty promised from the balcony of the town hall to bring the Reds straight back to Wembley the following season – a brave pledge.

Hopes that United would once again challenge for the league title were soon dashed when the Reds failed to win a First Division match for eight games between mid-October and Christmas 1976. Significantly, skipper Martin Buchan was out injured for all but the last of them. With the defence clearly troubled and needing quality back-up, Docherty returned to the transfer market for the first time in a while – and signed a forward. Brian Greenhoff's elder brother Jimmy joined from Stoke, on £50 a week less than he'd been paid in the Potteries. He was widely regarded as one of the best forwards never to play for England and, although he helped United get back on track, linking up brilliantly with Pearson, the team were never in the hunt for the title. His arrival meant that Sammy McIlroy was moved back into midfield, and Daly began to be edged out of the line-up before Docherty moved him on. Docherty also tried to sign Peter Shilton as a replacement for the ageing Alex Stepney. The fee was high, £275,000, but it was the goalkeeper's wage demands, which would have put him above anyone else on the club's books, that prevented a deal going through. United had remained, ever since Busby's day, one of the poorest payers, and they weren't about to change things now.

So, as was to become familiar for much of this period, United focused instead on the cups – and this time there were three to aim at, as Old Trafford prepared to host European football for the first time in the 1970s. To prevent any danger of a pitch invasion, and the possible consequences from UEFA, the fencing was extended round the entire perimeter of the pitch. In the UEFA Cup, the Reds' first opponents were Ajax, who had won the European Cup three times in succession earlier in the decade. After a 1–0 defeat in Amsterdam, a passionate crowd of just under 59,000 turned up at Old Trafford, under the new floodlights installed for that season, to roar United on to overturn the deficit, thanks to goals from Lou Macari and a late winner from McIlroy, set up by emergency striker Brian Greenhoff. A similar number came to watch a cautious and defensive Juventus side beaten 1–0 in the first leg of the second round, their tactics getting a very hostile response from the Stretford End. But the Italians had all the European experience in the world, and left the field smiling, knowing they'd done enough. They won the return leg comfortably – it was United's least successful European campaign to date.

The League Cup, despite coinciding with much of United's poor run, did bring about an incredible 7–2 victory over Newcastle United, before Everton ended all hopes of a run to Wembley. So, by Christmas, United had just the FA Cup left to aim for: the trophy Docherty had said he would win. Fortunately, the team's injury woes were largely over and, as in the previous cup run, there was just one change to the side the entire campaign, when young Albiston had to step in for Stewart Houston in the final.

Old Trafford hosted every round before United reached the semifinal. Third Division Walsall were seen off 1–0 in the third round, and then came Queens Park Rangers who, like United, had not continued their league form from the previous season. A Macari goal on a frozen late January afternoon was sufficient to help the Reds on to meet their previous nemesis, Southampton, in the fifth round. A battling effort at the Dell saw United back to Old Trafford for the replay, where Jimmy Greenhoff scored twice to make it five goals for him in three home matches.

By a strange quirk of the fixture list, United were in the middle of a run of seven home games out of eight played, during which time just under 395,000 fans came to share the joy of the Reds' regained enthusiasm and flair. A series of grudge matches came and went: Liverpool were held to a draw, Newcastle succumbed to a Greenhoff hat-trick, title-chasing Manchester City were thoroughly outplayed as United completed the double over them (had City won either, they would have been champions), there was the revenge act against the Saints, and then a declining Leeds lost 1–0.

It was breathtaking, exciting stuff, and for the crowds that flocked to watch it was always unpredictable. As the authors say in *The Red Army Years*, this was a time when fans 'felt and truly believed that their vocal efforts would help script and direct the drama they had paid to see'. Or, as Cliff Butler comments, speaking of a slightly earlier period: 'I went to participate; I was part of something. Sometimes I'd go home and I'd probably be more tired than some of the players, because I'd put so much into the game, especially the years when I was on the Stretford End . . . You were never still; you were continually swaying and moving, when a goal was scored you'd surge forward. It was utterly dangerous, but there was an excitement about it. You were part of a tribe.'

The next in the run of home matches was the quarterfinal tie against Aston Villa, where the Reds had to recover from an early goal conceded, but a Houston free kick and a strike from Macari late in the second half ensured United were through to the semifinal, where they were drawn to face Leeds. Since returning to the First Division, Docherty's side had beaten their Yorkshire rivals four times out of four, as the Revie era faded from memory. But Leeds had won the past two semifinal meetings between the sides, back in 1965 and 1970, and there is no such thing as an easy game against the team from the wrong side of the Pennines. Unless, that is, Jimmy Greenhoff and Coppell both score in the opening minutes to knock the stuffing out of them.

With a Cup final to prepare for, United's league form deteriorated as players saved themselves for their big day out at Wembley.

Waiting for them were newly crowned champions Liverpool. In this different era, United played twice in the week before the final, but selected the same side as would turn out in North London on both occasions, barring Stepney who was forced to miss one game. With Liverpool soon to join United as the second English side to win the European Cup, only the Red Devils stood between Bob Paisley's side and an 'impossible' Treble. The goals in United's 2–1 win came in a five-minute spell in the second half, with Jimmy Case's equaliser sandwiched by Pearson's precise shot and Jimmy Greenhoff's deflected winner. The match was played in a sporting atmosphere, with both teams applauding each other at the end, and the fans of both sides were on their best behaviour. Buchan, who had kept Kevin Keegan quiet while carrying an injury picked up earlier in the week, hobbled up the steps at the end of the game to lift the FA Cup.

For fans of a certain age, this was the first major trophy they'd ever seen United win, coming nine years after their previous piece of silverware, and it remains up there with the very best. During that period, the club had had four managers, been relegated and promoted, and missed out in one of the biggest Cup final upsets in history. But they'd also seen a close-knit team play an exciting, attacking style of football that was utterly irresistible to watch. This United *deserved* to win something; the fans deserved to see it happen, and it certainly helped that to do so they'd had to beat their Merseyside rivals against the odds. Could Docherty now go on and emulate Busby after 1963's FA Cup triumph and take the next step to league success? As he celebrated on the Wembley turf with the team, it seemed possible. However, before the decade was out, five of the twelve United players on show that day would have left the club, and before the summer was over the manager had been sacked.

Docherty brought on the beginning of the end himself, when he announced to the press that he had left his wife and was in love with Mary Brown. By 1977, divorce was increasingly common, but what made the situation more delicate was the fact that she was the wife of the club's physio, Laurie Brown. Docherty had told chairman Louis Edwards the news immediately after the Cup final before it became public knowledge. Clearly one of Brown or Docherty had to go, as it would be impossible for them to continue to work together in such circumstances, and the manager was certainly the harder man to replace.

But Docherty had made enemies behind the scenes at all levels at Old Trafford. The *Daily Express* reported: 'Directors' wives at the club, which is proud of its family image, helped force him out.' Sir Matt Busby certainly did not like this sort of publicity attaching itself to the club, and there were plenty of his former players who had grievances they were more than willing to air to him about Docherty. Even one of the club barmen had got into an argument with the manager over what appeared to be a case of Docherty selling FA Cup final tickets. In the end, it was a case of whether the club wanted to be one that took the easy option and stuck by a successful manager, or if they wanted to take a principled stand on the basis that United could not be seen to condone such behaviour on a range of issues. Once it came to that, Docherty was finished, and on 4 July 1977, at a meeting of the United board in Edwards' house, he was sacked.

As United had done the previous time, when Docherty succeeded O'Farrell, so once again the board decided to appoint a man who was as different as possible from the manager they had just sacked. Dave Sexton was a quiet, studious manager, renowned as an excellent coach. He had managed Chelsea between 1967 and 1974, leading them to FA Cup and European Cup-Winners' Cup success, beating Real Madrid in the process, before moving on to Queens Park Rangers, where he had taken them to the highest position in their history, as runners-up to Liverpool in 1976. His salary, quoted at £20,000 a year, was £2000 higher than Docherty had apparently been earning before he'd started to renegotiate his contract. Despite interest from Arsenal in recruiting him, he said he took 'twenty seconds' to decide his future lay, for the first time in his career, in the north.

Given United's occasional tactical naivety, and the gung-ho approach that sometimes cost them points when dominating matches, Sexton seemed an ideal choice, the man who could put the finishing touches to the side the Doc built, securing the 1–0 victories that under his predecessor might have ended 2–3 instead. But Sexton's personality did not gel with the Old Trafford faithful as much as Docherty's had done. The Doc was flash, brash, loud and cocky, personifying the Manc attitude. As Cliff Butler says: 'Mancunians are fiercely proud of the city. Birmingham thinks it's the second city; we know we are.' Docherty was happy to be the Napoleon of the Red Army, ready to make the grand gesture or the bold move. Sexton was more of a quiet strategist working behind the scenes in the bunker. If his approach had worked, and he'd brought trophies to the club, it would not have mattered what his personality was like or how the team played. But, crucially, he didn't.

At first, little seemed to change, though there was more tactical planning ahead of games and the training sessions were more structured. Sexton had, by and large, kept Docherty's backroom staff. The roles of Hill and Coppell became a little more withdrawn, so they were required to give support to their full-backs, something Hill found difficult to adapt to. It was hardly a drastic transformation, but the results were not good, despite the occasional highlight, such as the 2–0 victory over new European champions Liverpool, which was ecstatically greeted by the fans.

Soon, Sexton began to change the make-up of Docherty's squad, recognising the need to increase the size of it. Centre-forward Joe Jordan was signed from Leeds on 6 January 1978 for a record fee for United of £388,888; the record lasted barely a month before Sexton crossed the Pennines again to bring in centre-half Gordon McQueen for £450,000. Like his predecessor, his first moves were to buy up Scottish stars. Both proved excellent buys, but Jordan's arrival was the beginning of the end for Stuart Pearson, who seemed increasingly prone to injury and was eventually sold. However, when fans see a hero being edged out, the pressure is always going to be on the newcomer – especially when he comes from Leeds. But Jordan's commitment to the cause soon won over the Stretford End. Likewise, McQueen was a vital recruit; in Docherty's last season, when Buchan was injured, United's defence had been alarmingly porous. The tall Scot gave extra strength to the rearguard, but it meant that Brian Greenhoff had to be accommodated in midfield or at full-back instead, and eventually he too was sold.

Albiston highlights the difference in style that the players had to adjust to: 'Tommy's great strength was man-management and getting the best out of his players by motivating them. Dave was more of a coach and interested in improving players' technique.' In this new world of player responsibility and teamwork, one man was quickly deemed a luxury: Gordon Hill. Many of the players shared Sexton's view on this point. The fact that he scored seventeen league goals from the left wing in Sexton's first season, easily more than any of United's forwards, was irrelevant. The Stretford End favourite, and team jester, was distraught when he was told he was to be sold off to Derby County – and Tommy Docherty. His replacement, Mickey Thomas, brought more discipline to the role on the left side of midfield, but a goal tally of 15 in 110 games for United (as opposed to Hill's 51 in 134) immediately reveals one thing, among many, the Reds would miss. Of all the players in United's side, Hill was the one the fans most identified with, and he reciprocated: 'You're playing in George Best's shirt. If you've done that, it doesn't matter what you do after, does it?'

Sexton's first season was always going to be a period of re-adjustment. Some, like Coppell, were able to adapt to the more cautious approach and evolve their game; others, as we have seen, were moved on. The results were disappointing: United slipped from sixth to tenth in the league. In fact, the home fans had to put up with something new – losing. In 1977–78, United lost six league games at Old Trafford, more than in the previous three seasons put together. There were no significant cup runs to speak of, and in the Cup-Winners' Cup, United again could not get beyond the second round. To make matters worse, the Red Army caused so much trouble in their first-round away leg at St Etienne that United were banned from playing the return leg within 300km of Old Trafford, having managed to escape UEFA's original threat to ban them. Over 31,000 still made it to Home Park in Plymouth for the 'home' tie played furthest away from Manchester, while thousands more watched the game on closed-circuit TV back at Old Trafford.

But when United were beaten 4–0 in the second round at Porto there was no coming back, despite a heroic effort at Old Trafford where Coppell inspired the Reds to a 5–2 victory, but a 6-5 aggregate defeat. Despite the fact that there seemed no hope, 51,831 fans were there to roar their team on. That was real support. Indeed, United's crowds at Old Trafford stayed pretty constant that season, dropping only slightly from the previous campaign, reflecting a general fall in attendances among all clubs.

During the summer, more work was carried out at Old Trafford – this time on the pitch itself, where 230 tons of sand and gravel were dug into trenches to help the drainage and so improve the quality of the playing surface. However, during the cold winter that followed, the frost made the pitch cut up badly, but there was little that could be done about it at that stage. (It wasn't until the summer of 1981 that the top layer of the pitch was torn up, a bed of sand weighing some 1200 tons deposited on it and a new pitch laid on top. As the old pitch was discarded, many fans came to the ground to take away a piece of the abandoned turf for posterity.)

In 1978–79, with Stepney, the last of the European Cup winners, finally let go, attendances fell off more dramatically, averaging just 46,573, the worst since the relegation campaign. After the New Year, only once did Old Trafford accommodate more than 50,000 for a league match, and several times fewer than 40,000 turned up. This was because there was little sign of any improvement on the pitch, and the swagger and style of Docherty's side had gone. On occasion, boos were heard as the team left the pitch at the end of a game. The *Daily Express* published an article headed 'Cold Trafford' from a fan complaining that the stadium was 'bleeding to death with boredom', while letters to the *Manchester Evening News* berated the manager's tactics. Whatever Sexton was trying to do, it didn't seem to be working, and he certainly wasn't able to get the crowd behind him. He was a man under pressure, especially given the economic impact of losing up to 20,000 fans every game. There was the highlight of beating Leeds 4–1 on 24 March 1979, thanks largely to an Andy Ritchie hat-trick, the youngest United player to achieve this feat at Old Trafford, at 18 years and 118 days. But such moments seemed few and far between.

In the aftermath of the UK's IMF bailout and with industrial unrest an increasing problem, economics were to the forefront of the board's minds, particularly so for the Edwards family. Louis Edwards' butchery business was struggling, and the fall in United's attendances had hit revenues, which meant that the club had slipped into making a loss in 1978. He decided that a rights issue was the way forward to raise revenues for the club, as he wanted to boost the transfer fund and continue to develop the Main Stand, planning to extend the cantilever roof to the Stretford End and provide more hospitality boxes as well as doubling the size of the Executive Suite. At a cost of £1.5 million, the new corporate hospitality area of the Main Stand eventually opened in December 1980, incorporating five function rooms and an expanded membership scheme for 700 people, who now paid £360 a year. Prices for everything were increasing rapidly in those inflationary times.

There was some internal opposition to the rights issue, but Edwards and his family controlled the board and ensured the process went ahead. In the end, each of the shares previously in existence was replaced by 208 new £1 shares in United. By the time of the rights issue, Edwards and his family owned 74 per cent of the shares, and afterwards the Edwards family still retained control of the club while bringing in new money. It could certainly be argued it was a good deal for the club; but it was definitely a good deal for Edwards.

As had happened frequently in the past, a run in the FA Cup

was to save United's season, and arguably Sexton's job. Three London sides came up to Old Trafford in 1979 to try their luck: relegation-bound Chelsea were beaten 3–0 in the third round, Second Division Fulham fell 1–0 in a replay in the fourth, and Spurs lost 2–0 in a replayed quarterfinal to set up a semifinal date against Liverpool. If Liverpool had been favourites for the final two years before, they were arguably even more fancied this time, as they closed in on another title, with a record haul of sixty-eight points. When United had met them at Old Trafford on Boxing Day, they'd been overwhelmed 3–0, their worst home defeat of the season. It took a replay to do it, but United took a positive approach, which paid off when they won 1–0, and the Reds were back at Wembley for the third time in four seasons.

In the final, United were lacklustre against Arsenal, who with 86 minutes gone led 2–0. Twenty seconds later, McQueen pulled a goal back, and after a further 115 seconds United were level thanks to McIlroy. It took only 55 more seconds, and Arsenal were back in front – one of the most routine Wembley finals had been transformed into one of the most dramatic. Almost immediately, the final whistle blew, and United had lost.

Sexton, recognising his side had fallen short again, cleared out more of the Docherty team over the summer: Pearson, Brian Greenhoff and David McCreery were all on their way, and in their place came a young England midfielder from relegated Chelsea, Ray Wilkins, for a club record fee of £777,777. It was his only major signing, and yet it seemed to bring about the right results, as Sexton's United finally clicked into gear in 1979–80.

The main improvement came in defence. Gary Bailey had emerged as Stepney's true successor during the previous campaign, after Paddy Roche failed to nail down the position. For the next six seasons, the big, blond goalkeeper was a virtual ever-present. At right-back, Jimmy Nicholl played every game, while on the left Stewart Houston and Arthur Albiston shared the role. In the centre, Buchan didn't miss a game and McQueen had an able young deputy in Kevin Moran. The result was United conceded just thirty-five goals all season in the league – the best ever performance by a United defence in the top division to that date.

It gave United a solid base to work from, and a chance to win the league. With the side performing steadily, if not entirely spectacularly, the crowds came flocking back. Attendances at Old Trafford were up by more than 10 per cent on the previous season, and fans saw only one home league defeat in the entire campaign. Goals proved more difficult to come by, however, with Jordan leading the way with just thirteen. Many fans still felt they weren't getting the style of play they loved to watch, and the players accepted the criticism, McQueen commenting: 'If I'd been watching some of our games, I would have been complaining as well.'

The battle for the title developed into a two-horse race between United and reigning champions Liverpool, with the Red Devils always lagging just behind. However, a dramatic 2–1 victory over the Merseyside team in early April, helped on by an ecstatic Stretford End, ensured that things would go to the wire. Jimmy Greenhoff, making his first start of the season after a long injury that threatened to end his career, scored the winner that day with a header from two yards, showing how much he'd been missed. The pitch, however, looked little better than a ploughed field in some places, so it was hardly a surprise when Alan Kennedy's hamstrings pinged trying to keep up with Coppell. The game also featured one of the great misses of all time, when Alan Hansen lobbed the charging offside ploy of United and ran half the length of the pitch for a one-on-one with Gary Bailey, only to decide to pass to Kenny Dalglish. He was actually in an offside position, so it wouldn't have counted, but he still managed to miss the empty net. Two Liverpool heroes had displayed their feet of clay in front of the whole of Old Trafford. United won their next five games to keep the pressure on, but Liverpool didn't relent and had the advantage of a hugely superior goal difference. By the time United went to Leeds for their last game, Liverpool were effectively champions, barring a miracle result, and the team couldn't summon up a last effort to draw level on points.

There had been some off-the-field distractions, too. In January, Granada's *World in Action* ran a story looking into Louis Edwards' business affairs, but while the story was still rumbling on, Edwards died at home of a heart attack on 26 February. Under Edwards, there had been much work done on modernising the facilities at Old Trafford, and the team had achieved its greatest goal in winning the European Cup.

The following month his son Martin took over as club chairman and chief executive, bitter that the television programme had, he believed, caused his father's death. The 34-year-old immediately began to improve the administration of the club, ensuring there were proper budgets for the first time. Sexton was given a new contract after the improvement shown in his third season. Now, perhaps, with its young chairman and a manager who was finally beginning to deliver, Manchester United could go one step further and win the league.

10

The Ron Times

Having run Liverpool so close the previous campaign, there was a real hope that this time United could go one better in 1980–81, but three wins in the first twelve games soon left the Reds out of contention. The defence remained resolute, but it was at the other end that the problems lay: in fifteen league matches that season, United failed to score. For fans brought up on the exciting attacking football of the Busby Babes, the glory years of the 1960s and Tommy Docherty's cavalier approach, this was unacceptable. In the top half of the table, only Leeds United scored fewer goals, and being marginally more exciting than Leeds was hardly a recommendation to the fans on the terraces.

Dave Sexton tried to remedy the problem of who should play alongside Joe Jordan, now that Jimmy Greenhoff's career at United was winding to a close. Many fans hoped that Andy Ritchie would finally get the run in the side that his strike rate seemed to deserve, but the local boy was sold to Brighton for £500,000. Instead, in October, Sexton plunged into the transfer market to make a new club record signing, paying £1.25 million for a young striker who had won the European Cup with

Nottingham Forest: Garry Birtles. However, in twenty-eight appearances that season, Birtles scored just one goal – ironically in the FA Cup against Brighton, where the fans' favourite Ritchie was now turning out. To make the point even more forcefully, the immutable law of the ex applied, and Ritchie couldn't stop scoring against his old team.

With United failing to get past their second round in any of the three cup competitions (they had also qualified for Europe, but were knocked out of the UEFA Cup by Widzew Lodz on the away-goals rule) and crowds falling back again to an average of just over 45,000, this was not good enough. A late rally, when United won the last seven games of the season (albeit scoring just ten goals in the process), including one at Anfield, helped the team up to eighth in the league. But it was too late; the board had already decided that Sexton had to go. He had spent a net amount of £2 million on the team, reached one FA Cup final, seen crowds fall and fail to get excited by what they saw. He wasn't particularly good with the press, either, which meant that the newspapers were less willing to give him the benefit of the doubt than they had been for Docherty.

The board was well aware of all this; they were inundated with letters complaining about the football being played. They saw the declining attendances and revenues. It wasn't good enough, especially when Birtles, Sexton's record signing, was failing to find the back of the net. On 30 April, Sexton and his assistant Tommy Cavanagh were let go because, according to the official statement released by the club: 'The team's performance had failed to live up to the high standards of football entertainment expected of Manchester United.' The board's emphasis on entertainment, as opposed to results, was crucial. Whereas Frank O'Farrell had gone for failing to match up to the incomparable Sir Matt Busby, Sexton went because he couldn't move out from the shadow left by Tommy Docherty.

Now the club was in search of a manager once again. Only this time, it was clear that it was no longer the job they all wanted.

Lawrie McMenemy and Bobby Robson both turned it down, so too did Ron Saunders, who had just won the league with Aston Villa and was looking forward to what would be a successful European Cup campaign, even though he didn't stay to see it through. The United job had become a daunting challenge because of the huge levels of expectation that came with the role: seven wins on the trot hadn't saved Sexton, because he wasn't winning with flair. The manager also had to have a big personality, as quiet men such as Sexton and O'Farrell had been swallowed up by the intense scrutiny on United.

One man who did have the confidence and showmanship to take on the position was Ron Atkinson. As manager of West Bromwich Albion, he had kept the usually unfashionable team in the top half of the First Division, finishing above United three times in the previous four seasons. His sides played good, positive football, just like the Stretford End demanded; he enjoyed very good relations with the press; he even looked a bit flash and stylish, with his smart suits and chunky jewellery. And so the post-Busby yo-yo effect continued, and United reverted to a big personality as manager, in the style of Docherty.

Like so many managers before him, and since, Atkinson believed the club he inherited needed major surgery. He changed most of the backroom staff: Eric Harrison was recruited from Everton to head up the youth system, and soon found he had some gems coming through. But for Jack Crompton, who had worked with the club almost continuously since the end of the war, the news wasn't so good. He was abruptly sacked, having just taken charge of a tour to the Far East.

On the playing side, some of the squad, such as Martin Buchan, Lou Macari and Sammy McIlroy, were just beginning to be past their prime, while others filled positions where Atkinson had his eye on someone else. Full-back John Gidman came in, and Mickey Thomas was on his way. Joe Jordan wanted to try his luck abroad, and was sold to AC Milan; in his place came Frank Stapleton, for £900,000 from Arsenal.

But it was in the midfield where the biggest deal happened. First Atkinson returned to his former club to bring in tough-tackling midfielder, Manchester-born Remi Moses, a lifelong United supporter, and then he broke the British transfer record to sign Bryan Robson for £1.5 million from West Brom. Sexton had tried to sign him a year earlier, and it had been Atkinson who had prevented that deal from happening. Busby was shocked at the price and resigned; Atkinson thought he had a bargain. In the end, it was the latter who was proved correct. Showing that he understood the importance of the grand gesture, Atkinson ensured the formal signing ceremony took place on the pitch at Old Trafford on 3 October 1981 in front of 46,837 fans before the match against Wolves kicked off. The man whose place was now under threat, McIlroy, scored a hat-trick as United crushed Wolves 5–0, but it wasn't enough to prevent him from being sold on to Stoke soon after.

The excitement was back in Old Trafford, with Atkinson's showmanship creating a buzz around the place once again. He said all the right things, a master of the sound bite: 'If the team bores me, it will be boring supporters . . . I will not allow these people to be betrayed.' He also commented: 'Old Trafford is a theatre for entertainment, drama and football spectacle.' Results certainly improved, and United finished third in the table, nine points behind champions Liverpool (this was the first season with three points for a win). But in actual fact, the better league performance was largely down to an improved defensive record rather than improved goal-scoring prowess. Atkinson himself wished that Dave Sexton could have remained part of the coaching staff, and behind the flash image was a man who cared deeply about the game. In short, Atkinson not only looked like a salesman, he was actually a very good one, too.

Despite all this, attendances at Old Trafford actually dropped slightly. But what had been unacceptable under Sexton the year before was no longer deemed a problem under Atkinson. This was because there was rapidly declining interest in football in general –

that season just over 20 million went to league matches, whereas only two years previously the figure had been 24.6 million. The trend of declining attendances would continue until 1985–86, the season after hooligan trouble at the European Cup final at Heysel and the Bradford City fire disaster. Between them, these two events in May 1985 resulted in ninety-five deaths. For many, whether it was hooliganism or unsafe stadiums, going to football matches was increasingly not worth the risk.

For Atkinson's second season, 1982–83, there were more changes to the line-up. Dutch left-sided midfielder Arnold Muhren joined from Ipswich. Unlike his predecessor as a foreign recruit, Nikola Jovanovic (a Sexton signing), he was used to the English game and brought a classy element to the team. But there was another player, who emerged from the junior ranks that season, who was to make an even greater impact.

In fact, Norman Whiteside had made his debut at the end of the previous campaign, becoming United's youngest ever scorer at Old Trafford at seventeen years and seven days on 15 May 1982, and he had impressed enough to be selected for Northern Ireland's World Cup squad that summer. Having beaten Pelé to become the youngest player ever to appear in the World Cup finals, he was in the strange position of having played more games in the World Cup than in club football. Inevitably, given his youth and his Belfast upbringing, he was compared to George Best, but whereas Best had looked as though he might blow away in the wind as a youngster, Whiteside was already enormous – more Duncan Edwards than Best.

Whiteside had been 'discovered' by Bob Bishop, the man who tipped off United about Best, during Sexton's time. He found the set-up at Old Trafford very welcoming, and when he had to be whisked into hospital to have his appendix out, he was visited not only by fellow Ulsterman Harry Gregg, who was part of Sexton's team, but also by the manager himself, even though he was still a schoolboy. When youngsters were separated from their families and stuck in hospital, the club understood the importance of being there to help. In his autobiography, Whiteside comments on how everyone from Busby to fellow Irish players like McIlroy, David McCreery and Jimmy Nicholl all provided help and support. When the time came to sign his contract, the club not only offered to put up his parents in a club house in Manchester, they also ensured that Whiteside's father was given the full stadium tour and could walk out onto the Old Trafford pitch – a dream fulfilled for the lifelong United fan.

United went the whole campaign without ever tasting defeat at Old Trafford, the first time the Reds had managed this since 1955–56. In league and cup, they played 29 home games, winning 21 and drawing eight in front of just under 1.2 million fans. Once again, Atkinson had done an excellent job in selling his side to their most devoted, but critical, audience. However, apart from the game against Liverpool, after Christmas Old Trafford never once attracted more than 45,000 to a league match. That fixture, however, caused problems for the club, as it was decided not to make it an all-ticket occasion, so many thousands turned up on spec, and the gates had to be shut well before kickoff, much to the irritation of those left stranded outside in the crush. The trend of declining crowds, coupled with the country being at the bottom of a deep recession, was partly to blame. But so too was the fact that United were off the pace in the league, so the fans' focus instead went to the knockout competitions, where United were regaining their status as a cup side.

In the League Cup, United played at home in each round, and as Wembley drew near the crowds increased. Over 56,000 turned out to cheer on the Reds in the second leg of the semifinal against Arsenal. In truth, the tie had more or less been secured at Highbury, where United had won 4–2. The fans saw Steve Coppell score his last ever goal for United. A few weeks later, the man who had been a model of consistency, setting a record of continuous appearances for the team, picked up an injury on England duty that ended his career. It was a sad and premature finish to the career of one of United's great players. But his goal ensured there would be no way back for Arsenal, and United had reached their first ever League Cup final. Despite an early goal from Whiteside, the youngest player to score in a League Cup final at just 17 years and 324 days, an injury-hit United lost against Liverpool, who went on to retain their league title as well.

The FA Cup had a happier ending, with United not conceding a goal until the semifinal. The quarterfinal against Everton attracted the biggest crowd of the season, 58,198, to Old Trafford and a last-minute Stapleton volley with the outside of his right foot from substitute Macari's knockdown proved to be enough. In the semifinal United again faced Arsenal, but this time it was the Londoners who took the early lead, before United eventually won through at Villa Park. Having beaten four First Division sides to get to Wembley, United faced a fifth in Brighton & Hove Albion, but the south coast side had just been relegated, eight points adrift of safety. As in 1976, United were massive favourites, but at 2–2, in the dying moments of extra time, Brighton had the opportunity to snatch an unlikely victory. Gary Bailey saved the day and United took their chance in the replay five days later, winning 4–0.

The one cup competition that didn't go well that season was the UEFA Cup, where United were knocked out in the first round by Valencia – the two matches were ill-tempered and there was crowd trouble at both. In the aftermath of the game in Spain, Martin Edwards decided that it was safer if the club did not take up any of its allocation of away tickets, as local fans and police seemed to believe United's travelling supporters were fair game.

However, the FA Cup win meant United went into 1983–84 in the European Cup-Winners' Cup. It was to be one of the club's most thrilling overseas campaigns. First up were the Czech side Dukla Prague, but they almost caused a huge upset and were heading for a victory that would have made them the first foreign side ever to win a European match at Old Trafford. Fortunately, in the last minute, Stapleton was brought down in the penalty area and Ray Wilkins converted the resulting spot kick. When United drew the away leg 2–2, they were through on the away-goals rule.

Bulgarian side Spartak Varna were next, and the Reds won through comfortably enough to ensure their involvement in Europe would continue into the spring. The draw finally gave the club a big name to take on: Barcelona.

In the first leg at the Nou Camp, United were missing key players such as Gordon McQueen and Whiteside. In were drafted Graeme Hogg and Mark Hughes, both of whom had made their debuts that season. In front of 70,000 and up against arguably the best player in the world, Diego Maradona, United held out well, but a late second goal for the Catalan side seemed to tip the balance of the tie firmly in Barca's favour, especially as they had never let slip a two-goal advantage in Europe. Until, that was, they arrived at Old Trafford on the evening of 21 March 1984, where they were greeted by 58,547 fans, paying record receipts of £200,000, who believed they could help the eleven men on the pitch overturn the deficit.

It proved to be a game that would go into Old Trafford folklore. World Cup and European Cup winner Sir Bobby Charlton later commented: 'The immense joy resulting from that victory surpassed anything I have ever experienced in the game.' Arthur Albiston, who played that evening, said, 'As the comeback unfolded, the atmosphere grew . . . until it felt like the place would explode . . . There were none so special [times] as that night.' Whiteside explained how the crowd inspired him: 'It almost lifted me off my feet so that I could play at the very limit of what my body was capable of doing.' Cliff Butler, who reckons he has attended more than half of all the games ever played at Old Trafford, picks this one out as having the best atmosphere of any: 'The noise – everyone believes that the noise helped us beat Barcelona. Their stadium holds ninety thousand, but they just couldn't cope with the noise.' Bryan Robson commented: 'They had the pitch actually shaking on that night.'

And it was to be Robson's night. What happened was this: early in the game, United's players made sure they put pressure on the Barca team. Whiteside, who had come in for some rough attention from José Alexanco previously, won a fifty-fifty tackle against the defender that resulted in the latter ending up in the perimeter boards, a classic Atkinson 'reducer'. Everywhere else around the pitch, roared on by the fans, United players were winning their duels – even Hogg and Moses had Maradona in their pocket. But, better than everyone else, Robson inspired all around him, and midway through the first half scored United's first with a diving header.

In the second half, kicking towards the Stretford End, United kept coming. Robson scored again after the Barca keeper failed to hang on to the ball, perhaps unnerved by the noise, then helped set up Stapleton, who crashed the ball home and sent United into the lead: 'I never really go mad like that, but the occasion got to me,' he recalled. There was still more than half an hour to go, and Barca knew that just one goal would see them through on away goals, but for a long while they were too stunned, and it was only towards the end that they began to mount a serious challenge. But, backed by a roar that seemed to get louder by the minute, United held on and won the tie.

The pitch invasion that followed was one of the last seen at Old Trafford, but an entirely, deliriously happy one. Robson, a true Captain Marvel that night, was carried off the pitch a hero: 'My back was slapped until it hurt. What a night!' No wonder Atkinson told the media straight after the match that when he got into the changing room he was going to 'have a cup of tea'. Albiston's comment that 'we enjoyed ourselves after the game as well' was probably nearer the mark. The next morning, United received a £3 million bid from Juventus for Robson, but they weren't selling at any price.

The season was promising to deliver much. United might have suffered early exits from the two domestic cups, but they were very much in the mix in the race for the league title. By that stage, they had gone sixteen games unbeaten in the league, and were three points clear at the top. That run came to an end the very next game, away to Atkinson's former club West Brom, and soon after that Robson picked up a hamstring injury that meant he missed six games, including both legs of the Cup-Winners' Cup semifinal against Juventus. During that time, United won just one match, against Coventry, which left them out of Europe and struggling to catch up Liverpool in the league.

For the first leg of the Juventus tie, at Old Trafford, United were not only without Robson, but also Wilkins (suspended) and Muhren (injured), so their midfield line-up was Paul McGrath, Mike Duxbury and Moses – hardly ideal when facing Michel Platini and half of the Italian World Cup-winning team. Gidman was injured early on, and soon United went a goal behind. Another crowd of 58,000-plus tried to do their best, but even when substitute Alan Davies scored, the self-belief was never quite there, and Juventus were able to win their home leg (albeit only narrowly) to go through to the final. From then on, all momentum dissipated from United's season, and the Reds did not win again, finishing in fourth position, six points adrift of Liverpool.

Despite the falling crowds in football, this was a time when some businessmen began to see an opportunity in investing in the sport, and the era of clubs being owned by local figures began to change. Partly this was due to the changing media world, and the increasing attention given to football. On 16 December 1983, Old Trafford hosted the first ever league match to be shown live on the BBC, with the Reds emerging 4–2 victors over Tottenham. Although the crowd was a disappointing 33,616, down by more than 14,000 on the figure for the same fixture the year before, clearly this was a way forward for football that would bring teams into the homes of millions. Indeed, United were even compensated for the lost revenues. 'Television rights' were about to start to play an increasing role in the balance sheets of football clubs.

Inevitably, United caught the eye of someone: Robert Maxwell. At the time, Maxwell rivalled Rupert Murdoch as one of the biggest media figures in the country; he owned the *Daily Mirror*, while Murdoch had the *Sun*. Early in February, the *Mirror* reported that Maxwell had offered £10 million to buy the club.

The Edwards family, with more than 70 per cent of the shares, considered the offer and seemed tempted, but believed they could get £15 million. Fans were horrified at the thought of an outsider coming in, and staged a protest against Maxwell, while local businessmen tried to put together a consortium to match any bid from the press baron. Given what happened within the next few years to the price of United's shares, even at the higher price Maxwell would have had a bargain, but he withdrew. How much Maxwell's bid was really serious (Martin Edwards has said it was not a realistic offer for the club) and how much was a combination of paper talk and the mogul's massive ego is perhaps a moot point, but clearly other interested bidders would follow in due course.

Atkinson could take much solace from his first three seasons at United: they'd won their first trophy in six years, each time the Reds had qualified for Europe, and the side had occasionally managed to top the table, but had been unable to sustain the effort. Over the summer of 1984, he lost one of his most influential players, Ray Wilkins, to AC Milan for £1.4 million. Wilkins may have been nicknamed 'The Crab', because of his tendency to pass sideways rather than forwards, but at least when he passed it the ball usually found its way to a man in a red shirt. As they did for England, he and Robson made an excellent partnership in the middle of the field. In his place came Gordon Strachan from Aberdeen and Danish star Jesper Olsen from Ajax, both of whom gave the team more width, as well as Alan Brazil from Ipswich. Brazil had been brought in to give competition up front to Whiteside and Frank Stapleton, but he and the Irishmen soon found they were battling for a place alongside Mark Hughes in the starting line-up, as the young striker emerged as a potent threat.

Meanwhile, further work was carried out on the pitch, with undersoil heating finally installed. Manchester United had been much criticised for not doing this earlier, as it had forced many games to be postponed over the years, though the club had always argued that it wasn't just a case of ensuring the pitch was fit for action, there was also the question of whether it was safe for fans to get to the ground if conditions were icy. When it was first used in anger, ahead of an FA Cup tie in January 1985, the system failed, needing emergency repairs to ensure the game went ahead after all.

United's new side started the 1984–85 season backed by packed crowds at Old Trafford, with the lowest attendance in their first six home games being 47,559. After the Reds beat Spurs on 20 October, they leapfrogged the North London side to go third in the table, behind Arsenal and Sheffield Wednesday. But in their next game, at Goodison Park against an improving Everton side, they were humiliated 5–0. The Merseysiders came to Old Trafford three days later and knocked United out of the League Cup, and suddenly the Reds were struggling and the crowds fell back. The visit of league leaders Arsenal was televised live, which was perhaps why just 32,279 came to see a scintillating 4–2 win. Old Trafford hosted crowds of 45,000-plus just twice more all season in the league.

Some of this fall-off in attendances was due to yet more re-development work, this time at the Scoreboard End, which required the temporary shuffling around of various administrative offices and the club shop. The inconsistency in the crowds was matched by inconsistency on the pitch, which meant United again fell short as Everton dominated the league, rarely losing top spot after they reached the summit at the beginning of November. The team picked up a series of injuries that marred their progress. Once again, United needed to be a good cup side to save their season; once again, they were.

The UEFA Cup campaign didn't have quite the same drama as the previous season's efforts. The nearest United came to meeting a 'big' club was PSV Eindhoven in the second round. There was the satisfaction of beating Scottish opposition in Dundee United, the first time United had ever taken on opposition from north of the border in an official match. But the European journey ended in the quarterfinals in Hungary when United faced their first ever penalty shoot-out – and lost – against Videoton, who had played negatively throughout both legs. For reasons beyond United's control, it was to be the club's last appearance in Europe until September 1990, for the season ended in the horrors of Heysel, when Liverpool took on Juventus. The actions of the hooligans that evening finally persuaded UEFA that they had had enough of the 'English disease', even if the contagion had spread to other countries, and all English teams were banned from European competition for five years.

So United's hunt for silverware came down to the FA Cup. The club was once again lucky with the draw, gaining home ties in three out of four rounds before they reached the semifinals, thanks to a Whiteside hat-trick and a goal from Hughes against West Ham. By then, the Ulsterman had been moved back into midfield (following an injury to Moses) where his competitive instincts, footballing brain and lack of pace could best be accommodated. As had happened once before, the game was covered by a documentary TV crew, though this time the cameras were following the Londoners' Inter City Firm, who were attempting (and failing) to 'take' Old Trafford. The cameras got what they were looking for, not least when Strachan was hit by a coin when attempting to take a corner. The issue of football violence was not going away, and later in the month Prime Minister Margaret Thatcher chaired a government committee that looked into the option of banning the sale of alcohol from football grounds. This was eventually put into practice.

In the semifinal, United needed a replay to overcome Liverpool and so set up a final against champions and newly crowned European Cup-Winners' Cup winners Everton, who were hoping for their own treble. Eight years before, United had prevented the other Merseyside team from picking up a treble, and they repeated the achievement this time, despite losing Kevin Moran, the first man ever to be sent off in an FA Cup final. Whiteside was again able to come up with the vital winning goal in extra time.

Because of the ban on English sides in European competition, United could no longer bank on the extra revenue that came from

Europe, and plans for further expansion at Old Trafford were put on hold. The new restrictions on selling alcohol at football grounds also hit United's balance sheet. However, despite these constraints, there was still room in the budget for further improvements in the catering and hospitality suites.

With Atkinson's sides having won two trophies in the previous three campaigns, reached the final of another, and finished in the top four for four consecutive seasons for the first time since 1965–68, there was real hope that United could bring to an end their long wait to win the league title when the 1985–86 season began. The Reds got off to a flying start, winning the first ten league matches on the bounce, conceding just three goals and scoring twenty-seven in the process (eleven different players were on the score-sheet). By the end of the first weekend in November, United had forty-one points out of a possible forty-five, while second-placed Liverpool were ten points behind. The crowds flocked to Old Trafford, the best attendances there had been in the 1980s.

But then the wheels began to come off the United machine. Between mid-October and mid-March, Robson played a full ninety minutes only once in the league because of hamstring problems, making three appearances in all. When he did reappear, in an FA Cup tie against Sunderland, he was sent off early in the game. Strachan dislocated a shoulder, Olsen was injured, and there were many other absences. It became almost impossible to select a settled side. Only five players managed thirty or more league appearances that season. Lee Chapman of Sheffield Wednesday ended United's unbeaten run at Hillsborough, and Fortress Old Trafford was finally breached just before Christmas by Arsenal's Charlie Nicholas. By February, Everton were top and the next month Liverpool overtook both United and then Everton as they went on an irresistible charge to the Double, dropping just two points in the last dozen games. Even West Ham passed United as they stuttered to the finishing line, taking just twenty-seven points in the second half of the season.

Atkinson searched for answers: Colin Gibson was signed from Aston Villa; Terry Gibson was bought from Coventry, with Brazil going the other way in part exchange; forward Peter Davenport was signed from Nottingham Forest to replace Hughes, who was on his way to Barcelona at the end of the season. None of these deals felt as though they were going to turn things round for United. The imminent loss of Hughes, a real favourite of the fans who did not seem to want to leave, was particularly crucial. The transfer was agreed but initially kept secret, at Barca's request, and this secrecy caused the Welshman to lose form. His sale not only suggested a lack of ambition from the club, it could have been avoided if he had been offered a decent contract by Atkinson (his wages were to go up from £200 per week to £300; Robson, by contrast, was on about £2000 a week). The fans blamed Atkinson for cashing in. The deal also demotivated the players, who believed they were being treated as commodities.

Questions also remained about United's susceptibility to injury, and the team's reliance on Robson. And there were an increasing number of stories around the drinking culture at the club, not least when a trip to Amsterdam ended in a series of player fines. This also reflected on the level of discipline that Atkinson brought to his dealings with the team. When Moses and Olsen were involved in a training-ground spat, Atkinson's attempts to sweep the story under the carpet did not look good. Both elements combined when, on a post-FA Cup tour of the Caribbean in 1985, Whiteside walked straight into a plate-glass door, thinking it was open. Assistant manager Mick Brown called him 'an absolute disgrace', while Atkinson told his deputy: 'You leave him alone and let him enjoy himself.'

With the World Cup looming, Atkinson tendered his resignation at the end of the season, according to Jim White's *Manchester United – The Biography*. He realised that he had lost some of his spark, but he was persuaded to stay on for another season, although he was told there was no more money for transfers (the lack of European opportunities was continuing to hit United's bottom line). One win in the first nine games did not suggest he'd rediscovered the key to success.

By now the fans were critical and many of them were staying away, despite the opening of a Family Stand at the start of the season. United had recognised the fact that the problems of hooliganism had deterred many from bringing their children to games – and certainly the days when young boys would go unaccompanied had long gone – and were trying to reverse the trend. In fact, this move reflected exactly the time when declining attendances would begin to increase once again, for 1985–86 saw record low crowds across the Football League. That United's efforts to stem the hooligan problem were working was evidenced by the fact that Manchester's chief constable often brought his counterparts to matches to show how well run things were at Old Trafford, where the combination of CCTV, police intelligence and good stewarding meant that United had about the lowest arrest rate per fan in the country.

The board were concerned by the combination of falling crowds and increasingly vocal criticism of Atkinson. There was also the first sign that Atkinson and his coaching staff were losing the dressing room, as the players began to complain about the training routines set up by Brown. Atkinson was clearly on borrowed time – as, in fairness, he had himself recognised in the summer – and the board had begun to prepare the way to bring in a replacement.

He stayed long enough to see the new floodlights used for the first time in October 1986. Instead of the traditional pylon system, Old Trafford now had lights all along the roof of the sides of the stadium. The 216 lights cost £170,000 to install and, with the cantilever roof now running round three sides of the ground, ensured that the stadium looked impeccably modern. But all of this was soon to be a thing of the past for Atkinson.

On 4 November, United lost 4–1 in the League Cup to Southampton, a side they'd beaten 5–1 at Old Trafford a few weeks before. It was the final straw: two days later he was sacked.

'Big Ron' to the end, he threw a leaving party at his house in Rochdale, perhaps to celebrate the record compensation he had received of around £100,000. Only a few of the players turned up, among them Strachan, who realised how much things would change when he heard who Atkinson's successor was. David Lacey, writing in the *Guardian*, said of his replacement: 'United have remained true to the Old Trafford management pendulum which for more than fifteen years has swung between roundhead and cavalier in a regular arc.' By this logic, the new man was to be another Frank O'Farrell or Dave Sexton, a methodical, dour organiser of sides that seek to be well drilled but often fall short on providing either entertainment or trophies. As predictions go, it wasn't to prove the most accurate.

11

The Govaner Arrives

In his autobiography, *Managing My Life*, Alex Ferguson explains how he was contacted by Martin Edwards on the day after United's defeat to Southampton. Edwards and other members of the board, including Bobby Charlton, travelled up to Glasgow to negotiate terms, and a deal was quickly agreed, even if the new manager was surprised to find that there was no money in the budget for transfers and that he would have to take a pay cut to come to Old Trafford. It was, he said, 'a dream opportunity to fulfil the grand ambitions I had nursed since entering management'.

In some ways in that statement lies a clue to Ferguson's greatness, for he had already proved himself to be one of the brightest young British managers. His most recent role had been as manager of Aberdeen, where he had taken charge in June 1978 at the age of thirty-six. It was already his third job in management, after a successful but fairly unspectacular career as a tough centre-forward. At the time he arrived at Aberdeen, the scene north of the border, then as now, was dominated by the Old Firm of Glasgow, Celtic and Rangers. Between them, they had won the league title every year since 1965, and missed out on the Scottish Cup just twice since 1962.

Under Ferguson, that all changed. Aberdeen won the Scottish title in 1980, 1984 and 1985; the Scottish Cup in 1982, 1983, 1984 and 1986; Ferguson even took Aberdeen to success in Europe, winning the European Cup-Winners' Cup in 1983. Add in the Scottish League Cup in 1986 and you clearly had a man who knew how to build a trophy-winning team against the odds. Prior to his arrival, Aberdeen had won the Scottish league title once in their history, in 1955, and the Scottish Cup twice, in 1947 and 1970. Since he left, they have won the Scottish Cup just once, and never been higher than runners-up in the SPL. It gives you some idea of just how special his achievements were, his impact at Aberdeen perhaps comparable to Brian Clough's at Nottingham Forest. Furthermore, in those days, Scottish football was something to be reckoned with, the national side boasting players of the calibre of Dalglish, Hansen, McCoist, Miller, Souness and Strachan among others.

Ferguson had recently stepped into the breach as Scotland manager, after Jock Stein's sudden death, and had turned down various attempts to lure him away from Pittodrie. But when United called, it was an opportunity too good to refuse. The Reds were already out of the running for the title, and so he knew they would finish the season twenty years without being champions. Five men had tried and failed to recapture the glory of the Busby era; now it was his turn. The chance to knock Liverpool off their perch was one he wanted to take on, a challenge every bit as daunting as beating the Old Firm.

As David Lacey's comment at the end of the previous chapter shows, Ferguson appeared very much in the 'roundhead' tradition of United managers when he arrived. Certainly, he wasn't flash like Ron Atkinson or a cheeky chappie like Tommy Docherty, but that did not mean he was daunted or overwhelmed by the role as some of his less showy predecessors had seemingly been, and nor was he a manager who organised his side in a cagey manner: he liked to play positive, attacking football in the Manchester United tradition. In fact, like Busby, he was a perfect blend of roundhead and cavalier – he had an aura and an authority about him that could be daunting and intimidating, demanding respect, but his players also had the freedom to play expansively for him.

After an embarrassing defeat away to Oxford United and a draw at Norwich, Alex Ferguson started his career in front of the Old Trafford faithful against Queens Park Rangers. A crowd of 42,235 showed up on 22 November 1986 to welcome him; it was one of the bigger attendances that season to date. John Sivebaek scored the only goal of the game (and the only goal of his brief United career) to ensure it was a satisfactory occasion. The new manager set out his stall in his programme notes: 'I am not really interested in what has happened in the past. I don't mean any disrespect. It's simply that now there is only one way to go, and that is forward.'

He spent the rest of his first season assessing the club from top to bottom, knowing there was little to play for once United were knocked out of the FA Cup early on. At least in that competition he had the satisfaction of beating local rivals City in the third round in front of 54,294, the biggest crowd at Old Trafford that season, although the game nearly had to be postponed when the undersoil heating again failed to live up to its billing. The team rewarded the home crowd by losing only twice in the rest of the campaign, having lost three of their first four games at Old Trafford, but their away form was dire: just one win all season, albeit against Liverpool. Eventually, United worked their way up to a mid-table position. There were no new signings all season, so everyone had the chance to prove what they could do and to respond to the messages the manager was passing on. Some of the players at the time have suggested he took a little while to adjust to the scale of the club, and the size of the task that awaited him: nothing can prepare you for the interest that United generates.

Ferguson quickly identified various areas of concern: there was too much of a drinking culture among the players; the levels of fitness weren't good enough, and some players lacked the physical attributes to stand up to a tough season; and there weren't enough good young players coming through to put pressure on the older ones. There was room for improvement in the scouting system and in youth development – United seemed to be missing out on some young local players, too many of whom for Ferguson's liking were ending up at City. All of these aspects were addressed, and in the meantime he made sure that he encouraged and involved the entire club, from the players to the caterers and the cleaners, in understanding how they could make a difference to the success of Manchester United. Interestingly, when Lee Sharpe came to United from Torquay for his first training session in 1988, it was the clean kit and fluffy towels immaculately laid out that made as much of an impression on him as almost anything else. For Ferguson, the team at Old Trafford was never just about the eleven men on the pitch; attention to detail applied to the whole club, and not just to match-day tactics. If United were to match its own appreciation of itself as the biggest and best club around, it had to get everything right – and start to prove it on the pitch, too.

During the close season, Ferguson identified his main area of weakness as being up front, where United had scored only fifty-two goals in 1986–87. Frank Stapleton would be thirty-one at the start of the new campaign, while Peter Davenport hadn't fully blossomed at Old Trafford after Ron Atkinson had signed him. Besides, having just two strikers on the club's books was never going to be enough, if one of them fell injured, though there was always the option of using Norman Whiteside in that role. So, in July, he returned to the Scottish football scene he knew so well and signed Brian McClair from Celtic for £850,000. The young striker had been a prolific scorer for the Glasgow side, banging in fifty-seven league goals in the previous two seasons. United hadn't had a twenty-goals-a-season man since George Best in 1967–68, and McClair would achieve that landmark in his first campaign.

Ferguson began to address his concerns about a general lack of professionalism by bringing in the experienced England full-back Viv Anderson from Arsenal. Bought for £250,000 and signed on the same day as McClair, another good, solid professional, Anderson had impressed the manager during a tempestuous game against Arsenal soon after he'd arrived – he was clearly a team man, and a strong character. The training regime was also tightened up, with the manager imposing greater discipline on his squad. Where Atkinson had been the players' friend, Ferguson had no qualms about shouting at them if he felt they had let him, and United, down. He wanted players who could not only respond to such treatment, but who cared as much as he did.

McClair settled straight into his new home at Old Trafford, scoring in five of his first six games there. However, it wasn't the first time he'd played at the ground: 'My first experience of playing at Old Trafford was for Celtic against Rapid Vienna [after UEFA had forced a replay following alleged trouble at Celtic during the European Cup-Winners' Cup campaign in 1984–85]. It was full to the rafters with Celtic supporters absolutely full of hatred for this Austrian team, who they felt had cheated, but the atmosphere was absolutely terrifying if you weren't a Scotsman. The major problem we found was that Celtic Park was always a good pitch but Old Trafford was terrible, and we couldn't play how we wanted to on the pitch and we lost the game one-nil. The pitch was so bad.' Indeed, so hostile was the Celtic support that on two separate occasions fans got onto the pitch and assaulted Rapid players.

There was another reason McClair felt immediately at home at United, where the Old Trafford crowd and the level of expectation can sometimes prove daunting for new arrivals: 'There's always been a close bond between Celtic and United – Sir Matt and Jock Stein, and how they wanted to play football. Born out of that was the expectation of people when they went to watch both clubs. It was nice to win games, but to win in style was paramount, and that entertainment was at the forefront. When I came, supporters loved their football, but loved a particular style of football, which was great because I've always been an attacking type of player.'

Ferguson's hopes of doing more business (he told chairman

Edwards that he needed eight new players) were constrained by the club's financial position. United were not entirely helped that season by inaugurating a membership scheme, so that only members could have access to certain parts of the ground. It may have cost only a fiver to join, but it meant that fans could no longer simply turn up if they felt like doing so. Inevitably, there was some confusion at the beginning of the season, when some arrived at the ground and couldn't get in. As the government soon started to support calls for an ID-card system for all football fans, this move, which wasn't exactly popular at the time, may have helped prevent something far worse from being imposed.

The club continued to look for new ways of bringing in additional revenue. One of the most significant links turned out to be with rugby league. The sport was going through something of a renaissance during this period, and although Wembley remained the home of its traditional knockout climax, the Challenge Cup final, it needed a venue close to its heartland of support that could also be 'special'. Although Elland Road, Leeds, was in rugby league territory, Old Trafford had a bigger capacity and was undoubtedly a ground with a greater history attached to it. So, on 25 October 1986, it played host to the first Test between Great Britain and Australia in front of a crowd of 50,583 paying £251,061 – then the biggest attendance for any tour fixture in Britain, and the highest receipts for any match outside Wembley in rugby league history. Australian centre Gene Miles scored the first Test try at the ground. The turnout was all the more remarkable given the atrocious weather that evening.

At the end of the season, on 17 May, Old Trafford was the venue for rugby league's Premiership final, the play-off tournament that was then contested between the top eight sides from the regular season. Again, despite the weather, the event was an enormous success, with the record crowd of 38,756 who saw Wigan overcome Warrington 8–0 almost treble that of the previous year's final. Gate receipts of £165,166 were another record. Joe Lydon had the honour of scoring the first try in a Premiership final at the ground. Once established, the idea that the rugby league season would climax at Old Trafford was a tradition that would survive even the move to a summer season and the arrival of the Super League. Now known as the Grand Final, it takes place every October and in 2006 attracted a record crowd of 72,582 for the match between St Helens and Hull.

Despite the financial constraints, Ferguson did manage to unlock the safe once more during the season to bring in Steve Bruce from Norwich for £825,000. Like McClair, the central defender proved to be one of Ferguson's best signings, even if he did give away a penalty and break his nose on his debut, revealing the whole-hearted commitment to the cause that impressed fans and the manager alike.

However, on the pitch it seemed as though things were looking much better once the season got under way. In the first fifteen matches, just one was lost (away to champions Everton), even if there were more draws than was ideal. But Liverpool went the first twenty-nine games of the season without defeat, as the side romped home to the title, inspired by John Aldridge, John Barnes and Peter Beardsley. In the end, United finished runners-up, nine points adrift, but Ferguson knew they were very much second best, as Liverpool had eased off late in the season with the league clearly theirs, and that more work needed to be done to improve the team. Liverpool were the side to aspire to, and Ferguson had them very much in his sights from the beginning – and he wasn't afraid to let them know he was coming. His antipathy to the team from Anfield was legendary. He used the Merseysiders to motivate himself and all around him in the same way he had used the Old Firm when at Aberdeen.

Ferguson continued the process of rebuilding during the summer of 1988. Most excitingly, Mark Hughes was brought back to Old Trafford for £1.8 million. The Welshman had never wanted to leave in the first place, and hadn't enjoyed his time abroad, so was delighted to return. In tandem, Hughes and McClair missed just two games between them over the next two seasons, and over the following four campaigns they scored 135 goals – it was the most settled and successful strike partnership United had had since the days of Denis Law and David Herd.

Also signed during the summer was Aberdeen goalkeeper Jim Leighton, while experienced defender Mal Donaghy joined from Luton early in the season. At the other end of his career, a seventeen-year-old winger from Torquay called Lee Sharpe joined the club. As Busby had done all those years ago with Harry Gregg (and others, of course), when Sharpe first got off the train at Piccadilly station to visit United, the manager was there to greet him. Ferguson took him round Old Trafford, showing him the pitch, the dressing rooms, the executive suites and restaurants, introducing him to all and sundry. He immediately felt part of the family.

Sharpe's signing also reflected another strand of the manager's strategy, again echoing Busby's approach, of bringing in young stars that he could hope to mould into the United way of doing things. The difference was, when Busby did it, he was already almost unsackable having built up the post-war side; Ferguson still had much to prove to the fans, who were yet to be fully convinced that a Scot with no track record south of the border could deliver. In short, signing players with a view to the future was the mark of a man with ultimate self-belief in what he was doing.

United's league form slipped back in 1988–89, however, with a noticeable lack of goals coming from midfield, but at least the defence was the second best in the league, showing that a secure base was being built. Indeed, the fans responded as though they did not believe that the league was where United's hopes lay: United's third biggest crowd of the season was in the fourth round of the FA Cup, against Second Division Oxford; the second biggest crowd was in the fifth round, against Bournemouth of Division Two; and the biggest crowd, 55,040, saw United knocked out in the sixth round by Nottingham Forest. That the fans set so much store by the FA Cup was to have a big bearing on the Reds' next campaign. By contrast, the league attendances dropped to the lowest since 1966 when just 23,368 turned up to see Wimbledon in early May.

At that time, ahead of a three o'clock home kickoff, the players' day followed a set pattern. They arrived at noon for an early lunch in the Grill Room in the Main Stand, eating simple, nutritious food such as pasta or chicken, before retiring to the players' lounge until 1.30, when the team meeting took place and the manager assessed the opposition's strengths and weaknesses, likely set-play moves and so on. The meeting tended to last about twenty minutes, and afterwards Ferguson usually left the players to themselves until just before kickoff. Usually players were told beforehand if they were going to be dropped or promoted (but for his debut, against West Ham in September, Sharpe recalls that he wasn't warned, to ease any nerves). Most players then took their time, used to the routine, before they were eventually allowed onto the pitch to warm up with about half an hour to go. Afterwards, the manager said a few words, and gave individual advice to some players about their direct opponents. Then, it was time for action.

At this stage, fans still watched their football from behind metal fences at Old Trafford, and most other major grounds. As that season came to a close, however, all that was about to change. Having beaten United in the quarterfinal, Forest took on Liverpool in the semifinal at Hillsborough on 15 April 1989. As the Liverpool fans piled into the Leppings Lane End, the problem with the fences that caged in supporters was about to become sickeningly clear – in the crush that followed, there was no way out; ninety-six people eventually lost their lives in the disaster. Old Trafford was selected as the replacement venue when the semifinal was eventually played three weeks later for what was a highly sensitive and emotional fixture.

The impact of what happened at Hillsborough changed football for ever. In the future, top-level football in England would soon be played in all-seater stadiums, with no perimeter fencing to keep fans from coming on the pitches, as had seemed necessary when hooliganism had been rife in the game. The tradition of fans standing together, surging down the terraces after a goal, was going to have to come to an end. In its place came a much more family-friendly brand of football where the whole experience of the occasion was given priority. For some, this loss of intense passion diminished the game. For others, the risk of repeating the horrors of Hillsborough was too great and change was not only inevitable but essential to save the popularity of the sport. The next few years saw as dramatic a change to football stadiums as in any other period in its history. United responded swiftly to the new requirements, and Old Trafford was soon to be transformed.

12

The End of an Era

During the summer break after Hillsborough, United's focus was not so much on the stadium but on the team. Alex Ferguson had brought in only a few players in his first thirty months in charge, and let go many more. Now was the time to take more decisive action to sort out the squad. By mid-September, five new players had been signed: Mike Phelan, from Norwich, and Neil Webb, from Nottingham Forest, were first to arrive. The latter was already Bryan Robson's regular partner in the England midfield, while Phelan was an adaptable player who could fill either a midfield or defensive berth.

Once the season got under way, in came Gary Pallister, signed from Middlesbrough for a British record fee of £2.3 million. Ferguson had created a strong spine: Hughes and McClair up front, Robson and Webb in midfield, and now Pallister and Bruce in the centre of the defence. He hadn't finished with the spending either, bringing in another midfielder, Paul Ince, from West Ham – Ince was not yet twenty-two and was signed after Webb picked up a serious injury early on in the season – and winger Danny Wallace from Southampton. In total, Ferguson had spent almost £7 million in a few months, a huge amount at the time. He also completed the clear-out of Atkinson's men, as Norman Whiteside and Paul McGrath were sold on, both of them a part of the alleged drinking culture that the manager had sworn to end. Only Robson, Clayton Blackmore and Mike Duxbury remained from the previous manager's era, as well as the re-signed Hughes.

Ferguson, who had said when he arrived that he needed to revamp the side completely, had finally got his way, and the last part of the spending spree had been concluded after remarkable events behind the scenes at Old Trafford. Indeed, not just behind the scenes, for a new man had come to take control of the club and he showed off some of his football skills on the pitch in front of the Stretford End just before United's first home fixture against champions Arsenal. Michael Knighton had arrived in the most showy of styles; the fans cheered his efforts, welcoming the man who promised so much. McClair echoes the thoughts of many on that day: 'Incredible! I couldn't believe that. I still can't. He'd have made himself an absolute fortune.'

Knighton was described by the *Manchester Evening News* as a 'millionaire property tycoon' from the Isle of Man. His offer for the club valued each share at £20, which meant that Martin Edwards would pick up £10 million for shares his father had bought for £20,000. At the time, and subsequently, Edwards said the reason he agreed to sell was that Knighton was also offering to spend £10 million on redeveloping the Stretford End, with his plans including building a hotel there, as well as making more money available for the transfer budget. Lord Justice Taylor had already produced his interim conclusions in the aftermath of the Hillsborough disaster, and it was clear that clubs were going to have to fund a lot of improvements in the coming years. As finances had been tight at United, Edwards believed that a sale now was the right thing to do for the club. Furthermore, the chairman felt he could never do enough to win over the support of the fans, and so he might as well give someone else the chance to do so.

At the time, United had already unveiled plans to redevelop the Stretford End, at a cost of £8 million, with executive boxes and seating forming a large part of the plans. The club also decided to reduce the capacity of Old Trafford by over 5000 to just under 51,000, about half of whom could stand while the rest would be seated, in the aftermath of Hillsborough, to avoid any chance of overcrowding on the terraces. With the costs of redevelopment allied to the fall in revenues from a smaller capacity, Knighton's timing seemed perfect.

Almost as soon as the deal had been agreed, however, the press started to ask questions about Knighton. It soon transpired that his bid of £20 million plus £10 million for stadium development was in jeopardy, after his financial backers pulled out. In the end, by early October, 'in the interests of United' he called off the deal and settled for a seat on the board. Edwards remained open to offers for the club, and at the AGM in December said that he would make a quick sale for £30 million – the price had gone up by 50 per cent already since August. A day later, Rupert Murdoch was reported to be looking at buying United so he could show their games on his new TV channel, Sky (a month earlier, Sky had offered the Football League £4.5 million over four years to screen the Zenith Data Systems Cup and the Leyland Daf Cup – it was a very different era).

Only full-backs Duxbury and Blackmore were not Ferguson signings for that first game against Arsenal, and in the second half United blitzed the north Londoners to win 4–1, with Hughes, debutant Webb and McClair all adding to Bruce's first-half goal in front of a crowd of 47,245, Old Trafford's biggest league crowd in almost two years. There was a terrific sense of optimism that day, and a feeling that United might go on to do well with their new squad. With the hardly daunting trio of Crystal Palace, Derby and Norwich next up, United had a chance to put down a marker to the other title contenders. Instead, they picked up just one point. After a defeat at Everton, United's next two games ended 5–1 – the first, against Millwall, featured a home hat-trick for Hughes, the second was a humiliating defeat at Maine Road where United were woeful. Robson and Bruce missed the debacle against City, while Danny Wallace made his debut. Ferguson called it 'the most embarrassing defeat of my management career'.

Suddenly, it seemed as though everyone was buckling under the pressure of the situation. The manager had spent a fortune on new players and needed them to prove themselves; for some, such as Pallister, it was hard to settle in immediately. His partnership with Bruce eventually became one of United's best defensive pairings, but with a record price tag on his head, he didn't find it easy. Even the fans were feeling the tension. It was the early days of fanzines at many clubs, the first opportunity most fans had ever had to get their voice heard in print. What they were saying in their pages, and on the terraces at Old Trafford, was not good. Some of them believed Ferguson had sold top players, such as McGrath, Strachan and Whiteside, and replaced them with ones not of the same standard.

After three years in charge, there seemed to be no real improvement on the pitch, and no great flair either. As if the humiliation against City wasn't bad enough, United soon went eleven league games without a win, sinking to seventeenth place by the beginning of February. And, as so often in the past, much of that run of poor form coincided with the absence of Robson, Captain Marvel. Ferguson couldn't put his finger on what was wrong and subsequently admitted: 'I was, for the first time, feeling uncomfortable about my position.' He was 'retreating into a cocoon of self-examination' to try to find the answers. Fortunately, his luck was about to change.

Many have wondered how close Ferguson came to being sacked in this period, but the board of the time have always said they did not consider that option. They noted his phenomenally hard work-rate. They saw the way that he was reviving all aspects of the club, even if the results of the first team hadn't yet reflected that fact. For example, he had continued to develop the youth aspect of United. He was keen to blood young players, not only bringing in Lee Sharpe, but also several others including Lee Martin and Mark Robins, who were to have crucial roles that season. Brian Kidd had been recruited as the youth development officer, and the scouting network was massively expanded. One scout, Harold Wood, had already tipped off the manager about a young United-supporting teenager who was playing for City. Ryan Wilson was therefore invited to train at the Cliff, and so impressed those watching that he was signed on schoolboy forms in November 1987 on his fourteenth birthday, with the manager himself going to his house to persuade him to sign. As Ryan Giggs, he was still playing for United twenty-three years later.

United's run to the FA Cup final in 1990 took place entirely away from Old Trafford. The Reds were drawn away in every round, starting with a tricky third-round tie against Nottingham Forest when United were without six first-team regulars. Mark Robins scored the crucial goal in a 1–0 victory, but the support the team received from their travelling fans gave the players a huge boost. Afterwards, they were lucky in one sense, as they didn't face top-division opposition until the final. At the semifinal stage they'd avoided Liverpool, who had previously that season beaten their opponents Crystal Palace 9–0 and seemed a certainty to reach a third successive final. United were clear favourites against Second Division Oldham, but Joe Royle's side had already reached one Wembley final that year so weren't to be underestimated. On 8 April the semifinals were two of the most dramatic games one could wish for, both shown live on television. Incredibly, Liverpool were beaten 4–3 in extra time, while United managed a 3–3 draw, before winning the replay, thanks again to Robins.

The final against Palace was another cracking game, when United were almost undone in extra time by substitute Ian Wright, until Hughes scored a late equaliser to earn a replay. Ferguson made the brave decision to drop keeper Jim Leighton after the first game, as his confidence and form seemed to have deserted him. Les Sealey stepped in and had a relatively easy time of it as United cruised to a 1–0 win, thanks to a goal scored by another of the Reds' youngsters, Lee Martin. The left-back had just won the first trophy of the Ferguson era. None but the most optimistic fan could have imagined how many more there would be, especially as United had finished the season in thirteenth place, with Liverpool again champions.

There was a feeling this time that success in the FA Cup really was the start of something bigger. Indeed, after the horrors of the 1980s – the Bradford fire, Heysel and Hillsborough – that summer's World Cup, with Gazza's tears and 'Nessun Dorma', had created a positive mood in the sport. Ferguson's signings had begun to gel together and settle into the unique pressures of playing for Manchester United. There was only one major new recruit for the 1990–91 season, Denis Irwin from Oldham, who had impressed during the FA Cup semifinal and would go on to be one of the club's most consistent performers throughout the 1990s.

Meanwhile, the impact of Hillsborough continued to rumble on. The Taylor Report insisted that all grounds of First and Second Division clubs had to be all-seater by 1994–95. One of the inevitable results of this was that the old-style Stretford End, the spiritual home of the loyal United fans, with a now-reduced capacity of 7168, would soon be no more. Rather than simply install benches on the terracing, the United board decided to revive the old plan of bringing the cantilever roof all the way round the ground, over the Stretford End. In short, the plan was to knock it down and start again. In the meantime, the United Road Paddock was converted to a seated area for over 6000 supporters. The fencing round the perimeter of the pitch was also lowered in response to the report.

But before any of that happened, there were rumours that Old Trafford could be abandoned entirely. Manchester was bidding to host the Olympics, and part of the plan was that afterwards the stadium would be used as the joint home for City and United, rather as happened in Milan. The idea of losing Old Trafford, as well as sharing with City, went down just as well as can be imagined among the fans. But property developers, who had noted Edwards' willingness to sell United, thought they saw an opportunity, especially given plans to redevelop Trafford Park. Fortunately, none of this was part of the plans of anyone at United.

Sadly, the growing self-belief didn't translate itself into a serious challenge for the league title, where Arsenal proved almost unbeatable, losing just once all season. United did at least improve enough to finish sixth. There was the consolation of a home derby win against City in early May, thanks to a winning goal from Ryan Giggs on his full debut. So, once again, United were a cup team. And this time Europe was back on the agenda, as the English teams' ban from foreign competition was finally lifted.

United reached two cup finals in 1991. First was the League Cup, and to get there United had to beat Liverpool, Arsenal and Leeds among others, three of the top four sides that season. Liverpool were undefeated all campaign when they took a full-strength side to Old Trafford for the third round, but came away beaten 3–1. In the next round, Lee Sharpe scored a hat-trick at Highbury in an unbelievable 6–2 victory, while Leeds were beaten home and away in the two-legged semifinal. The Arsenal game came soon after the infamous bust-up at Old Trafford between the two sides that led to both clubs being fined and docked points. Perhaps if United had faced another top side in the final, rather than Second Division Sheffield Wednesday, managed by their former boss Ron Atkinson, the result would have been different. But United lost 1–0 to a John Sheridan goal.

Being back in Europe, even if it was just the European Cup-Winners' Cup, was a massive boost: floodlit European games, young stars coming through – this was back to the good old days. Except that Pecsi Munkas and Wrexham were hardly Real Madrid or Benfica. There was an additional benefit from the visit of the Hungarians: ITV paid £300,000 to screen both legs –

more than United earned in gate receipts. United reached the quarterfinals without conceding a goal against either of those two not so illustrious opponents. Montpellier were next, standing between United and an eighth European semifinal. A controversial sending-off at Old Trafford during a 1–1 draw, when Hughes went down despite little contact from a head-butt that had been directed at him, ensured the away leg would be tense. A 2–0 away win in France set up a semifinal tie against Legia Warsaw. Trips east could always be tricky, but a 3–1 away win in Poland meant the task at Old Trafford was relatively straightforward. The final, however, was a European fixture worthy of the name: Barcelona in Rotterdam. And one man, Mark Hughes, had something to prove against the club that had dispensed with his services. His two goals ensured United had a second trophy under Ferguson, and a massive celebration when the team flew back to Manchester. In the aftermath, the manager was clear about his plans for the following season: the aim was to win the league.

Having signed the speedy winger Andrei Kanchelskis at the end of the season, that summer Ferguson made two major signings, one of whom was another candidate for the accolade of best transfer deal in his time at United: Peter Schmeichel joined from Brondby for a fee of about £500,000, and for the next eight years that he played for the club he was arguably the best goalkeeper in the world. Meanwhile, England international full-back Paul Parker joined from QPR for £2 million.

By this time, United had become a public limited company (PLC), after making a profit of £5.5 million in the previous year. Shares were issued at £3.85 each, valuing the company at £47 million (the rapid increase in the club's value since the bids of Maxwell and Knighton was clear). Edwards retained a sufficient proportion of the shares to maintain his control of the club, while the funds raised provided scope for more expenditure on the rebuilding of the stadium. Many fans became small shareholders in the club (as had happened at Tottenham, who had pioneered this approach), giving them a small but direct say in the running of the club. The club shop was getting increasingly busy and profitable, too. Furthermore, the Football Trust provided grants to cover some of the costs for the replacement of seating in the Main Stand, as well as new seats in the United Road lower terrace. Old Trafford even hosted a rock concert, headlined by Rod Stewart, during the close season. ITV signed a lucrative deal to show United's home European ties live during the coming season. As the money came flooding in to Old Trafford, and other clubs, another idea was launched.

That summer all the First Division clubs resigned from the Football League with a view to setting up the Premier League, under the control of the FA, for the start of the 1992–93 season. The big clubs saw how the trend was going, and wanted to ensure they kept more control of their own affairs and revenues than had been the case under the auspices of the Football League, where the aim was to share things out more equally among the ninety-two clubs under its auspices. The bigger clubs, who generated most of the revenues, wanted a greater share of the income.

Meanwhile, a Football Offences Act came into existence, which meant fans could be punished by fines or bans if they threw objects onto the pitch, ran on the pitch, or chanted racist or obscene slogans. The number of arrests and ejections from grounds had been diminishing, not just at Old Trafford but across the country, and this law was designed to continue that process.

Just before the season began, United played a match against a Republic of Ireland side to mark a testimonial for Sir Matt Busby. Some 33,410 fans turned up, paying £250,000, to see a 1–1 draw. Busby, now eighty-two, was truly the founding father of the modern United. It may have been James Gibson, Harold Hardman and Louis Edwards that had run the club's business in his era as manager, but there would hardly have been a business to run if Busby had not created a team that thousands had paid to come and watch week after week. He created the template, and now Ferguson was hoping he could replicate it.

United began the 1991–92 campaign like champions, not losing any of their first twelve games, and became embroiled in what was essentially a two-horse race for the title with Leeds, the Reds usually having the edge. Brian Kidd had replaced Archie Knox as Ferguson's assistant manager, and brought in new training ideas that inspired the squad. The Super Cup was won at Old Trafford, after United beat European champions Red Star Belgrade 1–0, thanks to a goal by McClair. According to Ferguson, United began to lose some of their rhythm when the pitch at Old Trafford deteriorated alarmingly midway through the season, making the team's passing game much harder to implement. Accordingly, that summer part of the roof of the Main Stand was replaced by translucent covering to help maximise the sunlight that fell on the grass and so help to improve the pitch conditions.

United's defence of the European Cup-Winners' Cup that season was short-lived – partly because of new UEFA regulations on the number of foreign players allowed in a side (and for these purposes, foreign meant any British nationals who were not English). Similarly, their FA Cup campaign was halted early on in historic circumstances in the fourth round at Old Trafford, after United became the first top-division side to go out on penalties, against Southampton. Despite these early exits, the club faced huge fixture congestion for the title run-in. Partly this was caused by success in the League Cup, where United once again reached the final, this time beating Nottingham Forest 1–0 thanks to another trophy-winning McClair goal. In the middle of April, United played four games in six days, five in ten; the team picked up just one win in that time, and lost three games. The final match of that sequence, a 2–0 defeat at Anfield, meant Leeds claimed the title.

For the players, there were painful reminders of what it meant to lose. A picture of the agonised faces of Ferguson and Kidd after

Bruce missed a chance at Old Trafford against Forest was pinned up in the dressing room afterwards. While at Anfield, a few Liverpool fans asked some of the players to sign their autographs, before tearing them up in front of their eyes and declaring them losers. The press accused the players and the manager of bottling it – the pressure of winning the league after twenty-five years had, they claimed, got to United. If there were any truth in that, the result was to provide a powerful motivating force in the future: losing was too painful.

But there was little time to look back. The Premier League had arrived, and with it came an incredible £304 million TV deal with Sky and the BBC over five years, announced in May 1992, allowing the satellite broadcaster to air sixty live games per season. At the time, a poll reported that only 3 per cent of non-satellite owners were prepared to buy a dish to watch their football, but Murdoch's gamble was that they would eventually come round to his way. What's more, he was able to tip the scales in his favour: his newspapers, including the *Sun* and *The Times*, gave the Premier League massive coverage. Football was going to become an essential part of life if the media mogul had anything to do with it.

However, for the fans, and for many associated with the ground, there was one very poignant reason to look back: the Stretford End was pulled down at the end of the 1991–92 season, bringing to a close an era and a way of following United that could never be replaced. Cliff Butler, then the club's official photographer, watched on as the demolition firm Connell and Finnigan went about their work: 'I was there the day they pulled down the Stretford End. They pulled the pillar out; there was a cable attached round the uprights and they burned off the bottom and the top and just pulled it out and the roof just thudded to the ground. I could hardly focus that day because I was crying.' Old Trafford would never be the same again.

Indeed, during the previous season there had been a great deal of concern that not only would the ground be different, it would be difficult to get in, as thousands were sometimes locked out, even before rebuilding work had begun. Once the stand was rebuilt, the capacity of Old Trafford was going to be just 43,000, and during the start of the rebuilding process it was even lower, at around 33,000. For a club that not long ago had regularly attracted crowds of up to 60,000, this meant there was a real danger that some fans could lose the habit of going to watch football at Old Trafford entirely. At the time the board felt there just wasn't the scope to expand the stadium beyond the proposed figure. It was clearly to no one's benefit for thousands of fans to be turned away, but there seemed to be no solution to the problem.

Unsurprisingly, there was even more criticism from the fans when it was announced that the cheapest seats for the new season were going to be £15, up from £11 the year before, to preserve revenues. To try to placate fans, Edwards floated the idea of banning away supporters during the rebuilding, which would not only improve the capacity of the ground, as there would be no empty seats for segregation purposes, but ensure that as many United fans as possible were able to get into the ground. Perhaps inevitably, some feared that other clubs would take reciprocal action against United and they would miss out on following their team home and away. Whatever one did in this transitional phase, someone was bound to be upset.

The old Stretford End had been given a long farewell. First, United beat Spurs 3–1 in their last league match of the season on 2 May 1992 in front of 44,595 fans, with Hughes scoring United's last official goal. Then came a testimonial for Norman Whiteside against Everton, to which just 7434 turned up. Whiteside had hoped the game would be played in the afterglow of a championship-winning season, but instead found that the disappointment of missing out meant that few felt inclined to support their one-time hero. Almost exactly double that number, 14,681, came along on 15 May to see United's youth side, holding a 3–1 advantage from the first leg, beat Crystal Palace 3–2 to win the Youth Cup for the first time since George Best's day back in 1964. In the side that day were David Beckham, Nicky Butt, Ryan Giggs and Gary Neville. Perhaps it was time to look towards the future, after all?

13

The Home of King Eric

When the Premier League kicked off on 15 August 1992, pre-season title favourites Arsenal lost 4–2 and Liverpool lost 1–0 in the first live televised game on BSkyB. United had the opportunity to steal an early advantage but also lost, 2–1 at Sheffield United. When Old Trafford hosted its first Premier League game on 19 August, Everton cruised to a 3–0 victory. For a side bent on banishing the embarrassment of slipping up the season before, it was the worst possible start. Brian McClair remembers what it was like playing at a ground where one end was occupied by builders' rubble: 'At the start of the season, we were poor. The stadium was being redeveloped, and there was a difficult period because part of the stadium wasn't there. It did make a difference. Looking back on it, until we got into the swing of it, it was a very tricky time.' Fortunately, in November, the first 2500 seats in the new stand became available, and Old Trafford began to look less like a building site.

Alex Ferguson had been convinced that one reason United's title challenge had faltered the previous campaign was due to the lack of a big target man, to compensate for the difficulty of the

Old Trafford playing surface. In the summer he had signed Dion Dublin to fulfil that role, but early in the season Dublin broke his leg, and the manager was forced to go looking in the transfer market again. It is meant as no disrespect to Dublin to say that his misfortune was to set in motion something that brought delight to United fans the world over, for the new man was to prove the final piece in the jigsaw. The deal came about almost by chance, when Leeds contacted chairman Martin Edwards to inquire about signing Denis Irwin; the manager, who was there as well, turned it down flat, but asked about one of their stars. To his surprise, Leeds were open to the suggestion and a deal was done on 26 November for a bargain £1 million. His name? Eric Cantona.

Many players come to Old Trafford and find themselves daunted by the prospect of living up to the expectations of the fans or the distinguished names that have gone before them. Cantona almost seemed to wonder if United could live up to him. The Frenchman was instantly at home at United. Collar raised, he strutted round the pitch as though it was his plaything. His confidence and swagger rubbed off on those around him. And what's more, he delivered the performances his attitude required. He also provided an example on the training ground, too, inspiring others to work hard on improving themselves. From his very first day at the Cliff, he asked to stay and do extra work on his skills after the formal training session was over. For some of the young players coming through the ranks, his influence was immense and his example one to be followed.

Cantona made his debut as a substitute at Old Trafford on 6 December, helping United secure a 2–1 victory over neighbours City in front of 35,408 fans. Later that month he scored his first goal at his new home ground, a penalty in United's 5–0 crushing of Coventry. By the end of the Reds' next game, a 4–1 win over Spurs featuring another goal from Eric, they were top of the table. Their rivals in the race to become the first Premier League champions were Aston Villa and Norwich City.

United won their last seven games, which, for those who don't remember the title run-in, suggests that they cruised home to title glory. But it didn't feel like it at the time. The Old Trafford match against Sheffield Wednesday on 10 April stands out in many people's memories as the time the Reds showed they weren't going to stumble this time round. After ninety minutes, Wednesday were leading 1–0, but Steve Bruce equalised in front of the new Stretford End and then scored the winner six minutes into added time. Ferguson and Brian Kidd ran onto the pitch to celebrate, while the crowds in the stands went wild. Kidd recalled how the manager had been trying to downplay the pressure: 'He was trying to be Mr Cool then; nothing's going to get to him. And then when he legged it out of the dugout, all of a sudden he must have realised it: "I'm Mr Cool" and toddled back in there.' Happily, as the old Stretford End was being rebuilt, the capacity of Old Trafford was increasing, and for the first time that season more than 40,000 were packed into the ground. Eventually, at a cost of around £10 million, the 10,500-seater new stand, glistening in red and white, with its forty private boxes and all the usual extra facilities, was completed. Those who feared that the atmosphere would vanish from the stadium once the terraces had gone realised they had little to worry about on special moments such as this.

The link between the fans and the players at such times is so important, as McClair comments: 'Sometimes the nervousness [in a big game] can go both ways between the players and crowd. The more you're involved in situations like that the more you get used to it. But we never do things the easy way, as when Steve Bruce scored two goals in injury time versus Sheffield Wednesday, so there's a kind of pleasure and torture going on at the same time. We almost take things to the wire. It's called the Theatre of Dreams, but some of those dreams have been unpleasant.'

As the season came to its penultimate weekend, Aston Villa remained the only threat, but when they lost to Oldham on

2 May, United were champions by default. Lee Sharpe went down to Old Trafford and found a huge crowd gathered outside to celebrate. Eventually, he had to be rescued from the fans by the club's security as he was thrown in the air in the excitement of it all. Most of the players partied into the early hours at Bruce's house before joining the adoring masses at Old Trafford for the game against Blackburn. At the manager's house, another party was going on, as he celebrated becoming the first man to win the title north and south of the border.

On the day of the match, Sir Matt Busby was there (doubtless having come down the newly named Sir Matt Busby Way, in place of Warwick Road North), and so were many of the stars of United's previous title-winning side from the 1960s. Running out from the central players' tunnel (now the only remaining part of the ground that dates from the original 1910 construction, although it is no longer used by the players) for the last time, United were unsurprisingly slow out of the blocks and fell behind, but soon order was restored and the carnival atmosphere continued right up until Gary Pallister secured the 3–1 victory with a goal from a free kick, his first of the season. Bruce and club captain Bryan Robson lifted the new trophy together, as the celebrations took off to an even greater level. However, as McClair remembers, it was one of the most special occasions of his time as a player: 'Winning the Premier League title for the first time, the hairs on the back of your neck stood up. There was great joy and relief, as well. It made it even better because we had floundered in the final furlong the year before, and we'd been written off.'

Now United had the opportunity to go even further. Just as the club had been the star attraction at the dawning of the TV age of *Match of the Day* in the mid-1960s, now in the 1990s, with the Premier League and Sky, they were the best side in the country. Not only that, they had the game's most charismatic figure in Cantona and the sport's brightest young star in Ryan Giggs, who had retained his title as PFA Young Player of the

Year. The club had been offering tours of the stadium and a club museum since 1986 – now both had been expanded to cater for the increasing interest. The club shop was no longer owned by the Busby family, as had been the case for many years, but Edward Freedman had been brought in to make it a proper commercial concern. Now with 3000 square feet of retail space, it quickly became the hub of a huge merchandising operation that could generate as much as £20 million per year in revenue. Cliff Butler had warned one of the club's directors during the rebuilding of the Stretford End that the stadium would not be big enough if United had any success; his warning was about to be put to an ever greater test.

That summer Ferguson made just one foray into the transfer market, but although it would break the English record by a distance, at £3.75 million, the signing of Nottingham Forest's young Irish midfielder Roy Keane would prove to be another of the manager's masterstrokes, and Keane ended up being a bargain even at that price. With Robson nearing the end of his remarkable career, here was a ready-made successor. What made it all the more sweet was that Kenny Dalglish, now the manager of Blackburn, thought he was going to win the race for Keane's signature.

This time, there was no slow start to the season: United were top by the end of August, and stayed there for the rest of the campaign thanks to a 22-game unbeaten run, finishing eight points clear of runners-up Blackburn Rovers, who faded at the end. The defence of Peter Schmeichel in goal, full-backs Paul Parker and Denis Irwin and centre-backs Steve Bruce and Gary Pallister missed just six appearances between them all season. At Old Trafford there was just one defeat, against Chelsea in the league, in front of sell-out crowds in every match. Once the work on the Scoreboard Paddock and South Stand was complete, at a further cost of £5 million, the stadium had an all-seater capacity of just over 44,000, and thereafter attendances only twice slipped below 44,000.

This side was one of United's all-time greats. They dominated domestic football, reaching the final of the League Cup, where they lost out to Ron Atkinson's Aston Villa. They were formally crowned champions again on 2 May, and, just as had happened exactly a year before, they did it without playing, as Blackburn's defeat cost them any chance of the title. United then had two home games to celebrate, beating Southampton and drawing with Coventry – the latter game marking the league debut of Gary Neville as well as the last appearance for Robson, who joined Middlesbrough as player-manager the next season, the former captain handing on the baton to a future one. They rounded off the season in the FA Cup final with a 4–0 trouncing of Chelsea, who had done the double over United in the league. Their FA Cup run had largely taken place away from Old Trafford, except for a 3–1 win over Charlton in the quarterfinals. For the first time in their illustrious history, United had done the Double of league and FA Cup titles.

Only in the Champions League – the new name for an expanded European Cup, now in its second season – was this United side found wanting. After beating Kispest Honved, they let slip a comfortable lead at Old Trafford against Galatasaray, and ended up having to rescue a 3–3 draw, before going out after a goalless draw in the intimidating return leg in Turkey that ended in great controversy with the local police striking out at some of the United players. UEFA rules limiting the number of foreigners United could play meant that a full-strength side could not be selected. One foreigner who did play at Old Trafford was Schmeichel, who was called into unorthodox action when two Turkish fans invaded the pitch, waving a flag. The Danish keeper, according to Robson, 'didn't mess about' and wrestled one of them to the ground before picking him up and throwing him into the advertising hoardings.

Old Trafford itself went through a whole range of different experiences, from the violent to the sombre. The ground had previously played host to a range of other sports, not just both codes of rugby, cricket and baseball, but now boxing. A record crowd of more than 40,000 for a British boxing bout turned up on 9 October 1993 to watch Nigel Benn take on Chris Eubank in a rematch of one of the most intriguing rivalries in the sport. A rather disappointing fight was judged to be a draw, much to Benn's disgust.

Then, on 20 January 1994, Sir Matt Busby died, aged eighty-four, and Old Trafford became a place of pilgrimage. Busby's dignity and devotion to United were without equal. Two days later, Everton were the visitors and on an emotional day a lone bagpiper set the tone, leading the players out onto the pitch, before a minute's silence was perfectly observed. Sometimes on such occasions, these preliminaries can prevent a side from playing to their potential, but that day the Reds performed in a manner Busby would have been proud of and excited by. Giggs may have scored the only goal of the game, but it could have been many more. A few days later, the funeral cortège passed the ground, stopping for two minutes while the mourners bowed their heads in silence.

By now, the momentum behind United seemed unstoppable: the club had over 100,000 official members, and ticket applications were running way above the capacity of Old Trafford. With England once again soon to be the host of a major football tournament, and Old Trafford one of the designated venues for Euro 96, the board decided to start planning to knock down the old cantilever stand that had been built for the 1966 World Cup, and replace it with a new North Stand that would have three tiers. However, it wasn't just because of the one tournament that this decision was taken: the stadium clearly wasn't big enough for everyone who wanted to come, and it made no sense to be turning away thousands of people every game. In 1994–95, with the capacity a few hundred lower than in the previous season, United's league attendances varied between 43,120 and 43,868 – every match was essentially a full house. Demand for all things relating to the club just kept on growing. United's new

Megastore was opened on 3 December 1994, and immediately proved a huge financial success.

On the pitch, however, things weren't running quite so smoothly. Newcastle set the early pace in the league, before Blackburn overhauled them, with United in close pursuit. Defender David May had joined from Blackburn over the summer, but the biggest transfer came midway through the season when Ferguson signed centre-forward Andy Cole from Newcastle for a record deal valued at £7 million in January 1995. Both May and Cole boosted the England contingent for European competition. United weren't exactly struggling to score goals at the time – they'd beaten City 5–0 in the derby on 10 November, with an ecstatic Old Trafford crowd celebrating as the pace of Andrei Kanchelskis and Giggs, prompted by Cantona, cut them to pieces. But they had fallen short again in the Champions League, failing to qualify from a tough group and hampered by the rules on foreign players and a ban for Cantona that meant he missed the first four games.

The Cole–Cantona strike pairing made its debut at Old Trafford on 22 January against Blackburn, when a goal by the Frenchman helped narrow the gap on the league leaders. But their second game together, three days later at Selhurst Park, saw Cantona sent off for the fifth time at United, and then launch an extraordinary 'kung-fu' assault on an abusive fan: United's talisman was banned from all football until October. At one stage, he was set to go to prison, but on appeal the sentence was reduced to community service, coaching kids in Manchester. But the Reds continued their challenge for another Double. On 4 March, Cole showed just what he was about: goals, and lots of them. He hit five as United crushed Ipswich 9–0, team and individual achievements that have never been bettered in the Premier League. In the end, the Reds fell just short, missing out on the title by a point to Blackburn and losing 1–0 to Everton in a forgettable FA Cup final.

But as the season wore on, there were signs that something

was changing. Several of the players that had come through the United youth system started to make their way into the side. Nicky Butt and Gary Neville had already made their first appearances in the league before, but both were much more regular participants this season. Paul Scholes made his home league debut in the Manchester derby, while Phil Neville was given his league debut in the even more pressurised atmosphere of the away derby match, and finally David Beckham made his league bow at home against Leeds. Ferguson clearly not only had confidence in these kids' ability, he knew they had the personality to stand up to the toughest of challenges.

The fact that they all came through unscathed gave the manager the confidence to pursue a summer policy that had fans baffled: Hughes, Ince and Kanchelskis were all sold off. Three of the key figures in United's Double side of 1994, who had just missed out on another Double in 1995, were gone. Cantona was still banned, and there were fears either that he might leave or that he might return a diminished player. In place of these experienced, battle-hardened internationals, he signed no one. In the first game of the new season, Butt, Scholes and the Neville brothers all started, Beckham and twenty-year-old John O'Kane came on as substitutes, and United lost 3–1 at Villa. BBC pundit Alan Hansen had already seen enough to make the declaration that would haunt him: apparently, 'you can't win anything with kids'. Many United fans thought he had a point, much though they loathed agreeing with the former Liverpool man, and a poll in the *Manchester Evening News* (doubtless boosted by many City fans) suggested a small majority of its readers thought Ferguson should go.

United dropped just four points in the next ten games. In the middle of that run, there were two significant events. On 26 September, United's proud record in Europe, undefeated at Old Trafford in all games, seemed likely to come to an end in the second round of the UEFA Cup against Rotor Volgograd – and Schmeichel was the hero who prevented it. Surprisingly, this wasn't a last-minute penalty save to stop the Russian side from winning. Instead, the Reds were losing 2–1 going into added time, when Schmeichel came up for a corner, and powered home a thumping header to spare United's blushes.

More significantly in the long term, on 1 October, his ban completed, Cantona returned to action at Old Trafford as United faced old foes Liverpool. With the North Stand having been knocked down over the summer, the crowd was just 34,934, and United fans welcomed back their hero (away supporters were not allowed at this time, because of the reduced capacity). Almost immediately, he provided the cross for Butt to score. In a compelling game, Liverpool then scored twice, but it was inevitable that the Frenchman should have the final word. He scored from the penalty spot to equalise, before celebrating like a man who had waited eight months to return home. It was not the last impact he had on the outcome of the season; he was going to show everyone what they had been missing and lead his young side to triumph. A few weeks later, against Southampton, Giggs scored the fastest goal on record at Old Trafford, timed at just thirteen seconds, to set up a 4–1 win.

In what turned out to be one of the most compelling title races for years, Kevin Keegan's Newcastle opened up a twelve-point lead over United, and then saw their advantage gradually whittled away. In four league games in March, starting with a crucial game at St James' Park, United won three of them 1–0 and drew the other 1–1. Cantona scored all four goals, but the defence proved just as crucial as the Frenchman in United's quest. That month, as more and more of the new stand was opened, crowds topped 50,000 for the first time since April 1987, and by now United had overhauled Newcastle.

For the final home game of the season, United piled the pressure on with a stunning 5–0 victory over Forest. Newcastle, with two games in hand, were six points behind and their goal difference was seven worse. The previous game United had battled hard to overcome Leeds, and afterwards Ferguson expressed his hope to the TV cameras that United's old foes didn't fold against the Geordie side, who they were due to play the day after the Forest game; Keegan's emotional response the following day has never been forgotten by United fans, who still hope for him to cheer up. The Reds went to Middlesbrough knowing that a win would secure the title, and for the third time in four years United were champions after their 3–0 victory. Never before had the club won three titles in such quick succession. And, as with the Babes forty years before, 'Fergie's Fledglings' still had youth on their side.

Their FA Cup run had included another victory over neighbours City (when the first executive boxes in the new stand were opened). By the quarterfinal against Southampton, the second tier was open, as was a new pedestrian bridge over the Bridgewater Canal. United then beat Chelsea before they met Liverpool in the final. A poor game was brightened merely by Liverpool's cream suits and yet another Cantona goal in yet another 1–0 victory. It was the double Double. The press, many of whom had suggested he should have been booted out of the country after his attack at Selhurst Park, now voted him their Footballer of the Year. In truth, it was hard to imagine there being another candidate.

By the end of the season, the new three-tier North Stand was complete. Designed by Atherden Fuller (as the original 1960s firm Mather and Nutter had been renamed), the stand was 114 metres long and 45 metres high, with the biggest cantilever roof in Europe. At a cost of £28 million (£9 million of which went on buying the additional land required), it held 25,258 supporters and contained two tiers of executive boxes and numerous executive suites (the Red Café would open there in October 1996, and it would give a new home to the Museum from April 1998). Demolition work to knock down the old stand took just three days, and some 3500 tons of steel and 4500 tons of concrete were used to build the new one. Construction had been complicated by the problem of United

Steve Coppell shields the ball in his last-ever game at Old Trafford, against Coventry on 2 April 1983. That season United went undefeated in twenty-nine home games. *(Mirrorpix)*

In one of the best-ever atmospheres at Old Trafford, Bryan Robson scores the first goal of the night against Barcelona in the European Cup-Winners' Cup quarterfinal, 21 March 1984. *(Getty Images)*

Two men on the pitch: (*Above*) Alex Ferguson makes his Old Trafford debut as manager on 22 November 1986, the first of some 650 games in charge at the ground by November 2010. While (*below*), a less-expected sight, as Michael Knighton shows some ball-juggling skills in front of a surprised Stretford End, having just announced his plans to take control of the club in August 1989. (*Getty Images/Press Association*)

Steve Bruce sets Old Trafford alight with a second goal in injury time to win the game against Sheffield Wednesday in April 1993 and put United on the way to their first title in twenty-six years. *(Press Association)*

The funeral cortege of Sir Matt Busby pauses outside Old Trafford in January 1994, as United fans the world over mourned the loss of their founding father. *(Press Association)*

Old Trafford isn't just for football . . .

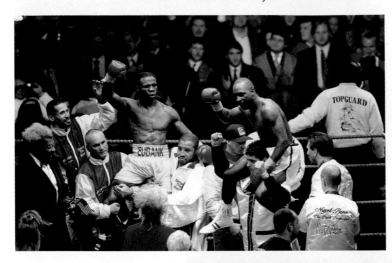

Chris Eubank and Nigel Benn both celebrate as 'Judgement Day' is called a draw, 9 October 1993. *(Getty Images)*

A very different No 11 was running down the wing in November 1997: All Black rugby union star Jonah Lomu is hardly Ryan Giggs, much to the England defence's regret. *(Getty Images)*

St Helens and Hull take to the field for rugby league's Grand Final in October 2006 in front of a record crowd. *(Getty Images)*

The return of the King: Eric Cantona celebrates with Roy Keane after scoring the equaliser against Liverpool in his first match back after a nine-month ban. *(Press Association)*

The new North Stand, completed in time for Euro 96, looms in the background as Ryan Giggs takes a corner against Spurs in March 1996. *(Press Association)*

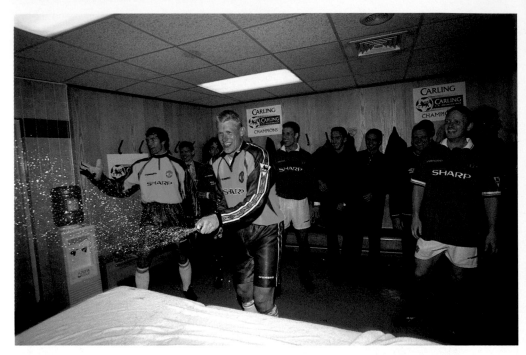

Peter Schmeichel leads the celebrations in the Old Trafford dressing room after United have beaten Spurs 2-1 to secure the first leg of a unique Treble in 1999. *(Manchester United)*

David Beckham celebrates scoring England's late equaliser against Greece to secure their qualification for the 2002 World Cup – Old Trafford proved a very lucky venue for England while Wembley was being rebuilt. *(Mirrorpix)*

Wayne Rooney clashes with keeper Brad Friedel during United's 4-1 win over Blackburn Rovers on 31 March 2007. The crowd of 76,098 was a club record attendance. *(Manchester United)*

A lone piper leads out the two sides for an emotional derby match on 10 February 2008, when Old Trafford marked the fiftieth anniversary of the Munich disaster. *(Manchester United)*

Paul Scholes fires home the winner against Barcelona in the tense Champions League semifinal of 2008, to set up United's third European title. *(Manchester United)*

The 'United Trinity' statue of Best, Law and Charlton, created by Philip Jackson, looks at the image created on the East Stand to mark Old Trafford's centenary. *(Manchester United)*

The families of the original team bury a time capsule by the old players' tunnel (the only surviving part of the original stadium) on 14 March 2010, when United celebrated 100 years at Old Trafford. *(Manchester United)*

Head groundsman Tony Sinclair stands on his immaculate turf in front of the Stretford End, May 2010. *(Author)*

Road, a public highway that had to remain, so the stand had to be built over it.

With Euro 96 about to come to Old Trafford, United ensured that everyone arriving at the ground knew who the club's founding father was, as an eleven-foot bronze statue of Sir Matt Busby, by sculptor Philip Jackson, was unveiled on the forecourt. This time, Manchester's famous stadium was going to play a far larger part in the proceedings than had been the case in 1966: not only would Old Trafford co-host Group C with Anfield, the ground was going to be used for one of the quarterfinals and a semifinal.

On 9 June, 37,300 saw Germany beat the Czech Republic 2–0 as the tournament got going. The second game, however, was thrown into question when the IRA exploded a huge bomb (about 1500kg) in the city centre the day before. Fortunately, no one was killed, but more than 200 people were injured and the cost of repairing the damage was estimated at around £700 million, with about 400 businesses affected by the blast. The game did go ahead after all, and the Germans beat Russia 3–0 in front of 50,760; finally in Group C, Germany and Italy played out a goalless draw, watched by 53,740, that resulted in Italy going out. Germany were back in the quarterfinals to beat Croatia 2–1 in front of just 43,412. The semifinal, played on the same day as England's fateful tie against Germany at Wembley and attended by 43,877, saw France and the Czech Republic draw 0–0, with the latter winning the penalty shoot-out 6–5. Old Trafford's first game in the tournament was therefore a preview of the final, with Germany winning both games. One of the Czech stars, Karel Poborsky, soon became a lot more familiar with the stadium after Euro 96 when he joined United.

The 1996–97 season got under way with Beckham's famous goal from inside his own half against Wimbledon that announced his special talent to a wider audience. Over the summer, Paul Parker and Steve Bruce had decided to move on, and Ferguson brought in Ronny Johnsen from Besiktas as Bruce's replacement, while Poborsky and Jordi Cruyff also joined to give further strength on the flanks, and soon after Lee Sharpe departed for Leeds. Ferguson was also looking for a new striker, but his attempts to sign Alan Shearer failed, so instead he landed Ole Gunnar Solskjaer.

After three successive autumn defeats, United then went on a sixteen-game unbeaten run in the league, by which stage they were four points clear of Liverpool, with Arsenal and Newcastle also in contention. During that time, the Old Trafford crowd witnessed one of the all-time great goals at the stadium, a sublime chip by Cantona from the edge of the penalty area against Sunderland. He turned round to look at the entire ground, as if in awe at his own skill.

In the end, the Reds' fourth Premier League title in five years came in the first week of May, with two games to spare. On 5 May, in front of a passionate crowd of 54,489, United came back from 3–1 down against Middlesbrough to equalise. Gary Neville, scoring his only league goal to date, started the comeback, and Solskjaer finished the job, but despite all their efforts they couldn't find a winner. The next day, both Liverpool and Newcastle failed to win, and the title came home to Old Trafford yet again without the side having to play. On the final game of the season, United paraded not only the Premier League title, but the reserve team were the winners of the Pontin's Premier League, and the A and B sides won their leagues too. United had won all four leagues they had entered sides into. But within a fortnight the joy of United fans was tempered by the announcement that Cantona was retiring from football, just a few days short of his thirty-first birthday. In total, he had played 185 times for the Reds, scoring 82 goals, but his impact on the team's self-belief and dedication was far beyond those numbers.

Following a series of disappointments in Europe, United finally had a Champions League run worthy of the name, but it was a curious campaign. For the first time, the limit on foreign nationals in a side was removed, as a result of the Bosman ruling, enabling Ferguson to pick the team he wanted at last. Never previously having lost at Old Trafford, United beat Rapid Vienna 2–0 in their first home tie, but then lost 1–0 to both Fenerbahce and Juventus. The game against the Turkish side was the fifty-eighth home European tie. Qualification for the quarterfinals depended on United going to Vienna and getting a win, and hoping that Fenerbahce lost at Juventus, who had already won the group. Fortunately, goals from Cantona and Giggs did the trick. The quarterfinal, against Porto, was virtually decided at Old Trafford, when United cruised to a stunning 4–0 victory. In the semifinal, Borussia Dortmund were lucky to win 1–0 in Germany, but in the return leg, missing Keane, United failed to take their chances after Dortmund scored early on through Lars Ricken, and a great chance to reach the final was gone.

The year of United's double Double had seen the passing of a link with the pre-war era when Alan Gibson, son of former chairman James, died. The role of the latter was marked by a plaque in the players' tunnel area, with another unveiled to commemorate United's other saviour, John Davies. Where so many other clubs (such as Derby, who moved from the Baseball Ground in 1997 after 102 years, or Middlesbrough, who left Ayresome Park in 1995 after 92 years) had taken the opportunity of the Taylor Report to relocate, United had stayed loyal to its base in Old Trafford, and to the history that it brought with it.

The result was that Old Trafford got to host two internationals in six months. The first, not so surprisingly, saw England's footballers take on South Africa in a friendly on 24 May 1997. It was the first time Old Trafford had hosted an England game in seventy-one years. Led by Stuart Pearce, England won 2–1 with goals from Ian Wright and Rob Lee. Glenn Hoddle picked local boy Phil Neville at right-back to win his second cap, but among his substitutes were Beckham winning his sixth, Butt (second) and Scholes, making his debut.

The second international was rather more surprising, and took place on 22 November. New coach Clive Woodward's England rugby union side took on the All Blacks. The famous New Zealand side had of course played at Old Trafford between the wars, so it could be argued they had more experience of the venue than England! However, for rugby union to leave its southern heartland in Twickenham was even more unusual than England's footballers venturing north from Wembley. It was a fiery occasion from the start: England hooker Richard Cockerill kicked away one of the Kiwis' scrum caps before they started to perform their haka. During the match, Kiwi Ian Jones scored the first try, Martin Johnson punched All Black skipper Justin Marshall, while Phil de Glanville, England's recently deposed captain, scored the home nation's only try in a 25–8 defeat. To the derision of the New Zealanders, England's beaten players went on a lap of honour to thank the fans for turning up in such good numbers: 55,243 attended. The huge and vocal support England received was in marked contrast to what they were used to at Twickenham.

Even for the New Zealanders, it was something special. Legendary bulldozing wing Jonah Lomu was hugely impressed by the place. He recalled how one of the security guards told him about Vinnie Jones putting a stereo system outside United's dressing room before a match and blasting out the Wimbledon theme tune. Woodward, a football fanatic who would eventually go on to have a coaching role at Southampton, was also excited by the opportunity. He was thrilled to visit the boot room, and to hold Beckham's boots.

He also got to learn something about the professionalism of the set-up at Old Trafford. Two days before the game, he wanted to train on the pitch, but in the heavy rain, he expected to be told it would damage the pitch too badly. Certainly, this is what he felt he would have been told at Twickenham. Groundsman Keith Kent had no problems with it, however, and England duly carried out their training session and churned up the pitch. Immediately they left, he recalls, 'an army of men came on and replaced all the divots, sorting it all out quickly and without fuss'. Perhaps it was no great surprise, therefore, that Kent was subsequently brought in to work at Twickenham. But of greater importance now to United was how they were going to get used to life without Cantona.

14

United on the Treble

The man given the impossible task of stepping in to Eric Cantona's boots was Teddy Sheringham, who was signed from Tottenham for £3.675 million. Undoubtedly one of the most intelligent forwards in the game, he not only scored goals but made them for others. His partnership with Alan Shearer in Euro 96 had been very potent. However, it wasn't just what he did on the pitch that had made Cantona so special to United fans, it was how he did it and his unique individualism that made him stand out. While Sheringham could hope to emulate the Frenchman on the football field, he had little chance of matching him in other ways. In truth, no one could. So United had to learn how to win again without their hero.

As Manchester continued the rebuilding process after the bombing, and would emerge a stronger, brighter city as a result, so United also began its rebuilding process. By 2000, the city, the team and the stadium were all, it was argued, better than they had been before. It just didn't seem to be heading that way in 1997.

At first all seemed well, as the Reds took up their customary position at the top of the Premier League. In the autumn, United were flying: Barnsley were smashed for seven at Old Trafford, with Andy Cole hitting a hat-trick and Ryan Giggs scoring two, Paul Scholes and Karel Poborsky scoring the others. The following week, Sheffield Wednesday lost 6–1 in Manchester, with two each for Sheringham and Ole Gunnar Solskjaer and Cole netting again, after an own goal had opened United's scoring. After that, a defeat at Highbury didn't seem to matter too much, but Arsenal had closed the gap to just one point. They were in the process of becoming United's main rivals, and the next seven league titles would be won by one team or the other. In the end, Arsenal could afford to lose their last two games of the season and still win the league by a point, before going on to complete the Double.

There wasn't any compensation in the domestic cups, but Europe was becoming something of an obsession for United and Alex Ferguson: to prove yourself as one of the truly great sides, you had to win the Champions League. In the group stages, United faced Kosice, Feyenoord and (again) Juventus. The Slovakian team were beaten 3–0 home and away, but it was Juventus who drew in a crowd of 53,428 to Old Trafford for the key tie of the group. A year before, the Italian giants had beaten United home and away: this was United's chance to show how far they had come. In a thrilling game against the side that had reached the final for the previous two years, United fell behind in the first minute but had the courage to recover and hit back with goals from Sheringham, Scholes and Giggs, the latter with one of his best strikes. Zidane pulled a goal back in the final minute, but it was a triumph for the Reds and a sign of the team's growing maturity, especially as they were without Roy Keane, whose cruciate ligament injury was to keep him out for the rest of the season.

By the time of the return leg, United were the favourites to win the whole thing according to some bookmakers and already through as group winners, so the resulting 1–0 defeat mattered little to United but kept Juve in the tournament. In the knockout stages of the Champions League, United faced Monaco for the first time. A cautious 0–0 draw on a dodgy pitch in the principality seemed to have set up the Reds for the semifinals, but when an injury-hit United side (missing Peter Schmeichel, Gary Pallister, Keane and Giggs, and with Gary Neville and Scholes both unable to complete the match) went a goal behind early on to an unstoppable shot from David Trezeguet, it left them with a lot to do. Solskjaer pulled a goal back early in the second half, but it wasn't enough, and they went out on the away-goals rule.

As the season drew to a close, on 11 April, Old Trafford had a special visitor: Pelé had come to open the new club museum, which had been built at a cost of £4 million. Then, as now, it was the starting point for the stadium tour, and was a treasure trove for anyone wanting to understand more about the history of the club, and to see the trophies won by United or the different kits that had been used down the years, among much else besides. Over the close season, the Old Trafford pitch was relaid and the drainage and undersoil heating improved.

Having failed to win anything in 1998, amazingly Ferguson had to face a lot of questions from some, despite his proven track record: although his signings had usually been good, no one recently had come in and dominated the place like Keane or Cantona; his age was beginning to be mentioned as an issue by some media critics, who seemed keen to push him into retirement. According to this theory, the new approach, personified by Arsene Wenger at Arsenal, was said now to have the upper hand over his supposed old-style methods. In his autobiography, Ferguson subsequently revealed that relations with the board were not smooth over the summer either.

To make matters worse, one of his young stars, David Beckham, had become Public Enemy Number One after he was sent off in the World Cup following a harmless flick at Diego Simeone. The response to this from all connected with United was remarkably supportive: the club backed him with a reported £5 million five-year contract; he played in stunning fashion during the season that followed, backed by the United fans, who were not going to accept other fans' criticisms of their No. 7 (a pattern that repeated itself a few years later after another World Cup). In short, the club pulled together against all outsiders to show just what it was made of.

As ever, Ferguson responded to all this criticism by trying to find a way to make United even better. The previous season, a run of injuries had hit United just as the campaign was building up to a climax; he realised that to compete on several fronts, the club needed to have greater strength in depth, enabling him to develop a squad rotation system. Ferguson was apparently told he had a spending budget of £14 million. He must have had some persuasive words with the board, as he went out and bought centre-back Jaap Stam from PSV Eindhoven for £10.815 million to replace Gary Pallister, winger Jesper Blomqvist from Parma for £4.4 million and centre-forward Dwight Yorke from Aston Villa for £12.6 million. It was his biggest spending spree yet: over £27 million.

But this spending was soon put into context on 7 September when BSkyB put in a bid to buy United, valuing the club at £575 million. A couple of days later, the board accepted an improved bid of £625 million, and there was talk of rival bidders threatening to come in with even higher offers. Given that Michael Knighton's bid less than a decade before had valued the club at £20 million, he and the investors who'd failed to support him at the time must have been kicking themselves. Fans, who had reacted with horror at the possibility of Robert Maxwell taking control of the club in the 1980s, were just as concerned about Rupert Murdoch this time, and organised themselves to stop him. Although the deal eventually fell through in April 1999, after Peter Mandelson referred it to the Monopolies and Mergers Commission, it reflected the fact that, according to accountants Deloitte & Touche, United was now the richest club in the world, with a turnover of almost £88 million.

At the same time as all this was happening, on 10 September 1998, MUTV went on air for the first time, showing exclusive behind-the-scenes programmes about life at United. United was the first club to have its own in-house TV station, and ownership was shared equally by the club, Granada and BSkyB.

With all this going on, it was easy to forget the main purpose of the club: to win football matches. And perhaps the off-field distractions were behind the Reds' poor defeat at Arsenal, though the sending-off of Nicky Butt didn't help either. In November, Schmeichel announced he was going to leave United at the end of the season. Then, early in December, Brian Kidd left to become manager at Blackburn, eventually to be succeeded in February as Ferguson's assistant manager by Steve McClaren. With the new pitch proving a liability, it was dug up again in mid-November and replaced, with a view to starting again after the season was over. In January, for the match against West Ham, an electricity cable was cut outside the ground, causing problems inside that led to difficulties for fans when they were trying to leave in semi-darkness. All in all, things weren't really clicking into gear, it seemed.

Aston Villa were the surprise pace-setters in the Premier League, heading the table for much of 1998, but after United and Arsenal suffered defeats in mid-December, both went on exceptional runs: United were unbeaten in eighteen league games, dropping just ten points, while Arsenal dropped eight points in nineteen games. With two matches to go, both sides had identical records: 75 points and a goal difference of plus-42. Arsenal then lost for the first time since December, at Leeds, while United failed to make the advantage tell by drawing at Blackburn the following day, in so doing relegating the Lancashire club along with his former assistant Kidd.

A crowd of 55,189 packed into Old Trafford on 16 May 1999 knowing that a United win would give them the Premier League title. After twenty-four minutes Les Ferdinand put Tottenham in the lead. With Arsenal only drawing, United were still on course to win the title, having scored more goals during the season, but Beckham's equaliser from a Scholes pass just before half-time made everyone breathe a little easier. Soon after the break, substitute Cole, on for Sheringham, scored a superb goal to make it 2–1. A few minutes later, at Highbury, Kanu scored to ensure a nervous finish, for a Spurs equaliser would have handed the title to their North London rivals. It can safely be said that the fans of both teams in Old Trafford that day did not want to see that happen, and when the final whistle blew, United were champions again, for once winning it in front of their own delirious supporters.

And it wasn't simply because United were champions that the celebrations were so ecstatic – they were now just two games away from a unique Treble. The Reds had got to the final of the FA Cup the hard way, even if they had been helped by being drawn at home all the way to the semifinal. All bar one of their opponents were Premier League sides, the exception being a Fulham team who were on their way to getting there. First up it was Middlesbrough, managed by United old boy Bryan Robson. Boro took the lead early in the second half, before Cole, Denis Irwin and Giggs hit back in the last quarter.

If fans felt United left it late, they were about to get used to a recurring theme of the season in the fourth round, when old foes Liverpool came to Old Trafford. Another packed house saw Michael Owen score an early goal for the Merseysiders and United then laboured to get back into the match. By the end, United had just three defenders on the pitch, while strikers Cole, Solskjaer and Yorke had support from Giggs and Scholes, not to mention Beckham and Keane. In the end, the pressure had to tell and Yorke scored with a tap-in from a Cole knock-down with two minutes remaining to ensure a replay. But United weren't finished, as substitutes Scholes and Solskjaer combined for the latter to drive home the winner from the edge of the box in the final minute. The Norwegian described it as 'one of the greatest feelings I've ever had. I used to be a Liverpool supporter and to be able to score against Liverpool the winning goal in injury time . . . it was a very good feeling.'

There were no late dramas against Fulham, when a Cole goal midway through the first half was enough. In the quarterfinal, Chelsea held out for a draw, but at Stamford Bridge Yorke scored twice to guide United into the semifinal, where the Reds faced

Arsenal at Villa Park. After a goalless first encounter, the two sides met again in Birmingham three days later. At 1–1, first Roy Keane was sent off late in the second half and then Schmeichel saved an injury-time penalty from Dennis Bergkamp. In extra time, substitute Giggs scored one of the most memorable goals in FA Cup history, his slaloming run from the halfway line ending with an unstoppable shot past David Seaman from a tight angle.

With substitutes having won the game to secure the Premier League and scored vital goals to get United to Wembley for the FA Cup, there was a pattern emerging to United's season. Almost inevitably, when captain Keane went off early in the first half of the final, substitute Sheringham scored soon after to give the Reds the lead against Newcastle, and Scholes added a second to claim United's third Double in five years. Now United had four days to wait to see if they could win the Champions League.

United couldn't have had a much tougher group in Europe, after they'd qualified for that stage by beating LKS Lodz, with Bayern Munich and Barcelona joined by Brondby. The latter were always likely to be the makeweights, despite winning their first game against Bayern. The Reds showed it was going to be an eventful campaign when they threw away a two-goal lead to draw 3–3 with Barca in the first game. After two draws, home and away wins over Brondby, including a 5–0 romp at Old Trafford, put United in a strong position, so a draw against the German side in M16 ensured the Reds went through as league leaders.

In the quarterfinals, United met Inter Milan (and Beckham encountered Simeone again) and a couple of early goals from Yorke enabled them to hold off late pressure from the Italian side. In the return at the San Siro, a 1–1 draw and a fine defensive stint from Henning Berg took United into the semifinals. For the third season in a row, United then came up against Juventus and were lucky to escape from Old Trafford with a 1–1 draw, thanks to a Giggs goal in the last minute, set up by substitute Sheringham. The real drama came in Turin, however, when Keane carried his team through to the final with an inspirational effort (all the more impressive as a booking meant that he would miss the final) to help United win in Italy for the first time, by 3–2, after they'd gone 2–0 down in ten minutes. There were echoes of Robson's efforts against Barca in 1984.

And so it was that huge swathes of Manchester travelled to the Nou Camp, Barcelona, for the Champions League final on 26 May, where Bayern Munich were again the opposition, the nineti-eth anniversary of the birth of Sir Matt Busby. Munich scored early, and for much of the match United struggled to find their best rhythm, the wear and tear of the sixty-third game of the season perhaps beginning to show, as well as the absence of not only Keane but also Scholes from central midfield. But Ferguson's close-season strategy to bolster strength in depth, the team's never-say-die attitude, and successful substitutions once again all combined to play their part, as first Sheringham then Solskjaer scored in the dying moments to ensure United were crowned European champions for the second time in the club's history.

Within a few days, it was Sir Alex Ferguson, as the manager was knighted in the Queen's birthday honours list, due recognition of his remarkable and unique achievement, not to mention his ability yet again to bounce back from the criticism he had faced only a few months previously. Early in the new season, he was granted a testi-monial by the club, and a full house turned up to see United stars past and present, as well as many who never wore the red of United, put on a great show. And at the end of February 2000, he was granted the freedom of the city of Manchester. Having achieved all there was to achieve, Ferguson's task with the team was to go out and do it again, though this time there was another competition to throw into the mix, the FIFA Club World Championship, held in Brazil.

The summer of 1999 was relatively quiet as far as rebuilding the team was concerned; Mark Bosnich came in to replace Schmeichel. But the club had been planning further expansion to Old Trafford, and building work had begun on a new two-tier East Stand, with plans for expansion to the West Stand afterwards. Happily, this work could be done without restricting the numbers piling in to the stadium to watch the team that won the Treble.

The second tier of the East Stand was filled to capacity for the first time in January 2000, when a crowd of 61,267 saw Beckham score a late winner against Middlesbrough. The new Megastore, with Sir Matt's statue now situated above the entrance, was moved to the East Stand as well, enabling work to get started sooner than expected on the West Stand. The club also incorporated more space in the East Stand for supporters with disabilities, as well as the additional office space required for the burgeoning empire that was Manchester United. The success of the business side of United was confirmed during the season when the club agreed a £30 million-plus four-year shirt sponsorship deal with Vodafone, and the share price took the value of the club to more than £800 million by February 2000, an increase of more than 25 per cent on BSkyB's offer just eighteen months before.

On the pitch, United got off to a great start, typified by a 5–1 hammering of Newcastle, with Cole scoring four goals, and away wins at both Arsenal and Liverpool. By the beginning of October, United were top, but then came a shocking 5–0 defeat at Chelsea. Leeds were the new pace-setters, and were still top of the table when United flew out to Brazil. As the tournament overlapped with the early rounds of the FA Cup, United were excused their participation in the world's oldest competition by the FA, who were keen to bolster England's chances to host the World Cup of 2006. It was a decision that brought much criticism of United, but the club was left with little choice in the matter, however much many of those within the set-up would rather have participated in defending one of their three trophies.

While United were in Brazil, their title rivals all dropped points, so from having been seen as a distraction that could cost the team dear, it proved to be a useful break from the winter in England. The Reds dropped just nine points in their last nineteen games in a stunning run of form that marched them to the title with almost embarrassing ease, eighteen points clear of second-placed Arsenal. United finished with 91 points and scored 97 league goals, Yorke leading the way with 20, followed by Cole with 19. But it was Keane who deservedly picked up the PFA and Football Writers' awards as the footballer of the year, due recognition of his key role in United's triumph, and his insatiable drive to win. The title was officially secured with a 3–1 win at Southampton on 22 April; there were still four games to play.

Utterly dominant at home, the focus was back on Europe to provide a challenge. United's group was much easier than the one they'd faced the year before, with Croatia Zagreb, Sturm Graz and Marseille hardly a daunting prospect. But when United could only draw 0–0 at Old Trafford against the Croatians in the first game, there was a swift and early warning against complacency. That season, the first group stage was followed by a second group phase involving Bordeaux, Fiorentina and Valencia. Again, United got off to a poor start, losing 2–0 in Italy, but recovered to ease through the group again as league leaders.

Their opponents in the quarterfinals were none other than United's traditional nemesis: Real Madrid. A solid defensive performance in Spain saw United return to Old Trafford with a goalless draw, a decent result but one that always puts the pressure on the home side not to concede an away goal. When Roy Keane put through his own goal after twenty minutes, United were up against it, and the tie was almost over when Raul netted twice early in the second half. The Reds fought back valiantly, scoring twice, but were still two goals short when the final whistle blew. That Madrid went on to win the Champions League was small consolation for all those who had hoped United could retain the biggest trophy in football.

But United did now at least have the opportunity to become only the fourth club ever to be champions three seasons in a row, after Huddersfield Town (1924–26), Arsenal (1933–35) and Liverpool (1982–84). To help secure this, Ferguson signed French World Cup-winning goalkeeper Fabien Barthez for a record £7.8 million from Monaco, but his hopes of bringing in striker Ruud van Nistelrooy were put on hold when the Dutchman collapsed with a serious knee injury. One of the most important changes took place away from Old Trafford, as United moved its training facilities out to Carrington and away from the long-standing base at the Cliff. The new venue has unrivalled facilities, both in terms of playing surfaces to train on and equipment indoors for fitness work, treatment of injuries and anything else a footballer could require to maximise his potential. Hidden away from prying eyes, it is a perfect base for the players and ensures that their focus is not distracted by anything while they are there.

In the boardroom, there was an important change, as Martin Edwards retired from day-to-day control of the club to become life president, Peter Kenyon succeeding him as chairman and chief executive on the football side. For thirty-five years, the Edwards family had run United, but now as the club approached a billion-pound enterprise, things were moving on again. The men in the boardroom rarely receive any credit, but the Edwards family had not only overseen huge success on the pitch, they had also rebuilt and developed Old Trafford twice to make it one of the world's most impressive and famous stadiums. It was quite a legacy.

The hat-trick of league titles was rarely in doubt. After going top early in September 2000, United stayed there for the rest of the season, except for a brief period in October when a defeat at Arsenal allowed Leicester City to head the Premier League for a fortnight. Coincidentally, United travelled to Filbert Street for their next game, and won 3–0 to reclaim the top spot. Arsenal were again United's closest rivals, but they came to Old Trafford and lost 6–1, with Yorke scoring a hat-trick in the first twenty-two minutes – the race was that close. Coventry City were the visitors to Old Trafford on 14 April, and when the Reds won 4–2, with two goals from Yorke and late contributions from Giggs and Scholes in front of 67,637 (the highest of the season), they were champions again, this time with five matches to spare.

Old Trafford played to full houses every week that season. In the league, the lowest attendance was just 190 below the highest – you simply could not cram any more people in there. The redevelopment of the stadium had been completed during the previous summer when the West Stand had a second tier added. The cost of the work on both stands was estimated at £30 million, but the extra capacity of almost 13,000 fans would soon pay for the cost.

But there were beginning to be some complaints about the atmosphere in the ground. Post-Taylor Report, there had been strict enforcement by the stewards against people standing up to watch the matches. Partly this was a question of politeness – if the person in front of you stands, then you can't see – but partly it was something that Stretford Council's safety officers wanted to enforce, even threatening to close down parts of the stadium if fans did not listen. The trend had been developing since the end of terracing, and there was no doubt it altered the atmosphere. As Brian McClair, who played before and after the redevelopment, comments: 'Of course it [changed things]. You can ask anyone who spent time on the Stretford End. Just being there and being able to meet your mates, stand at the same bit and get involved in the tribal thing to now having to sit. You can still get some really great atmospheres at Old Trafford, particularly on European nights, but it is going to change things. It's now a more pleasant environment; you get more families going now. There's no menace now, because it's well stewarded.'

The issue received its most famous airing after the final game of United's first-group-stage matches. Drawn alongside Anderlecht, Dynamo Kiev and PSV Eindhoven, United had made relatively heavy weather of things, and went into their match against Kiev in third place, knowing they had to win to qualify. For a club that had grown up on 'great European nights', after an early goal by Sher-ingham, it was a relatively quiet atmosphere, despite the fact that if United conceded a goal they would be out of the tournament. A 1–0 victory duly secured in front of 66,776 fans, captain Keane decided to have his say about the fans who 'have a few drinks and probably their prawn sandwiches and they don't realise what's going on out on the pitch'. For the hard core of fans who were frustrated at the number of irregular supporters who came to Old Trafford for a day out, and loaded up their cars for the journey home with merchandise from the Megastore, it was just what they wanted to hear. But in truth, there is room for both types of fan, and a club with millions of supporters around the world cannot afford to exclude those who can't be there every week. But Wilf McGuinness, who often works in United's hospitality suites, has a different take on this: 'The people in the boxes and hospitality, when I talk to them, say, "We're Stretford Enders who've done well in business and I am able to sit here, and I still shout like when I was in the Stretford End."'

In the second stage, United's group comprised Panathinaikos, Sturm Graz and Valencia, which again proved relatively straightforward. But the same could not be said of the quarterfinals, where Bayern Munich again lined up against United, seeking revenge for United's late steal in Barcelona. At Old Trafford, United failed to spark, but seemed to have done enough to go into the return leg with a goalless draw, which they knew from painful experience could be a useful result. However, in the last few minutes, Sergio scored for Bayern to give them a 1–0 victory, and United could not pull things round in Germany. Once again, the Reds had fallen short abroad while dominating at home.

There was more drama at the end of the season, when Sir Alex, who had earlier announced that he was planning to step down as manager after the 2001–02 season, decided that he would quit United entirely after his final campaign. With the Champions League final scheduled to be held at Hampden Park in Glasgow, there was an obvious target to aim for as a final send-off. Soon after, the board came up with some new proposals for Sir Alex, including a generous pay rise, and the continuing involvement of the most successful manager in English history beyond May 2002 was confirmed. Indeed, Sir Alex was soon having second thoughts about whether he had made the right decision at all as he began to prepare for what lay ahead.

The new board was certainly willing to back Sir Alex with money for transfers. The deal to sign van Nistelrooy finally went through after he made a full recovery from his knee injury, and the prolific Dutch goal-scorer arrived for a fee of £19 million; classy Argentine midfielder Juan Sebastian Veron was signed from Lazio for £28.1 million. Then, as the season got under way, Stam was moved out to Lazio and veteran French World Cup winner Laurent Blanc joined on a one-year contract. The latter signing marked a new departure for Sir Alex, and one he would occasionally repeat in the future, bringing in very experienced players for a short-term role when most needed.

It took a little longer than usual, but by the start of 2002, United moved to the top of the Premier League, sparked by a sudden flurry of goals from van Nistelrooy, who scored ten in eight successive games, including a hat-trick in a 6–1 thrashing of Southampton at Old Trafford. The fans had a new goal-scoring hero, which was vital now that Sheringham had gone and Cole and Yorke were on their way out, too. But as the season drew to its climax, United could do nothing about the stunning run put together by Arsenal, who won their last thirteen games of the campaign, claiming the title with a game to spare at Old Trafford when they won 1–0, before going on to claim the Double. Even had United beaten Arsenal, they would have still been relying on an upset in the final game to have a chance. Even more disappointingly, for the first time in the Premier League era, United finished in third place, overtaken at the end by Liverpool.

But there was plenty of good news for Old Trafford. With Wembley being rebuilt, United's stadium was selected as the venue for England's final World Cup qualifier and a crowd of 66,009 turned up to see the crucial game. Manager Sven-Goran Eriksson ensured there would be passionate backing for his side, with Beckham continuing as captain and Gary Neville, Scholes and Cole all playing their part. Needing at least a draw, England went behind in the first half and had to wait until midway through the second half for a Sheringham equaliser, but almost immediately fell behind again. Playing like a man possessed, Beckham drove on his team and in the final minute hit an unstoppable free kick to ensure the game finished 2–2.

Just as exciting was the fact that Old Trafford was selected as the venue for the 2003 Champions League final. Whether the prospect of challenging for the Champions League on home turf also played any part in Sir Alex's decision to stay on is not clear, but in February 2002 he commented on how his family had persuaded him to continue as manager. Although he had just passed his sixtieth birthday, he was in excellent health and certainly not ready to put up his feet. As always for him, there were new challenges to take on, and he did not want to leave unfinished business.

In the Champions League, United stuttered slightly through their first group stage, losing home and away to La Coruna, but in the second stage, alongside (inevitably) Bayern Munich, Boavista and Nantes, they were undefeated. The highlight was a comprehensive 5–1 victory over Nantes at Old Trafford on 26 February, soon after Sir Alex's confirmation that he would be staying. In the quarterfinals, United again met Deportivo La Coruna. After losing to them twice earlier in the campaign, a 2–0 win in Spain set them on their way, before they finished the job with a 3–2 victory at Old Trafford. In the semifinals, United avoided Real Madrid and Barcelona to get the seemingly easier tie against Bayer Leverkusen, who had just put out Liverpool. In Manchester, United led for much of the match but it finished 2–2, and Gary Neville was out for the rest of the season after breaking his foot. In Germany, United took the lead, but were unable to hold on, and so the opportunity of a big day out in Glasgow was lost.

So United ended the season without a trophy for only the third time in thirteen years. Captain Keane suggested that some of the players might have grown too complacent. (He was never one to mince his words – he uttered some much harsher criticisms of the Ireland set-up just before the 2002 World Cup started, before walking out of the squad.) Certainly, for United, the defence needed tightening up, after conceding forty-five goals in the league, and over the summer Rio Ferdinand joined from Leeds for a record fee of £30 million. With Steve McClaren having gone to Middlesbrough in summer 2001, a new man was brought in as Sir Alex's assistant: Carlos Queiroz, who not only proved himself an excellent coach, he brought a different range of contacts to the club.

At first, the improvements weren't obvious, as United lost five games in the Premier League by Boxing Day. The key target was to overhaul Arsenal, and a 2–0 win at Old Trafford in early December was a big help in that direction. But after Boxing Day, in the eighteen matches that remained, the Reds dropped just six points and didn't lose once. The crucial period came in fourteen days in April, when United faced Liverpool, Newcastle, Arsenal and Blackburn in quick succession, four of the top six sides. First up were Liverpool, who were stunned 4–0 in front of 67,639 at Old Trafford. Next United travelled to St James' Park, where some rash comments had been made about Scholes by one of their players, questioning the midfielder's ability. His reply was a masterclass in all the arts of midfield play, as he not only scored a hat-trick but pulled all the strings in a 6–2 victory. United had finally hit top spot. A trip away to nearest rivals Arsenal ended in a 2–2 draw, with Keane in fine form after an injury, and then the Reds were back at Old Trafford to beat Blackburn 3–1, with van Nistelrooy on the score-sheet (he was in the middle of another purple patch, scoring thirteen goals in eight successive games). United finished the season five points clear of Arsenal to secure their eighth Premiership title; Sir Alex's decision to keep going had been fully justified.

In the Champions League, with the lure of an Old Trafford final, United first of all had to qualify for the tournament proper after their third-place finish the season before. Zalaegerszeg of Hungary were their opponents, and even surprised everyone by beating United at home; the return leg at Old Trafford did not prove a problem and the Reds were through to the group stages. Bayer Leverkusen, Maccabi Haifa and Olympiakos Piraeus didn't provide the strongest challenge, and United won their first four games to qualify. A slip-up away to Haifa was put right with a final victory over the German side to ensure United qualified as group leaders.

The second group stage, with Basel, Deportivo La Coruna and Juventus, was much more challenging, but United again won their first four games (including a remarkable 3–0 victory in Turin that suggested the Reds could beat anyone) to ensure qualification to the quarterfinal stage. Van Nistelrooy was on fire in this tournament, too, scoring six goals in the second group stage. He finished the season with an incredible forty-four goals, second only to Denis Law's record forty-six in 1963–64.

In the quarterfinals, United faced Real Madrid but lost in Spain 3–1. For the return leg, Sir Alex left Beckham on the bench, and played Veron. United slipped further behind, as Madrid's Brazilian striker Ronaldo scored a brilliant hat-trick. Paul Tomkinson remembers how a couple of United fans near him were giving the Brazilian lots of abuse, until they were told to quieten down by others who knew they were witnessing something special. At the end, Ronaldo was applauded off the pitch by the Old Trafford faithful. They almost got something even more special, when Beckham came off the bench and scored twice to help United to a 4–3 lead on the night. But it wasn't enough.

Real Madrid didn't even go on to return to Old Trafford for the final. Instead, the game was contested by two Italian sides, Milan and Juventus. Sadly, the event did not live up to the prospect of the two best sides in Europe coming together. A 0–0 draw was followed by a penalty shoot-out – and even then neither side was particularly proficient at putting the ball in the back of the net, as Milan won the shoot-out 3–2.

However, the Real Madrid match was significant in one other way: it was the game when Beckham says he felt his days at United were drawing to a close. The manager had been concerned at the possibility that Beckham's celebrity lifestyle was distracting him from the main business, and a row earlier in the season after Arsenal came to Old Trafford and knocked United out of the FA

Cup showed that the bond between the two men was not as close as it had once been. Real Madrid, with their celebrated line-up of *galacticos*, was the obvious destination, and that summer Beckham became the first of the Fledglings to leave the Old Trafford nest when he was sold for £25.8 million.

Beckham's replacement that summer was Ronaldo, but it wasn't the man who had just destroyed United's Champions League dreams, but a young Portuguese winger, born in Madeira, who had the United players recommending that Sir Alex sign him up immediately, after a pre-season friendly against Sporting Lisbon. At the time, he was the world's most expensive teenage transfer at £12.24 million. In fact, this was only a small part of the reorganisation of the side initiated by Sir Alex: Veron was sold and replaced by the Brazilian Kleberson; Barthez was also moved on, and in came the American goalkeeper Tim Howard. In each case, the manager was bringing in a younger man as he looked to build for the future, showing that his 'retirement' was not merely on temporary hold – he was thinking long term. At the time, the riskiest move seemed to be the signing of Cristiano Ronaldo but, of all of them, he was the one who went on to have the greatest impact.

All this transfer activity, however, was not the most significant business of the summer. As the Premier League continued to draw in unheard-of riches, football was coming to the attention of many from outside the game, and indeed from outside the country. It was no longer the case, either, of media moguls looking to add football to their portfolios; now it was sometimes people one had never heard of coming in from far-away countries. To a degree, United, as a PLC and the most famous and successful team in the Premier League, were always liable to attract new investors. Among those buying shares in the club around this time were John Magnier and J. P. McManus from Ireland; Dermot Desmond, the owner of Celtic; John de Mol, the Dutch creator of *Big Brother*; and Malcolm Glazer, the American owner of the Tampa Bay Buccaneers.

However, none of them took complete control of the club at

this stage. But in West London, there was a Russian revolution taking place: in June 2003, Roman Abramovich paid Chelsea owner Ken Bates a reported £140 million for the club. With a fortune that ran into the billions, here was a man who had almost unlimited funds to make Chelsea whatever he wanted. For the past seven years, the Premier League had often come down to a personal duel between Sir Alex's Manchester United and Arsene Wenger's Arsenal. If Abramovich had anything to do with it, all of that was going to change. As a statement of intent, he soon poached Peter Kenyon from United to run his club.

15

Building the Quadrants

United's campaign to remain the dominant force in the Premier League in 2003–04 now faced a double threat from Arsenal and a newly wealthy Chelsea. The Reds actually started the season well enough, but their plans were thrown into confusion when Rio Ferdinand was banned from all football for eight months after forgetting to turn up for a routine drugs test. There were also too many slip-ups against some of the lesser lights of the league: even Wolves, who finished the season in bottom place, managed to beat United, and there were home defeats to Fulham, Middlesbrough and Liverpool. Given all that, it was hardly surprising that United fell short. What was a surprise, however, was the form of Arsenal, who went the entire Premier League season undefeated, a unique achievement since the Preston Invincibles way back in the 1880s, at the dawn of the Football League. Meanwhile, the growing threat from Chelsea was visible for all to see, as they rose to finish second in the Premier League and were clearly going to get stronger. The men from Old Trafford had it all to do now if they were to reclaim their crown as the leading side in England.

One way of helping to ensure that United could set the standards their rivals could only dream of was by continuing to develop
Old Trafford. Yet again, even though United finished fifteen
points behind Arsenal, the stadium was full to capacity every
match with crowds of about 67,500 and thousands of unsuccess-
ful ballot applicants unable to attend. In October 2003, the
United board asked the club's property manager, George Johnstone, to look into the feasibility of developing the quadrants at
the north end of the ground, as the club wanted to plough some
of its profits into improving the stadium. By January, having
worked with architects, structural engineers, quantity surveyors
and mechanical and electrical engineers, Johnstone had the plans
ready to present to the board. Unusually, the first visualisations
were the ones that were essentially what we see today. A couple of
months later, United officially announced they were looking to
expand Old Trafford again, subject to planning permission, the
new quadrants adding at least 7500 seats to the capacity.

By that stage of the season, United knew they had just one
route still open to them to win some silverware, as another
European campaign had come to an end. In the group stages, the
Reds had been in good form, particularly at Old Trafford where,
in three games against Panathinaikos, Glasgow Rangers and
Stuttgart, United had scored ten goals without conceding one,
with eight different players getting on the score-sheet, showing the
all-round threat the team posed.

The format of the Champions League had just been changed to
its present incarnation, where it moves straight from the group
matches to the Round of 16, and United's foes this time were
Porto. The UEFA Cup holders and Portuguese champions had
already proved themselves to be a very decent side, but United
went into the tie as favourites. Having lost 2–1 at the Estadio do
Dragao, the return leg at Old Trafford was finely balanced. Paul
Scholes gave United a 1–0 lead that would have put them
through, before having a second goal wrongly disallowed for offside. Soon after, Porto equalised and their manager went racing

down the touchline to celebrate the goal that had effectively put them through to the quarterfinals. It was Jose Mourinho, making his first impact at Old Trafford. His team went on to win the trophy, beating Monaco 3–0 in the final, and soon after he moved to Chelsea to replace Claudio Ranieri as manager.

So the focus was on the FA Cup instead. After away wins against Aston Villa and Northampton, the fifth-round draw brought an enticing tie to Old Trafford: neighbours Manchester City. In the late 1990s, City had slumped to the third tier of English football, but, with their new stadium in Eastlands that season, were now in the process of re-establishing themselves as a Premier League side. The previous campaign, United had dropped five points against City, but had beaten the Blues 3–1 in December. If the game needed any extra spice, Robbie Fowler and Steve McManaman, formerly of Liverpool, were able to provide it in front of 67,228 very noisy fans. Gary Neville was sent off relatively early in the match after the gentlest of head-butts to Scouser McManaman, but even with ten men United were still too good, as Ruud van Nistelrooy scored twice, Scholes once and Cristiano Ronaldo got the other in a performance that showed just why Sir Alex had been willing to pay out so much to bring him to Old Trafford.

There was less drama around the next round, as Fulham were beaten 2–1 in Manchester, and so United were through to yet another FA Cup semifinal, where their opponents were the 'Invincibles' of Arsenal. The other semifinal, between Sunderland and Millwall, took place at Old Trafford, where Theo Paphitis, now best known as one of the dragons in *Dragons' Den* but then the chairman of the south London club, was in the process of having one of the best days of his life, as Millwall qualified for the final. His experience of the ground showed that all the work that had gone into making it a special venue had absolutely paid off. For him, 'The biggest day was not the Cup final; the biggest day was that semifinal.'

The other semifinal, at Villa Park, was arguably the game that many neutrals would have wanted to be the final. Backed by the passionate support of their fans, United put in a terrific performance, with Scholes deservedly getting the winner, to take his side through to the final at Cardiff's Millennium Stadium. The Reds had already played there once previously, losing the League Cup final to Liverpool the season before. This time defeat was always unlikely, and there were no surprises as United strolled to a 3–0 victory, their eleventh FA Cup success. There was a slightly low-key feeling to the whole day, almost as if it were a small consolation prize, but that was largely because so much had gone into getting to the final in the first place.

Although preparations for developing the quadrants at Old Trafford were under way during the summer of 2004, planning permission still needed to be granted, so the most significant piece of rebuilding undertaken was with the team. Nicky Butt was sold to Newcastle, becoming the second of the Fledglings to leave, having made 387 appearances for United. Combative Argentine defender Gabriel Heinze was signed to strengthen the defensive options, but it was Everton's teenage prodigy Wayne Rooney who really hit the headlines. He had been on United's radar ever since he had impressed against their youth team when aged just fourteen. He had gone on to score a thumping winning goal against champions Arsenal when only sixteen (then the youngest Premier League goal-scorer), before having an inspired tournament in the 2004 European Championships until the moment he broke his metatarsal. If United wanted to sign up the best young English player around, they could wait no longer, and for a reported fee of about £25.6 million he was on his way to Old Trafford. Ronaldo's record as the world's most expensive teenager had lasted just a year.

Rooney was soon in action at Old Trafford, not only for United but also for England, as United's ground was chosen to host four out of five of England's home World Cup qualifiers, due recognition of the stadium's status as the biggest and best in the country while Wembley was being rebuilt. First up, on 9 October, was Wales. A crowd of 65,224 saw England record a 2–0 victory thanks to goals from Frank Lampard and David Beckham. As well as Rooney, England's line-up also featured Rio Ferdinand and Gary Neville, with new signing Alan Smith coming on midway through the second half. For Wales, Ryan Giggs ensured there was local support for both sides. Next, on 26 March 2005, it was another of the home nations: Northern Ireland. This was a much more emphatic result, as England won 4–0 in front of 62,239, with Joe Cole, Michael Owen (with two goals) and Lampard all scoring in a fifteen-minute burst early in the second half. Ferdinand, Neville and Rooney were again all in the team that started.

The final two qualifying games both took place in October 2005, with Austria the first to try their luck. Lampard was again on the score-sheet in England's 1–0 victory, but England made it hard for themselves after Beckham was sent off early in the second half for two bookable offences within a minute of each other. Subsequently, Ferdinand and Kieran Richardson came on as substitutes. Four days later, on 12 October, Poland came to Old Trafford as group leaders, so an England win was vital if they were to top the group. Owen scored just before half-time, but Poland equalised almost immediately, and it was left to Lampard to secure a late winner that sent the crowd of 65,467 home happy. Ferdinand and Rooney were restored to the starting line-up, and Smith came on again as a late substitute. Four wins out of four meant that Old Trafford had been a perfect venue for England, even if no United player had managed to score a goal.

After falling short the previous season, United wanted to get the 2004–05 campaign off to a good start, but the injury-hit squad began with a Charity Shield defeat to Arsenal and a Premier League defeat at Stamford Bridge to Chelsea. By 15 August, it was already clear that the two London sides were going to be formidable foes.

Having lost their first game, United were defeated only once in the next thirty Premier League matches – an excellent run of form, slightly marred by the number of draws. In the autumn, Liverpool were beaten 2–1 at Old Trafford, with Mikael Silvestre the surprising scorer of both goals, and then Arsenal came to visit on 24 October. The Gunners had continued their unbeaten run from the previous season well into the new campaign; it now stretched for forty-nine games. Sir Alex had decided that the best approach was to try to knock Arsenal off their rhythm, and the Reds set about the task with gusto in a spiky encounter that United ended up winning 2–0, notching up their 1000th Premier League point into the bargain, thanks to goals from van Nistelrooy (from the penalty spot, gaining revenge for a miss in the same fixture the previous year) and Rooney (scoring on his home Premier League debut).

In the aftermath of the game, there were reports that Arsenal players had thrown pizza at the United manager. Other managers were quick to notice how Sir Alex's tactics had worked, and the Gunners lost four more times that season. United even completed the double over them at Highbury, when the build-up to the game was enlivened by an eyeball-to-eyeball confrontation between captains Roy Keane and Patrick Vieira. Even if Arsenal did finish above United in the table that season, it could be argued that those two matches shifted the psychological balance between the clubs firmly back in United's favour.

But that still left Chelsea. Although they were beaten once, they still amassed more points (ninety-five) than any side in Premier League history, with United eighteen points adrift. By the time they came to Old Trafford for the penultimate game of the season, they were already champions, and Sir Alex told his players to form a guard of honour as their opponents ran out onto the pitch. It was the sort of experience, just like the one when Liverpool fans had torn up the autographs of 'losers' more than a decade before, that no one wanted to have to go through again. United's defence had had its joint best campaign ever, conceding just twenty-six league goals, but there had been a shortage of goals scored – fifty-eight was the worst tally since 1990–91. Partly this was because van Nistelrooy had missed much of the season, but also the support strikers, Smith, Louis Saha and David Bellion, were not scoring enough goals. And nor were the wide men, Giggs and Ronaldo, with ten between them.

In the Champions League, the biggest highlight was a stunning 6–2 victory over Fenerbahce at Old Trafford. United had again had to qualify for the tournament proper, beating Dinamo Bucharest in the process. But it was their first home tie in the group stage against the Turkish side that marked the debut of Rooney after his injury in the European Championships. He celebrated the occasion in the most spectacular fashion, scoring a hat-trick. His first came from a through ball by van Nistelrooy, then he scored from way outside the box with an unstoppable shot, before earning the match ball early in the second half when he scored from a free kick. There was clearly not going to be any need for a settling-in period for the teenager. In the next home game, the Dutchman showed he was still top dog when it came to Europe, as van Nistelrooy scored all four (a joint record in the tournament) in United's 4–1 victory over Sparta Prague. In the final home group game, against Olympique Lyon, the Reds won 2–1 to ensure that Sir Alex's thousandth game in charge of United was a happy occasion. Perhaps inevitably, van Nistelrooy was one of the scorers; slightly less expected was the fact that Gary Neville also scored. But, once more, United couldn't get past the first knockout round, when AC Milan were 1–0 winners home and away.

So, yet again, United's hopes of silverware depended on the domestic cups. In the League Cup, the Reds managed to defeat Arsenal at Old Trafford only to draw Chelsea in the semifinals. A 0–0 stalemate at Stamford Bridge gave them every chance of proceeding to the final in the return leg, especially as Sir Alex had never lost a domestic semifinal since arriving at United – a run of nineteen fixtures. United fell behind, but backed by the passionate support from the stands at Old Trafford managed to pull a goal back, thanks to a superb lob from Giggs in the middle of the second half. It wasn't to be enough, sadly, as Damien Duff scored a late winner to end the manager's record. Mourinho famously turned up with an excellent bottle of wine to share with Sir Alex after the game. It may have helped ensure that the two men had a good relationship; it did nothing to compensate for the defeat.

In the FA Cup, United had the embarrassment of a 0–0 home draw against Exeter City in the third round, before going through in the replay. Middlesbrough were beaten 3–0 in the next round, and then United were off on their travels for the rest of the competition, before meeting Arsenal in the final. With his side weakened by injuries, Arsene Wenger sent it out to play cautiously, and they ended up getting the goalless draw that had seemed to be their aim from the start. But in the penalty shoot-out, it was the Gunners who hit the target most frequently to leave United with a rare empty trophy cabinet.

By then, United had new owners. Ever since the Glazer family had first begun buying up United shares in earnest in 2003, they had continued to pick up more and more. At one stage, it had seemed as though it was going to develop into a straight fight for control between Malcolm Glazer and the Cubic Expression investment vehicle of J.P. McManus and John Magnier, perhaps with neither giving way, but in the end the American won through at a price of about £800 million. As with all the previous potential outside buyers of the club, there were protests from fans, worried about what the new owners would do, the level of debt they had taken on to fund the purchase, and many alarmist stories and rumours that spread via the internet and elsewhere that have proved to be wildly inaccurate. In truth, once United had become a publicly quoted company then, like any other PLC, it became available on the open market to anyone with the desire and the wherewithal to buy it. With the Glazer takeover, United reverted to being a private limited company. Some fans might have wanted the club to be owned by a group of philanthropic multimillion-aires who had grown up on the Stretford End, but in the real world of global sporting brands, which United had become and where the likes of Abramovich operated, this was not going to happen. The proof now was going to be in the results that United achieved under Glazer and his family. The next few years were to see many more Premier League clubs bought by foreign owners.

As soon as the season ended, United also began work on building the two new quadrants in the northeast and northwest corners of the stadium that were to raise its capacity to 76,000. The quadrants effectively ensured that Old Trafford would have a bowl shape, which George Johnstone said would 'allow noise to roll around the stadium' better than was currently the case. The towers for the quadrants were designed to have the maximum visual impact, making the ground look as modern as possible. As building work continued during the new season, there was no reduction in the numbers of fans that could get in to watch the action. The hope of everyone was that they would have plenty to cheer this time round.

Since Peter Schmeichel had left United in 1999, Sir Alex had employed eight different keepers in the Premier League by the start of the 2005–06 season. Finally, in Edwin van der Sar, he had someone who could make the position his own. Signed from Fulham for a reported fee of £2 million, the Dutch keeper was massively experienced and, having played for the likes of Ajax and Juventus, was not daunted by the pressures of Old Trafford. Otherwise, the only other major business done by the manager over the summer was the signing of South Korea's Ji-sung Park; he was confident that his developing side was only going to get better, and that in Ronaldo and Rooney he had two of the best young talents in the world. Another United stalwart was let go during the close season, as Phil Neville left for Everton, knowing he would get more starting opportunities there. After 386 appearances for United, he went on his way with the good wishes of all at the club.

United's form in the Premier League during the first part of the season was actually pretty decent, with only two defeats before the New Year, but there was a sense that things weren't quite right. Partly it was down to a hangover from the takeover, with fans still concerned about what it meant to the club. Partly the media kept

on saying that the current United side weren't really good enough
to take on Chelsea, even though United managed to beat them 1–0
at Old Trafford on 6 November, thanks to a Darren Fletcher goal
that ended the Londoners' forty-game unbeaten run in the Premier
League. That result moved United up to third in the table; it was
also the occasion of the home dressing room being bugged. When,
later that month, Keane articulated some of his worries about the
team on MUTV, the club decided not to air his comments, which
targeted several individuals. A few days later, Keane left United. It
was the end of an era, and the man who had personified not only
the team's drive, but was also widely seen as Sir Alex's embodiment
on the pitch, was gone. In truth, after 480 appearances for United,
injuries had left him with little still to give, and Keane played only
a few more games before hanging up his boots. Soon after, United
were out of the Champions League, failing to qualify from their
group for the first time – for once, the Reds seemed to lack firepower, failing to score in four out of the six games.

As if to add to the gloom, on 25 November 2005, George Best
died of multiple organ failure. Aged just fifty-nine, the United
legend's battle with alcoholism had been one hurdle he could not
overcome. The area outside the main entrance to the ground was
soon festooned in scarves and other memorabilia, as football fans
from around the world grieved at the loss of one of the game's
supreme talents. The opportunity for Old Trafford to pay tribute
to him came a few days later in the League Cup fourth round,
when West Brom were the visitors. Coincidentally, they were the
team he had played against when he made his United debut back
in 1963, and it was appropriate that the club should now be managed by another Old Trafford legend, Bryan Robson. Before the
game kicked off, there was a tribute from Sir Bobby Charlton, and
the two managers laid wreaths before everyone in the stadium fell
silent, holding aloft pictures of Best. United won the game 3–1,
with Ronaldo setting them on the way by converting a penalty he
had won. It was perhaps inevitable that the young Portuguese had
scored the goal, as he was a player whose skill Best hugely admired.

It was United's only home tie in the competition until the second leg of the semifinal, when Blackburn Rovers were the visitors, managed by another Old Trafford old boy, Mark Hughes. Having drawn 1–1 at Ewood Park, United took an early lead through van Nistelrooy before being pegged back. In a game littered with controversial decisions, there was no denying Saha's volley from a Rooney cross that ensured United had reached a cup final for the fourth successive season. The Reds won the final comfortably enough, beating Wigan 4–0, with Rooney (two), Saha and Ronaldo the scorers. At the end of the game, the players all put on shirts wishing Alan Smith a speedy recovery after his horrific broken leg in the recent FA Cup defeat at Liverpool. Sir Alex even had the opportunity to give two of his mid-season recruits, Patrice Evra and Nemanja Vidic, a late run-out as substitutes. The two defenders were a rare example of the manager using the mid-season transfer window to do some business and, after a relatively quiet summer in the transfer market, it was a sign that under the Glazers United would continue to invest in bringing in the best players. Sir Alex commented on how the fact that United was no longer a PLC meant that such deals did not have to be mentioned to the Stock Market beforehand, improving secrecy and the speed with which deals could be done.

Despite the fact that United had won a trophy and ended the season as runners-up in the league, many commentators believed it was Liverpool who would pose the greater threat to Chelsea in the future, after Jose Mourinho's side had again won the Premier League by eight points from United. The fact that Chelsea would continue to dominate was almost taken as a given by many pundits – but not by the men from Old Trafford, and certainly not by Sir Alex. After all, in his time at United he had seen off the challenges of Liverpool, Blackburn, Newcastle and Arsenal among others. He was confident in his squad. The League Cup trophy was, he believed, merely a portent of what was to come, and not, as some critics were saying, the limit of United's current ambitions. The blend of youth and experience was now coming to its peak, with the older players entering a golden autumn of their careers, while the younger ones – not just Ronaldo and Rooney, but also players such as Fletcher – had acquired greater knowledge and were able to take on more responsibility. So confident did he feel about this, he even sold the man who had been United's main goal threat for five seasons, van Nistelrooy. His strike rate of 150 goals in 219 games marked him out as the most prolific of all the leading goal-scorers in the club's history.

The redevelopment of the quadrants was now complete, giving Old Trafford a capacity of around 76,000. Towards the end of the 2005–06 season, more and more of the new seats became available, with the first crowd to top 70,000 turning out for the game against Arsenal on 9 April, when Park and Rooney were the scorers. The crowd of 70,908 broke a record dating back to 1920, but lasted only five days until the next home game, when more seats were made available. The total cost of the quadrants had been £46 million, and each one had ten restaurants, as well as executive boxes, hospitality lounges and just about any other feature one could wish for. For the best seat and hospitality packages within these areas, a season ticket cost £7500, more than ten times the top-priced regular season ticket. The lowest price for a season ticket was the equivalent of just £20.50 per game, among the lowest in the Premier League.

Building the quadrants had not been a straightforward matter, because the quadrants had to link in with the surrounding stands, which meant everything had to be done with minute accuracy. Frustratingly, as George Johnstone reveals, 'concrete floors projected six inches further than the drawings said they did, or steelwork that was supposed to be there wasn't there – lots of things like that. A real challenge.' Just as much trouble had been caused by planning issues relating in particular to the northeast quadrant, which had to be built over United Road. Although the last tenant had moved out of the area beyond, it was still a public highway, so the Open Spaces Society objected to its being closed while the building work went ahead, even though it was now a road that led nowhere.

So United went into the 2006–07 season with a spectacular newly completed stadium and one major new signing: Michael Carrick had joined from Tottenham for a fee of £14 million, rising to £18.6 million, inheriting Keane's No. 16 shirt. Not many gave them much chance of overcoming Chelsea, partly because the Londoners had just signed two of the world's most famous footballers in Michael Ballack and Andriy Shevchenko, but of more direct relevance had been events in that summer's World Cup. In the quarterfinal, Rooney had been sent off, and Portugal's Ronaldo had been caught on camera winking about the incident that led to the red card. Some pundits assumed the most likely response to the incident from Rooney was that in the first training session at Carrington he would punch his team-mate and hasten his departure from the club. Just how likely any of that was became clear in United's first game, at home to Fulham, when the two players combined to devastating effect, scoring three of the Reds' five goals. They looked unstoppable.

By 22 October, when United beat Liverpool 2–0 at Old Trafford, they were in a two-horse race with Chelsea, already eleven points clear of the Merseysiders, who were supposed to have emerged as the new contenders. Five weeks later, Chelsea could only draw at United, thus ensuring the Reds maintained their three-point advantage at the top of the table, and by the New Year the gap had grown to six points. With the early months of the year so crucial to United's three-pronged attack on trophies, Sir Alex brought in experienced Swedish striker Henrik Larsson on loan. Although he made just thirteen appearances, scoring three goals, he became an immediate hit with the fans at Old Trafford, giving the team new options and ensuring that no one up front became too overworked.

Larsson scored on his debut, a third-round FA Cup tie against Aston Villa. In each round United faced Premier League opposition, and Old Trafford played host in every round up to the semifinal, when United secured a place in the final at the cost of

Watford. With the Reds still in pole position in the Premier League, there began to be talk of another Treble, and the reason had little to do with the domestic situation and everything to do with a stunning performance in the Champions League quarter-final four days before United guaranteed they would be going to the new Wembley.

United had begun their European quest with their first ever competitive match against Glasgow Celtic. The two British clubs that had been the first to taste success in the tournament conjured up a real thriller, which United eventually won 3–2. The Reds then went on to win the next two, before losing the following two games, meaning that historic foes Benfica could knock United out of the tournament if they won at Old Trafford. The Portuguese side looked as though they would go in at half-time with a 1–0 lead until Vidic stepped up to head home emphatically, and after that there was only ever going to be one winner. Lille were seen off in the next round, and then it was the turn of Roma. In Italy, Rooney scored a vital away goal, but United still lost 2–1 – a tense night loomed at Old Trafford as United sought to overcome the deficit and reach the semifinals for the first time since 2002.

What happened next was as complete and stunning a performance as anyone had seen for many years. As Kevin McCarra reported in the *Guardian*: 'United obliterated Roma and all but erased the reputation of Serie A.' Within twenty minutes, Carrick, Smith (making his first start since his broken leg) and Rooney had all scored to give United a 4–2 aggregate lead. Ronaldo added a couple more either side of half-time, before Carrick made it six. Roma pulled a goal back, and soon after Evra got in on the act, almost as if to warn the Italian side about trying anything like that again: 7–1 was the final score. In the modern Champions League, it is rare to get a complete mismatch; by the quarterfinals it is almost unheard of. The fans chanted, 'Are you City in disguise?' while van der Sar commented: 'I have never seen a performance like this in my whole life.'

It surely couldn't get any better than that. Sadly, it didn't. United still managed to win the Premier League, six points clear of Chelsea. As Sir Alex had done before, Mourinho told his players to form a guard of honour as the new champions ran onto the Stamford Bridge pitch in what was now a meaningless end-of-season fixture. As the two sides were due to meet in the FA Cup final, neither manager wanted to show his hand ahead of that game. By then, United had fallen short in the Champions League after a thrilling 3–2 win over Milan at Old Trafford where Rooney was in stunning form. In the return leg, Kaka destroyed United's dreams of reaching another final. The new Wembley did not prove a happy place for United, either, as a tense, sterile game ended in a 1–0 defeat for the Reds.

The fact that there was disappointment in United winning just one trophy shows how far the side had progressed during the season. Arguably, this Premier League victory was one of the greatest achievements in Sir Alex's long list of remarkable landmarks. Until then, the combination of Abramovich's money and Mourinho's utter self-belief seemed to have the rest of the Premier League in thrall. For once, United were even the neutrals' favourites, as the 'plucky underdogs'. Only United and Sir Alex seemed to think Chelsea could be stopped, the players gave their all, and the fans realised they were seeing something special and were desperate to be a part of it all. On 31 March, they even created a new record that stands to this day, as 76,098 crammed into Old Trafford to see United beat Blackburn Rovers 4–1. After Rovers took an early lead, the Reds hit back with goals from Scholes, Carrick, Park and Solskjaer. It was the last goal the Norwegian legend scored for United, typically within five minutes of coming on as a late substitute. In 366 appearances for the Reds, almost half of them as a substitute, he had scored 126 goals, including a record 28 as a substitute. It was fitting that this moment should come in front of a record crowd.

Now, having re-established themselves as the team to beat, the next challenge for United was to see not only if they could repeat their success, but go one step further – particularly in Europe, where Sir Alex felt United hadn't fully done themselves justice in recent years.

16

The Red Army in Moscow and Beyond

Reinforcing from a position of strength has been one of Sir Alex Ferguson's consistent policies throughout his time at Old Trafford. In the summer of 2007, he did exactly that, buying in a blend of youthful promise along with more established stars. Twenty-six-year-old Owen Hargreaves joined from Bayern Munich for a fee of about £17 million. The highly regarded midfielder had been one of England's stars in the 2006 World Cup, and bringing him to United was a long, slow process, but well worth the effort. Joining on a two-year loan was Carlos Tevez, the Argentine forward who had done so much to keep West Ham in the Premier League the season before, not least in scoring the winner at Old Trafford in the last game of the campaign. The all-action striker gave the Reds a new threat up front.

At the beginning of their careers were Anderson, a Brazilian midfielder signed from Porto, and Nani, a Portuguese winger signed from Sporting Lisbon. Billed respectively by some as the 'new Ronaldinho' and the 'new Ronaldo', they both had much to live up to, but Sir Alex knew they would have time to deliver on their potential and was happy for them to be their own men, rather than echoes of others. Meanwhile, leaving the club were Gabriel Heinze, Kieran Richardson and Alan Smith. But all this work meant the Reds had a squad of such depth they could cope with competing across a range of tournaments – they were going to need it.

The Reds made an unspectacular start to the season, often winning 1–0, but importantly still winning. Crucially, they were given a boost when their main rivals, Chelsea, parted company with Jose Mourinho and replaced him with Avram Grant. The new manager's first game was the toughest of challenges, at Old Trafford, when United won 2–0 thanks to goals from Tevez and Louis Saha at the end of each half. That seemed to give United the extra boost they needed, and the goals were suddenly flooding in. In October, they scored four goals in four consecutive matches, while the defence was in supreme form – it wasn't until the end of that month that they conceded a goal at Old Trafford in the Premier League. Early in the New Year, Newcastle were hit for six when they came to Manchester. All the goals came in the second half, and Ronaldo scored his first hat-trick for the club, making it ten goals in six home league matches for the flying Portuguese star.

The season developed into a genuine three-way tussle for the title, with Arsenal and Chelsea the main rivals, but none of that mattered when Manchester City came to visit Old Trafford on 10 February. It wasn't the fact that United went into the fixture two points behind Arsenal and needing the win, nor the importance of local bragging rights that were at stake; instead, it was the occasion the club commemorated the fiftieth anniversary of Munich. The club did many things to mark the occasion, renaming the tunnel under the South Stand as the Munich Tunnel and putting on display there a permanent exhibition telling the story of the Babes. There was also a memorial service held in the Manchester Suite in the North Stand, with the survivors and their families all represented. But the main focus was on the derby.

There was much debate beforehand about whether the disaster should be commemorated with a minute's applause, as had become increasingly fashionable, for fear that some City fans might mar the ceremony in some way. But United, and key figures such as Sir Bobby Charlton, were very clear that a minute's silence was the appropriate thing to do. Within the stadium, the silence was complete, due recognition from all concerned that this was both a Manchester disaster and a sporting tragedy, rather than the occasion for petty local squabbles.

The spirit of the Busby era was evoked by United wearing a 1950s-style shirt for the match, with no sponsor's logos and the players' shirts numbered one to eleven; City too did not have any logos on their shirts. After what had gone before, the result was largely immaterial, though sadly United lost 2–1.

In early spring, Arsenal began to lose some of their consistency, while United went top in mid-March, scoring thirteen goals in five league games that month without reply, and were never caught thereafter. A 3–0 win over Liverpool at Old Trafford was received ecstatically by the 76,000 crowd, especially as Wes Brown was the surprise first goal-scorer for United (continuing a long tradition of United defenders hitting the target against the men from Anfield) and the Merseysiders' Javier Mascherano talked himself into a red card.

With only five games to go, Old Trafford hosted Arsenal in a match that could either bring the Gunners right back into the title race, or end their prospects. After the London side took the lead, United hit back with a Ronaldo penalty and a superb free kick from Hargreaves. But after a draw at Blackburn and defeat at Chelsea, United were left needing to win both their last two games to ensure the title remained at Old Trafford.

The first of those games was in Manchester, with West Ham the visitors. Although United have an excellent record against the Hammers, this rarely seems to apply during title run-ins. Fortunately, despite Nani being sent off, the Reds were able to win 4–1, with goals from Ronaldo (two), Tevez and Carrick (the latter two both West Ham old boys). With Wigan their final opponents, the 76,013 crowd believed they were saying farewell for the season to a side that would surely be champions. At Wigan, Ronaldo scored his thirty-first league goal of the season (twenty-one of them at Old Trafford), the most for United in a league campaign since Dennis Viollet's thirty-two in 1959–60. In all matches, he scored forty-two goals in the season and was close on unstoppable. Nominally played on the right, he was just as likely to turn up on the left or in the middle. He scored goals from free kicks that Beckham would have been proud of; like his other predecessor in the No. 7 shirt, Eric Cantona, he scored vital, match-winning goals; his pace rivalled that of Kanchelskis; he was as good as anyone in the air; and he had some tricks that George Best would have loved. He seemed the complete footballer. There was no surprise when he won both major domestic honours (PFA and FWA) as the footballer of the year, and then went on to become European Footballer of the Year, the first United player to win the award since Best forty years before.

But it wasn't just about Ronaldo and the other goal-scorers; the Reds' defence (usually Edwin van der Sar, Brown, Ferdinand, Vidic and Evra) had conceded just twenty-two league goals all season – a club record. United had secured their tenth Premier League title, but now they had other things on their minds, for a Champions League final beckoned.

United had started their European campaign in formidable form, winning their first five ties against Sporting Lisbon (where Ronaldo scored on his return to his former club), Roma and Dynamo Kiev. The front three of Ronaldo, Rooney and Tevez were in devastating form, scoring ten goals between them in the six group matches. In the first knockout round, United came up against Lyon and a 1–0 home win, thanks yet again to a Ronaldo goal, was enough to see them through to the quarterfinals after the first leg had been drawn. Amazingly, their opponents were again Roma, who they'd met at the same stage the previous season as well as in the group games. There were no 7–1 wins this time, but a 2–0 victory in Italy meant Sir Alex could rest one or two players for the return at Old Trafford, and Tevez ensured the tie was never in serious danger.

In the semifinal, United met Barcelona and held the Catalan side to a 0–0 draw in Spain. On a tense night at Old Trafford, the 75,061 crowd saw the Reds in resilient mood, looking to nullify the threat from Messi, Eto'o, Xavi and Iniesta, after Paul Scholes' superbly hit drive from twenty-five yards early in the first half. It was a thoroughly professional European performance, with resolute work from Patrice Evra to suppress Messi in particular. Unusually, United allowed Barca to dominate possession, confident they could hold out, but it did nothing for the nerves of the fans, worried that an equaliser would give the Spanish team the advantage with an away goal. But the supporters played their part, as Giggs recalls: 'Every time, the crowd were up, getting us little decisions.'

So it was that United reached their third European Cup or Champions League final, and their opponents in Moscow were all too familiar: Chelsea. A year before, the London side had prevented United from achieving a famous Double, but this time there were hopes the Reds could turn the tables. They had showed they could either attack with scintillating football, or defend solidly. Midway through the first half, Ronaldo put United into the lead from Brown's cross. But it wasn't enough, as Chelsea equalised before the break. That was all the goal-scoring in normal and extra time, so it went to a penalty shoot-out. United were the first to slip up, with Ronaldo surprisingly the guilty party, but John Terry missed the spot kick that would have secured victory for Chelsea. It went to sudden death. Giggs, who broke Charlton's appearance record in this match, scored United's last penalty. Then van der Sar saved Nicolas Anelka's effort to win the trophy. Two years before, Sir Alex's side were being written off; now they had won the biggest prize of them all.

With the Munich campaign having taken place fifty years before, the club invited the survivors to join them at their hotel in Moscow. It was a generous gesture, especially as the venue wasn't the easiest for people to get to otherwise. However, one of them, Harry Gregg, found there was no room for him and his wife. Ken

Ramsden, who'd stepped in as a fifteen-year-old to help Les Olive with the club's administration in 1960, came to the rescue again and found them a room on the ninth floor, the same level as the players. Gregg comments: 'And I watched the current United team doing the same daft, stupid things to each other that we did all those years ago.' It was a relief to him that the money might have changed, but the team spirit was just the same. United understands its history.

A few days later, on 29 May, forty years to the day since the Reds first won the European Cup, 'The United Trinity' statue of George Best, Denis Law and Bobby Charlton was unveiled by United's chief executive David Gill and Sir Alex in front of the East Stand. Built by the Inverness-born sculptor Philip Jackson, who was based in West Sussex and had recently completed the statue of Bobby Moore outside Wembley, it stood nine feet tall. Law, who was one of those present, commented: 'It's fantastic that we are facing Sir Matt Busby.' His statue, of course, stands right by the entrance to the East Stand.

During the summer, there was one major piece of incoming transfer business as Sir Alex signed Dimitar Berbatov from Tottenham for a club record fee of £30.75 million. One of the most stylish forwards in the business, he gave United's attack not only another creative force but also more physical presence and ensured that the club had arguably its strongest ever attacking line-up of Berbatov, Ronaldo, Rooney and Tevez. Meanwhile, one of the key pieces of business the manager did over the summer was preventing a transfer, as he held off the attentions of Real Madrid, who were desperate to sign Ronaldo. With Berbatov's arrival, Louis Saha was on his way to Everton, and Mikael Silvestre was sold to Arsenal. Arguably the biggest departure was that of Carlos Queiroz, Sir Alex's assistant, who had been an influential figure in the coaching set-up. Queiroz left to manage Portugal ahead of their World Cup qualifying campaign. Into his place stepped Mike Phelan, who had been first-team coach since 2001 and one of Sir Alex's early signings as a player back in 1989.

United's 2008–09 league campaign got off to a tough start, with early visits to Anfield and Stamford Bridge, and by the end of October the team were languishing in sixth place. On 15 November, Sir Alex marked fifty years in the professional game by watching United beat Stoke 5–0. Ronaldo scored two goals that day, the first of which was his hundredth for the club, while late on local lad Danny Welbeck scored his first for the Reds. The manager's belief in giving youth its opportunity had not dimmed over all his years in the game. Indeed, later in the season, another United youngster was to have a critical impact on the campaign.

Sir Alex's Christmas wishes must have all come true. After two wins over the holiday period, United then beat Chelsea 3–0, with goals from Vidic, Rooney and Berbatov, in front of 75,455 delighted fans at Old Trafford. The victory closed the gap on the London side, though Liverpool were still setting the pace. It was the start of an eleven-match winning streak in the Premier League that took United to the top of the table, during which just two goals were conceded. The run came to a shuddering end when Liverpool came to Old Trafford and won 4–1, despite United taking an early lead. And when the Reds lost again in the next match, at Fulham, the title race was back in the balance.

When Aston Villa held a 2–1 lead in the following game at Old Trafford with just ten minutes remaining, it seemed as though United were stumbling. Missing Berbatov, Ferdinand, Rooney, Scholes and Vidic through a combination of injury and suspensions, the pressure was on. Ronaldo then equalised with a terrific left-foot drive from twenty yards; he'd done little in the match – except score two excellent goals. Now United went all out for the winner, while Villa had opportunities on the counter.

As the final whistle drew near, Sir Alex threw on Welbeck to join seventeen-year-old Federico Macheda as United's centre-forwards, the latter making his first-team debut. It was an astonishing gamble. Then Giggs (who made his debut for United before his team-mate was even born) passed to Macheda on the edge of the box. He hit a stunning drive on the turn that flew past

Brad Friedel's outstretched fingers and into the corner of the net: 3–2 to United and a start to remember for a lifetime.

Yet again, United had done it right at the end. As Sir Alex has commented: 'Old Trafford has got that suction towards the goal when we are really in full flow and the crowd is really up for it. The ball just seems to get sucked towards the Stretford End. It's an amazing feeling. There are too many of these moments to mention where we decide games in the last fifteen minutes. It's not always entirely because of the team, it's because of the fans too. They make it happen. There's no better sight. Last-minute goals are not by accident. It's the nature of our stadium; it's the nature of the way we take risks to win the game.'

It was the kind of result that changes fortunes, and afterwards United dropped just two points in the remaining eight games. There was still time for the occasional alarm, however – it wouldn't be United without them. So Tottenham's visit saw the Londoners take a 2–0 lead into half-time, only for United to hit five in the second half.

The title was secured in the penultimate game with a 0–0 draw at home to Arsenal in front of 75,468 delighted fans. United finished four points clear of Liverpool, and seven ahead of Chelsea. It was the club's eleventh title in the seventeen years of the Premier League, and took the Reds to eighteen titles in all, equalling Liverpool's record. United also became the first club ever to win a hat-trick of championships twice, following their trio between 1999 and 2001.

The Premier League title meant United were able to contemplate an astonishing Quadruple. In April, there was even talk of a Quintuple. Back in December, United had won the FIFA Club World Cup, beating Gamba Osaka in the semifinal and LDU Quito 1–0 in the final in Japan. Next up was the League Cup. United were given home draws in every round, beating Middlesbrough, Queens Park Rangers and Blackburn Rovers (Tevez scoring four of United's five goals in this match) to get to the two-legged semifinal. Championship side Derby won 1–0 in their home leg, but in the return United eased through 4–2 to reach the final. Tottenham were the opponents, but a scoreless game was decided by a penalty shoot-out that was most notable for the fine form of Ben Foster in United's goal, enabling the Reds to win their second trophy of the season 4–1.

Tottenham were also the only visitors to Old Trafford during the FA Cup run that took United to a semifinal tie against Everton. Because of having so many key games in the Premier League and Champions League, Sir Alex rested several players for this fixture, which was held at Wembley. The stand-ins did a fine job, but couldn't force a winner, so the match ended 0–0, and this time the penalty shoot-out went the wrong way, preventing the possibility of a clean sweep for the Reds.

And so it was that everyone's attention swung back to the Champions League final, where United were bidding to become the first club ever to retain the trophy since it took on its new format. They had got there after a steady effort in the group stages, winning just two games and drawing the rest, which at least meant they equalled the record for unbeaten matches in the Champions League – nineteen so far.

The record was exclusively United's after they drew the first knockout leg, away at Inter Milan, now managed by Mourinho. In the home leg, Vidic and Ronaldo scored early in each half and the Reds eased through to the quarterfinals 2–0. There they met Porto, who had famously achieved a great result at Old Trafford in 2004 under Mourinho after scoring a late goal. Against a subdued United they did so again, netting the equaliser with only a minute left. The 2–2 draw meant United realistically had to win in Portugal, which they duly did, thanks to an early Ronaldo goal on his latest return to his home country.

This result set up a thrilling all-England semifinal against Arsenal. In front of 74,733 at Old Trafford, John O'Shea scored an early goal for United from a Carrick pass, and thereafter the Reds controlled the game without ever quite managing to put the tie beyond the Gunners. The prospects seemed good for the return at the Emirates, if the balance of power remained intact. The match was significant for another reason, as it marked the occasion of Giggs' 800th appearance for United. The man who ended the season with his eleventh league winner's medal was also named the PFA and FWA Footballer of the Year. It was overdue recognition for someone who kept on churning out brilliant performances. Later in the year, he surprised even himself when he became the BBC's Sports Personality of the Year, ahead of new F1 world champion Jenson Button.

If the first leg had suggested a United dominance, the return proved it, as the Reds scored twice in the first eleven minutes, thanks to Park and Ronaldo, to end the contest. Their opponents in the final were Barcelona, whom United had beaten in the semi-final the previous season. But this was a much-improved Barca team, and in the Stadio Olimpico in Rome the Spanish side out-played an off-key United for all but the first ten minutes of the game and won 2–0.

It was a frustrating and disappointing end to the season, and the news in the summer was even worse when Ronaldo was sold to Real Madrid for a world record fee of £80 million. Also on his way out was Tevez, after United decided not to take up the option to make his loan move a permanent one. In came Antonio Valencia from Wigan, for a fee reported to be £16 million, with the daunting challenge of replacing United's former No. 7. However, the man who took over that famous shirt number was Michael Owen, brought in on a free transfer from Newcastle.

The Tevez move was a sign of changing times in Manchester, for he'd headed across town to City, where the Abu Dhabi United Group had taken control of the club in September 2008. If Abramovich had seemed to have unlimited wealth when he took over Chelsea, City's new owners could have bought out the Russian with comfort. Clearly the Premier League was going to have another major player in future years. Because they had taken control of City right on the transfer deadline, they had been unable to do much transfer business at first, though the speedy signing of Robinho for a British record fee of £32.5 million gave an idea of what might happen. In the summer of 2009 (and again in 2010), there seemed no stopping their transfer activity. Undoubtedly, the Manchester rivalry was going to be given an extra edge.

United began the Premier League campaign looking for a unique fourth successive title, and soon found themselves in a familiar battle with Chelsea. But it was the visit of City on 20 September that was one of the most eagerly anticipated matches of the season. No United fan among the 75,066 crowd can have gone away disappointed by what they saw – it was a truly breathtaking game. At first, all seemed well when Rooney scored after two minutes from an Evra pass. City then equalised following a defensive mistake by the Reds. Inevitably, it was Tevez, who had received a hostile reaction from the United fans, who set up the goal. Early in the second half, Darren Fletcher headed United back into the lead, before City equalised again. Fletcher scored United's third, with another header, this time from a Giggs cross, but City were still not finished. They capitalised on another defensive mistake to bring the score to 3–3 as the ninety minutes were up. Was this a sign, as many in blue had hoped, that the balance of power in Manchester was changing? In the sixth minute of added time, Giggs spotted a run from Owen in the inside-left channel. His perfectly weighted pass split the defence; Owen opened up his body and curled his shot past the stranded Shay Given to ensure unbridled celebrations all around Old Trafford. United deserved the victory: they had dominated possession, territory and had the majority of the chances, but as so often they had kept their fans waiting until the very end for the moment of joy.

It was hard to follow that, and United's autumn became an injury-blighted period that reached its low point in December when Carrick found himself turning out in central defence along-side Fletcher at right-back; only Evra of United's first-choice defensive options remained available. After Christmas, the Reds were back on track and the race for the title became nip and tuck, although both United and Chelsea suffered the occasional unexpected hiccup. Fortunately, there was no mistake from United on 14 March 2010 for the visit of Fulham. This was the occasion the club had chosen to mark the centenary of Old Trafford, and a special day ended with the Reds 3–0 victors. Chief executive David Gill reflected: 'I think it was great. It shows what we can do in terms of events and recognising our history and heritage. Mike Bolingbroke did a great job overseeing the team on those events – the depiction on the front of the stadium; the actual game, where we invited representatives from the very first game to come along, and more besides. That was great to see them on the day, what it meant to them. It's what we do well. Ken Ramsden and his team are very good at that, and I think we understand that all those people played a great part in our history and it was important to reflect on that. Just to see how the stadium has transformed in that period is wonderful. As is the fact that we're still on the same site, we've still got all that history and heritage. It's a true asset of Manchester United.'

The visit of Chelsea to Old Trafford on Easter Saturday proved crucial, as the Londoners went into a two-goal lead, though one of the goals should have been given offside. If that had been the case, Macheda's late goal would not have been a consolation, but a vital equaliser. As United ended up losing the title by a single point, it could have made a huge difference, but it has to be accepted that Chelsea, now managed by Carlo Ancelotti, were worthy champions. Their 103 Premier League goals was a record.

United's FA Cup campaign never took off, as the Reds were beaten in the third round (for the first time under Sir Alex) at home to old rivals Leeds United, who also became the first team from a lower division to knock one of Sir Alex's teams out of the FA Cup. It was a painful experience that United were able to put right later that month in the semifinal of the League Cup, where they met Manchester City. The first leg at Eastlands had gone 2–1 in favour of the Blues, tilting the tie in their favour. United dominated much of the return leg, but had to wait until the second half before Scholes and then Carrick scored to give United a 3–2 aggregate lead. Tevez then pulled one back and, with United fans anxiously eyeing up the banner on the Stretford End that records the number of years City have gone without a trophy, extra time seemed inevitable. But in added time, Giggs crossed and Rooney headed in the winner to send the crowd delirious.

The England man was in extraordinary form, taking on the mantle of being the main goal-getter, and developing a new ability in the air that had rarely been seen before (scoring more headed goals this season than in his entire career to date). Giggs, too, was finding new ways to improve, commenting during the season on how he had been practising his free kicks now that he had more opportunity to take them in Ronaldo's absence. He even got to take a couple of penalties late on in the campaign, the first (shoot-outs apart) of his career.

United went on to win the League Cup, retaining the trophy for the first time, when they beat Aston Villa 2–1 at Wembley with goals from Owen and Rooney. For Owen, it was a bittersweet occasion, as the heavy pitch seemed to provoke an injury to his hamstring that ended his season.

After two successive Champions League finals, United wanted to make it three in a row. But the 2009–10 season saw a sudden swing in the balance of European power. In recent years, English teams had dominated the tournament, with United, Chelsea, Arsenal and Liverpool all regularly reaching the semifinals; but this time none got that far. United won their first three group games to make qualification almost inevitable, and ended up as comfortable winners of their group.

But it was the second-round tie that got all the attention, as United faced Milan. Of course, the meeting of two of Europe's biggest names was always likely to be high-profile, but the second leg at Old Trafford was something special, for it marked the return of David Beckham to the ground for the first time in a competitive fixture since he'd left the club back in 2003. He has commented: 'You can't explain stepping out at Old Trafford,' and by the time he came on as a second-half substitute, he knew the truth of his own words. The game was over as a contest, with United 3–0 up on the night and 6–2 ahead on aggregate, but his arrival on the pitch was greeted with a huge cheer. The fans recognised a man who has never lost his love for the club or his gratitude to all the staff who helped him on his way. His first touch, however, earned him ironic boos. Soon after, he hit a stunning shot that would have been one of his best ever goals had it gone in, but it wasn't to be.

Nor was it to be for United when they met Bayern Munich in the quarterfinals. Rooney scored early in the first leg in Germany, and although Bayern equalised it seemed the Reds would return home with a draw and a vital away goal. But in the last moments, Rooney picked up an injury and the German side scored a second goal. Both events were to prove crucial for the outcome of the season. The striker had been unstoppable until then, but never quite regained the momentum in the weeks that remained. In the return leg at Old Trafford, United swept into a 3–0 lead after forty minutes, with Nani scoring twice. But Bayern pulled back a goal before half-time, Rafael was sent off soon after the break, and the balance shifted. Former Chelsea star Arjen Robben scored the decisive goal with fifteen minutes to go. There was no coming back this time.

So the campaign in which United marked one hundred years at Old Trafford ended with another trophy in the cabinet, the sixth major award in four seasons. The Reds continue to plan for how the second century at the ground can be just as thrilling and dramatic as has been the case in recent years. They do so with a management team including Sir Alex Ferguson, Mike Phelan and Brian McClair who have some sixty years of Old Trafford experience between them, and three players – Ryan Giggs, Gary Neville and Paul Scholes – who have played over fifty seasons at United between them. But the commitment to youth and the future was clear from the signings made for the 2010–11 season: Chris Smalling joined from Fulham, Javier 'Chicharito' Hernandez from

Mexico and Bebe from Portugal. It summed up United: always aware of their history and their roots at Old Trafford, but always looking to the future, trying to ensure that tomorrow will add to the story just as today has done. It is a combination that has worked in the past, and a combination that those linked with Old Trafford will keep on striving to improve.

Afterword

For all the attention that is given to the team, Old Trafford is not just about the performance of the eleven men who get to run out on the pitch week in week out. Old Trafford is also about working on the pitch itself, to ensure the players can perform at their very best; it is about developing and improving the stadium all the time, and providing an excellent service, to make sure that the experience each fan has of their visit to the ground is as happy as possible. It is even about preparing the young players, so that when they get their chance to fulfil their dreams, and put on that famous first-team shirt and run out in front of 75,000 fans, they are ready for it.

The Old Trafford pitch of today is a marvel – not something that has always been the case, by any means. It is also flatter than it was in years gone by. In 1994, the camber on the pitch was shaved back, as it had got bigger and bigger over years of summer work. It had got to the stage where those sitting on the front row could see only from the waist up the players on the opposite side of the pitch.

Walking on to the turf, the first thing that strikes you is just how dense, lush and springy the grass is. Cut to a length of about two inches (it is allowed to grow slightly longer before a rugby Super League match), it feels almost as resilient as Astroturf, and it is easy to imagine the ball zipping across the top of it, rather than weighing down the grass. Standing in the centre circle, or the penalty area at the Stretford End – places where in the past one might have struggled to spot any grass at all once the season was a few weeks old – there is now solid greenery. Just occasionally, as one walks around, there is a bare patch, perhaps a few inches in diameter, but one could comb the entire pitch and spot only a handful or so of these. Generally, however, one wouldn't even know that there was any soil beneath the grass, so thick is it. And this is what it is like at the end of a season, after about eighty usages in the previous twelve months. Just imagine how much better it will be after the summer renovations.

Tony Sinclair is the head groundsman and the man responsible for its immaculate state. His offices and equipment are all stored in a building outside the southwest corner of the stadium, with easy access to the pitch via the players' tunnel. He joined United in 1989, as Keith Kent's assistant, before succeeding him in the top job when the latter took over the role at Twickenham. His enthusiasm and passion for his work are a pleasure to behold, and his commitment to providing the best surface possible is total. It is a year-long job, too. During the season, it needs nonstop maintenance, while the off-season is equally busy with repairs. No wonder he says, 'You've got to live this job.'

The problem he had to solve at Old Trafford was that in the seven years before 2003, eleven pitches had been laid at a total cost of around £2 million. What happened was that the grass was supplied on 50mm thick turf with an indigenous soil, and below it was 300mm of sand for drainage purposes, as it is obviously important for the pitch not to get waterlogged. The problem with this was that the roots would not grow down into the sand, so the turf was easily ripped up. Not only did this make it harder to pass the ball accurately, it meant there was an increased danger of injury. (If anyone ever goes down injured in a match at Old Trafford, Sinclair always checks the turf where it happened to ensure the pitch played no part in it.)

However, the current pitch was laid in 2003, so what did Sinclair do to solve the problem? First of all, the soil on which the grass is grown is made of fibresand, a mixture of coarse sand and polypropylene nylon, which feels something like horsehair. These two ingredients are mixed 75 per cent sand to 25 per cent fibre, to a depth of 400mm. The pitch is often watered as close to the start of a match as possible, and sometimes again at half-time, but because it drains so fast the watering simply helps the pitch to play better and reduces the number of divots created during the game.

Above the fibresand is a special blend of grass, Johnson's 100 per cent rye grass, using four different types of seed. Each type of seed has specific qualities that are wanted – good root structure, fast growing, and so on – so getting the balance right between the ingredients is as crucial as it would be in a cookery recipe. Sinclair has more grass-seed catalogues than most people have recipe books to make sure he gets the blend right. It has to be Michelin-starred seed.

In 2010, summer renovations began on 7 June, with overseeding to ensure the grass remained vigorous while the fibresand was kept wet, so that the new grass is encouraged to develop deeper roots. Each month throughout the year, soil samples are taken to check for any mineral deficiency that could damage the grass. There is a daily diary of exactly what has been done to the pitch, and the days ahead are also planned meticulously, though of course the amount of sun and rain (also monitored) has a bearing on what is needed.

The greatest difficulty comes during the winter months, when the height of the stands and the low, sporadic sun means that not enough light can get onto the grass. Without artificial help, some 10 to 15 per cent of the grass would die during January and February even without the additional damage caused by games being played on the pitch. To provide that extra light, United have some SGL (Stadium Grow Lighting) rigs that are moved about over various areas of the ground to give the grass the light it needs. Again, the positioning of each rig is noted and monitored.

Just as attention to detail with the surface is important on the pitch, some would be surprised to know how much thought goes into ensuring the surfaces are just right inside the stands. Property manager George Johnstone explains: 'Every year we're looking at improving the facilities around the stadium. One of the projects we did over a number of years was introduce the rubber stud flooring, because most of the floors were initially concrete, and so this makes it feel warmer; we've clad the steel columns in boarding so they look a lot more pleasant.' The addition of water fountains in the concourses was another small idea to improve things for everyone.

During the summer of 2010, Johnstone was at least not having to plan any further expansion to Old Trafford. While he says he has learned never to say 'never', he confirms there are no current plans to expand the ground again, despite gossip to the contrary about the possibility of a third tier to the South Stand. Chief executive David Gill echoes his thoughts: 'We've indicated that we have desktop plans to look at that and what can be done, but it's feasible. At the moment we're quite happy with a 76,000 capacity, though. To do anything with the South Stand has major implications with the local residents, transport issues and supply and demand. In order to have a payback, you would have a large mix of new executive seats, so all of these things are in the mix. At the moment we're comfortable with 76,000, there are no current plans to do anything.'

Instead of rebuilding a stand, Johnstone's main project was improving fifty hospitality boxes. When the first ones had been built at Old Trafford, before the 1966 World Cup, most people wanted to be shut away behind glass away from the rest of the crowd. Now most box owners say they'd far rather be much closer to the action and be a part of it all. 'The feedback was, "We feel disconnected from the crowd". So we had a little competition with three architects: we want a better connection with the crowd, put in the most up-to-date AV systems, gadgets and toys – give us your best shot.' The final results include: 'Touchscreen controls for all the room and so on, to make it a bit special and give a reason why you'd want to be there rather than somewhere else.'

Old Trafford becomes one of the biggest catering enterprises around on a match-day, averaging 4450 meals for each game. With some 1300 people employed on the catering side on the day, it is a huge operation. For those who go instead to the kiosks in the concourses, they are eating some 7500 pies, 4500 hotdogs, 1500 sausage rolls and drinking 17,000 bottles of beer. Contrary to popular reputation, no prawn sandwiches are served.

Unless, of course, they are on the menu in the players' lounge. This room where the players relax before a game is not particularly large, maybe twelve metres by five. There are ordinary burgundy chairs lined up under the international honours board that records the achievements of United players for their respective countries. It is a mark of the changing times that just off the lounge is a crèche for the team's children. Once again, the emphasis on family, and on getting the details right, is apparent. Across the corridor from the lounge is the home dressing room, which is slightly larger, wood-panelled, and all the players' seats are set up in a ring facing the white board where Sir Alex can make a few last points before the game begins. The corridor to both dressing rooms, home and away, and down to the players' tunnel is lined with big photographs of recent United successes: trophy-winning shots, goal celebrations. The players in red go onto the pitch knowing what they have to live up to and provide for the fans – it's inspirational positive reinforcement. For their opponents, it makes clear just what a daunting task lies ahead of them.

But, of course, it's not just about making things right for the old hands, the likes of Giggs, who has been turning out here for twenty years. It's about making sure that when a player takes his first steps onto the pitch, he is ready for the moment. For, as Giggs has commented, when asked about his greatest highlight in his trophy-laden career: 'My finest moment was my first appearance for the first team. Nothing has beaten that experience and nothing ever will.'

The responsibility for getting young players ready falls to Brian McClair, who explains what the club can do to help, while knowing that nothing can truly prepare someone for running out in front of 75,000 people for the first time. 'When I was coming to the end of my time here, I was playing in the reserves along with the likes of Gary [Neville], [Nicky] Butt and [Paul] Scholesy, and we played the first four and the last four games at Old Trafford, so at least those people had the flavour of playing there, even if there weren't lots of people there. That was a great thing to have, so even though you were coming into the stadium full, you had been on the pitch, and been used to playing on the size of the pitch, because the pitch is a big one.'

Nowadays, he says, the demands on the stadium mean reserve-team games are no longer played at Old Trafford. 'We are missing that. Sometimes, as Macheda did, you go straight into the side without having been on there. You can encourage them. The younger ones, from sixteen to eighteen, have all got tickets to go to the home games, so they can be part of what's happening there. And now the Academy kids will have a training day on the pitch, so at least they've been on there.'

And so it is that the entire machine of Manchester United works towards getting the best out of its players, to ensure they can perform to their maximum capacity. This, in turn, will give the fans the most pleasure, and everything else is laid on for them to make their experience a good one. Wherever you go, there are reminders of the past and a sense of what is to come. For everyone at Old Trafford knows that they work in the Theatre of Dreams, and they can make those dreams come true for millions around the world.

Bibliography

The Autobiography, by Jonah Lomu (Headline, 2004)

Back Page United, by Stephen F. Kelly (Queen Anne Press, 1990)

Charles Buchan's Manchester United Gift Book, edited by Simon Inglis (Played in Britain, 2007)

Determined, by Norman Whiteside (Headline, 2007)

The Doc: Hallowed Be Thy Game, by Tommy Docherty (Headline, 2006)

Engineering Archie, by Simon Inglis (English Heritage, 2005)

From Goal Line to Touchline, by Jack Crompton with Cliff Butler (Empire Publications, 2008)

George Best and 21 Others, by Colin Shindler (Headline, 2004)

Heading for Victory, by Steve Bruce (Bloomsbury, 1994)

The King, by Denis Law (Bantam Press, 2003)

Legends of United, by David Meek (Orion, 2006)

Managing My Life, by Alex Ferguson (Hodder & Stoughton, 1999)

Manchester, An Architectural History, by John J. Parkinson-Bailey (Manchester University Press, 2000)

Manchester United – The Biography, by Jim White (Sphere, 2008)

Manchester United, The Complete Record, by Andrew Endlar (Orion, 2007, 2008)

Manchester United in Europe, by David Meek and Tom Tyrrell (Hodder & Stoughton, 2001)

Manchester United Ruined My Life, by Colin Shindler (Headline, 1998)

Manchester United's Golden Age 1903–1914: The Life and Times of Dick Duckworth, by Thomas Taw (Desert Island Books, 2004)

My Idea of Fun, by Lee Sharpe (Orion, 2005)

My Manchester United Years, by Sir Bobby Charlton (Headline, 2007)

The Official Illustrated History of Manchester United, by Alex Murphy and Andrew Endlar (Simon & Schuster, 2010)

Old Trafford: 100 Years at the Theatre of Dreams, by Iain McCartney (Empire Publications, 2010)

The Red Army Years, by Richard Kurt and Chris Nickeas (Headline, 1997)

Red Dawn, by Brian Belton (Pennant Books, 2009)

Red Voices, by Stephen F. Kelly (Headline, 1999)

Rothmans Book of Football Records, by Jack Rollin (Headline, 1998)

Sky Sports Football Yearbook, edited by Jack and Glenda Rollin (Headline, various editions)

Winning!, by Clive Woodward (Hodder & Stoughton, 2004)

Numerous websites were also consulted, but special mention should be made of manutd.com and stretfordend.co.uk, the club's official statistics website.